IMAGES of America

LOOMIS

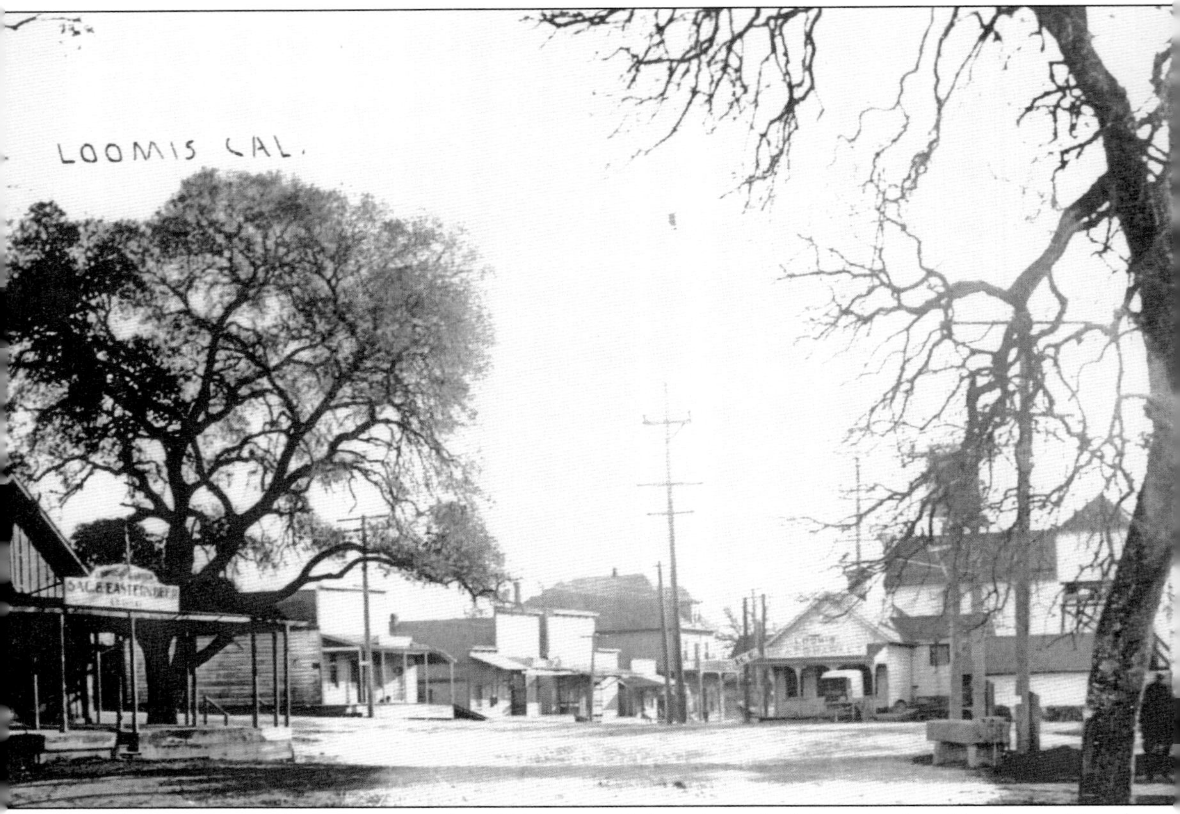

In this picture taken sometime after 1911, Loomis Saloon is on the left under the old oak tree. Brazel Misley's Market is in the front right. To the far right is Misley's Hall. The building in the back of the Meat Market is Dick Cook's Saloon. (Courtesy of the Loomis Basin Historical Society.)

On the Cover: The Loomis water tower was the pride of the community. Water was furnished by the Yuba Water Company. It was located near on Walnut, near Taylor Road close to the railroad crossing. This area later became the Loomis Lumber Company. The man in the buggy is Mr. Cook. James Oscar Loomis is the elderly man in the white shirt with suspenders. To his immediate left is Alex Scroggs, standing (dressed in black with white buttons on his shirt). Mr. Yarborough is the man with the gray beard and black hat. On Yarborough's left is Claude Hoffman, blacksmith, and his daughter Maggie. At Loomis's right elbow is Sabin Webb. The rest of the people are not known. The photograph was taken in 1881–1882. Sadly, the water tower never worked and was taken down.

IMAGES
of America

LOOMIS

Loomis Basin Historical Society

ARCADIA
PUBLISHING

ISBN 978-0-7385-7019-8

Published by Arcadia Publishing
Charleston, South Carolina

Printed in the United States of America

Library of Congress Control Number: 2009922888

For all general information contact Arcadia Publishing at:
Telephone 843-853-2070
Fax 843-853-0044
E-mail sales@arcadiapublishing.com
For customer service and orders:
Toll-Free 1-888-313-2665

Visit us on the Internet at www.arcadiapublishing.com

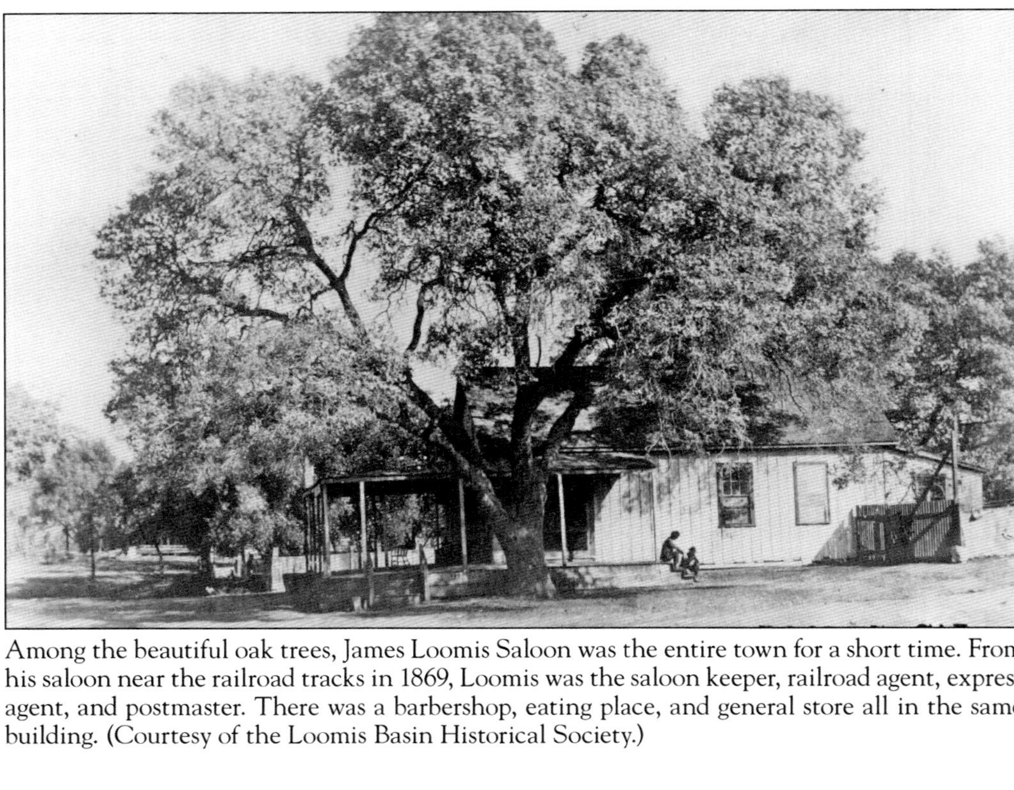

Among the beautiful oak trees, James Loomis Saloon was the entire town for a short time. From his saloon near the railroad tracks in 1869, Loomis was the saloon keeper, railroad agent, express agent, and postmaster. There was a barbershop, eating place, and general store all in the same building. (Courtesy of the Loomis Basin Historical Society.)

Contents

Acknowledgments		6
Introduction		7
1.	Influence of the Railroad	9
2.	Agriculture	15
3.	Street Scenes and Businesses	39
4.	The Fire Department	69
5.	Schools	73
6.	Homes	87
7.	Churches	109
8.	Organizations and Sports	113
9.	Quarries of the Loomis Area	123
Loomis through the Years		126
About the Loomis Basin Historical Society		127

Acknowledgments

Whether they lived and worked in Pino, Smithville, Pine Grove, or Loomis, early pioneers and settlers unwittingly formed the history of the area, starting families and a solid basis for future generations. They built the foundation so that we could enjoy and appreciate the past. The town changed names for various reasons, but the perseverance, integrity, and hard work of these settlers never changed. The multigenerational families are an indication of this spirit. I would like to specifically thank the past generations of pack rats. These include Barbara and Ken Mackey, who graciously shared labeled binders full of photographs from the Turner family who came to the area in the 1850s. Also, thanks to Vivian and Markey Rasmussen. Vivian compiled information from many residents and was able to write one book of local history. Their children have graciously donated much of her archives to the Loomis Basin Historical Society. Lloyd Gatt took many pictures of the town and shared them with the historical society. Alice Rippey Barnes and Barbara Leak were extremely helpful with photographs and information. There were many contributing families to this effort: Rippey, Barnes, Leak, Fieser, Owen, Taylor, Mehl, Sippola, Lopez, Day, Nute, Horton, Takemoto, Yokote, Struble, Hansen, Nelthorpe, Law, Larsen, and Quong are only a short listing. I thank my husband, Rod Enright, for putting up with my hobby, and apologize for thinking my parents were packrats. All that material and "stuff" was a great gift to leave for future generations. To the computer-savvy generation, thank you John and Lynn. I would also like to thank my grandfather, Porter Taylor, who left Slickrock, Kentucky, set out west, and eventually settled in the Loomis area. To Frank and Marge Nute, thank you for instilling a craving for family history. Marge was born in Loomis to Porter Lee and Allie Flesher Taylor. Frank came from Minnesota and after marrying Marge came to live in Loomis and raise their family.

To all the settlers and families who came from around the globe to settle in Loomis, thank you for establishing the small-town attitude of caring, generosity, and hope that still continues today, over 150 years after the first settlers came to the area. Unless otherwise noted, the images appear courtesy of the Loomis Basin Historical Society.

—Beth Nute Enright
Secretary
Loomis Basin Historical Society
March 2009

INTRODUCTION

An insight to the original settlement of this area is given in the history the First Congregational Church of Loomis, California, by Adaline Hansen. She states, "In 1851 two men, Smith and Hubble, by name, in their wandering for gold-diggings came to the intersection of the old toll road between Sacramento and Auburn, and the road which crossed the American river below the present Rattlesnake bridge, to Marysville. This was a point about one mile south of Loomis. It was named Pine Grove because of the heavy pine growth. As there was another Pine Grove Post Office in the Young State of California, it became officially known as Smithville. A schoolhouse was built which was used 'till 1925 when the school was moved to its present location in Loomis.

California was growing in population. By this time, a railroad was started from Sacramento, passed near Folsom, and progressed as far as Wildwood Station, near the present junction of Auburn Folsom Road with Brennan Road. The railroad company hoped to continue over the mountains. At that time, the government got behind the Central Pacific, and so 1863 saw another railroad coming through Roseville and Rocklin. At the point where the railroad crossed the Marysville Road, a station was built and an agent appointed. The station was named Pino. It was found that there was confusion between the names Reno, Nevada, and Vino, Tehama County, so the railroad authorities changed the name Pino to Loomis, the name of the first station agent, James Oscar Loomis."

This feeling of confusion was not limited to the railroad stations. Frederick Turner, postmaster of Pino, moved to make a change also. The post office was Pino, the school district Smithville, and the depot Loomis. On May 28, 1890, the town name officially became Loomis in honor of the first station agent. James Loomis had also been postmaster on December 6, 1869. Thus all the confusion was finally put to rest.

The area was diverse in population and economy. Gold mining had gotten many of the original settlers to the area, but as dredging and placer mining phased out or moved on, other resources had to be put to use. The Chinese had come to the area to help with the railroad, and many of them also moved on with the railroad and the search for gold. Emigrants from all over Europe came to the area. As the gold played out, the Mediterranean climate was put to good use with fruit ranching. Peaches, pears, plums, persimmons, grapes, strawberries, oranges, mandarins, and olives became the mainstay of this area's economy. The Japanese came to settle and work the crops along with Danish, German, Finnish, Spanish, Portuguese, and East Indians. The agricultural industry helped expand the town and the businesses needed to support the fruit, the railroad, and the people who lived in the area. At one time, this small town in the foothills of the Sacramento Valley boasted many fruit packing sheds. The crops from this area were known the world over. By railroad, the packed fruit traveled to markets in New York, Chicago, and other points east. In 2009, only two fruit sheds remain to give a hint at what the past was like.

Set among the oak trees that are common to the area, a saloon belonging to James Oscar Loomis was for a short time, the entire town. The saloon was near the railroad tracks, and in 1869,

James Oscar Loomis was saloon keeper, railroad agent, express agent, and postmaster. There was a barbershop, eating establishment, and a general store in the building. There were olive trees and a watering trough in front of the building.

On December 6, 1869, Loomis was appointed postmaster of the community, which at the time was still Pino. On May 28, 1890, the town officially became Loomis, named after the former Michigan entrepreneur. On June 17, 1895, the Placer County pioneer died, leaving a legacy that thrives to this day.

On July 12, 1915, Loomis was the victim of a fire that started in the middle of the night when there was no organized fire department, no water pressure, and no fire apparatus to fight the fire. The main portion of the business district was destroyed, with an estimated loss of more than $40,000. This fire struck at a time when most, if not all, of the buildings were wooden structures. Every building the fire touched was destroyed. Originally two men were suspected of setting the fire. They broke into Plaus Drug Store. Dr. O. L. Barton challenged their behavior, and they suggested they were just helping to get items out of fire danger. They were later arrested by Constable Newton as they were leaving town. It was later found that fire started from an oil stove in the resident portion of May's stable. Electric and telephone wires were down before the fire was discovered around 3:30 a.m. The town was destroyed in less than two hours. The businesses and residences were eventually rebuilt, but wood was not the material of choice. Granite, cement blocks, and other fireproof items were used. Shake shingles were also not used. By 1930, the Loomis Fire Protection District was formed, and William Dearborn was the president of the board. Thirty men signed on as volunteer firemen. The first fire truck was a 1930 Ford Model A pumper. By February 1945, a new Ford pumper was added. In 1951, the need for additional equipment prompted the purchase of a fire truck from the Mehl Chevrolet dealership in Loomis. The fire trucks were stored in several buildings around town, including the Reeves and Doty Ford Garage and an old blacksmith shop.

In 2009, much of the heritage of the original Pino/Loomis settlement is still visible. Much of the post-fire architecture still exists. The building owners and the businesses may have changed, but in viewing old photographs, it is clear that Christensen's Saddle and Supply is the Law Brothers; Nelthorpe and Son is the original Bank of Loomis; Main Drug and Cook's are the same building; and the Horseshoe Bar and Grill is in the original Gatt's Meat Market. Many of the old families still live in homes that can be traced back to early Loomis. There are many multigenerational families that can state that their ancestors helped settle the area. Many of the roads and streets are named after these families. There is a proud heritage in this small settlement that has its foundation in the agricultural industry.

One

Influence of the Railroad

In 1910, the future of the town of Loomis seemed assured and permanent when the Southern Pacific Railroad announced that it was going to build a new train depot. It was to be built 100 feet south of the old depot and designed somewhat along the lines of the Lincoln depot. The following item appeared in the *Placer Herald* newspaper of February 19, 1910: "Loomis was a sleepy hamlet 25 years ago. Today it is a booming fruit growing and shipping center. Its permanency as a railroad station is secured with plans for a new depot. It will be 2 stories high so as to provide a home for the agent. It will be the best arranged and handsomest depot in the County." The March 26, 1910, issue carried a follow-up article as follows: "The new depot is finished except for the painting. The telegraph and telephone wires are roughed in and the building will be ready for occupancy. It is 133 feet long and its overhanging roof makes it appear lower than it is. Never the less, it is an attractive building and well adapted to its purpose." The final article appeared in the April 16, 1910, publication of the *Placer Herald*. "Agent Aymer expects to take possession of the new depot in a few days. He had expected the S.P. Company would build so as to give him living quarters, but owing to a costly fire, having originated in the sheds from Agent Aymer's kitchen stove, housekeeping quarters were cut out and the depot is not a two story building." The railroad cars carried thousands of packed fruit boxes to the auctions of New York and Chicago. As time progressed, fruit ranching and shipping by rail became cost prohibitive. The mainstay of the area's economy slowly gave way to other endeavors. The depot has been has been refurbished and has become a community center.

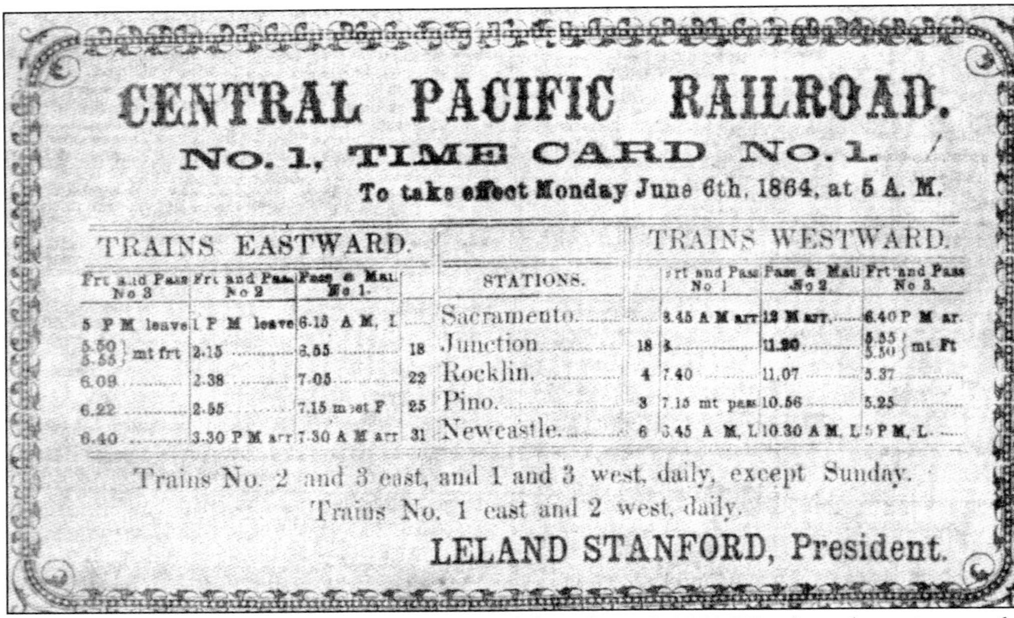

CENTRAL PACIFIC RAILROAD.

NO. 1, TIME CARD NO. 1.

To take effect Monday June 6th, 1864, at 5 A. M.

TRAINS EASTWARD.						TRAINS WESTWARD.		
Frt and Pass No 3	Frt and Pass No 2	Pass & Mail No 1.		STATIONS.		Frt and Pass No 1	Pass & Mail No 2	Frt and Pass No 3.
5 P M leave	1 P M leave	6.15 A M, L		Sacramento.		8.45 A M arr	12 M arr,	6.40 P M ar.
5.50 / 5.55 mt frt	2.15	6.55	18	Junction	18	8	11.20	5.55 / 5.50 mt Ft
6.09	2.38	7.05	22	Rocklin.	4	7.40	11.07	5.37
6.22	2.55	7.15 meet F	25	Pino.	3	7.15 mt pass	10.56	5.25
6.40	3.30 P M arr	7.30 A M arr	31	Newcastle.	6	6.45 A M, L	10.30 A M, L	5 P M, L.

Trains No. 2 and 3 east, and 1 and 3 west, daily, except Sunday.

Trains No. 1 east and 2 west, daily.

LELAND STANFORD, President.

Pictured is a Central Pacific Railroad time card from June 6, 1864. This lists the train stop for Pino. This was the name for Loomis prior to December 6, 1869.

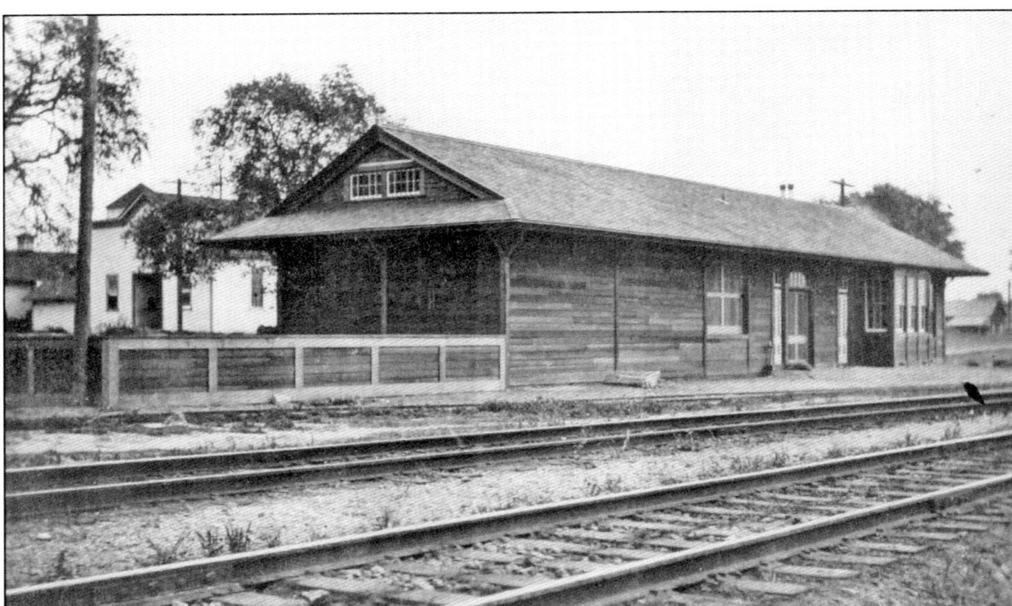

Pictured in the 1870s, this is the first train depot for the town. Misley's Hall is in the background.

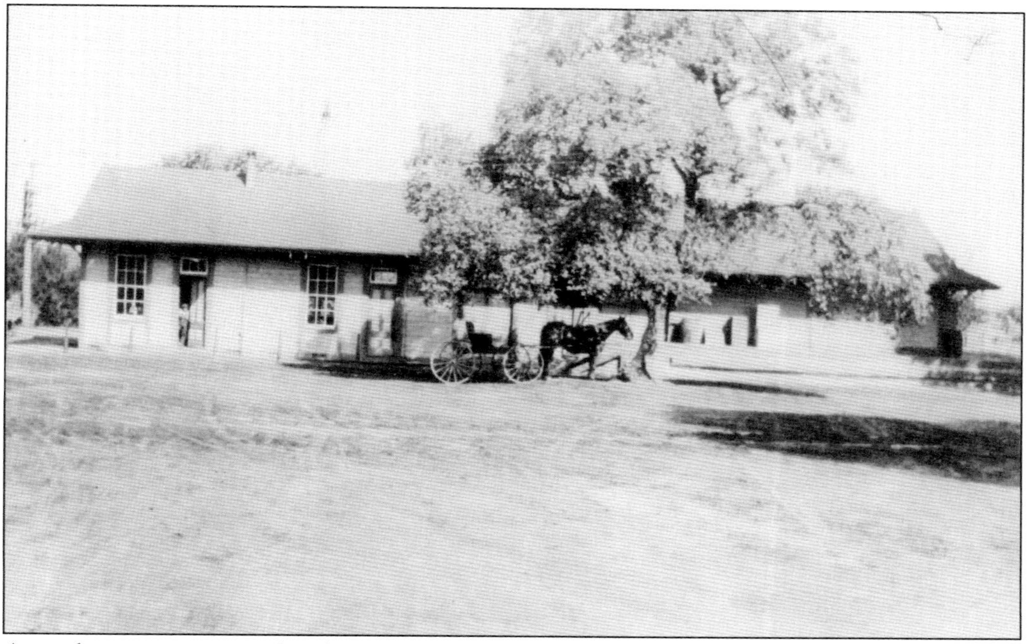

According to an item in the *Placer Herald* newspaper of February 19, 1910, "Loomis was a sleepy hamlet 25 years ago. Today it is a booming fruit growing and shipping center. Its permanency as a railroad station is secured with plans for a new depot to be built 100 feet south of the present depot and somewhat after the lines of the depot in Lincoln. It will be 2 stories high so as to provide a home for the agent. It will be the best arranged and handsomest in the country."

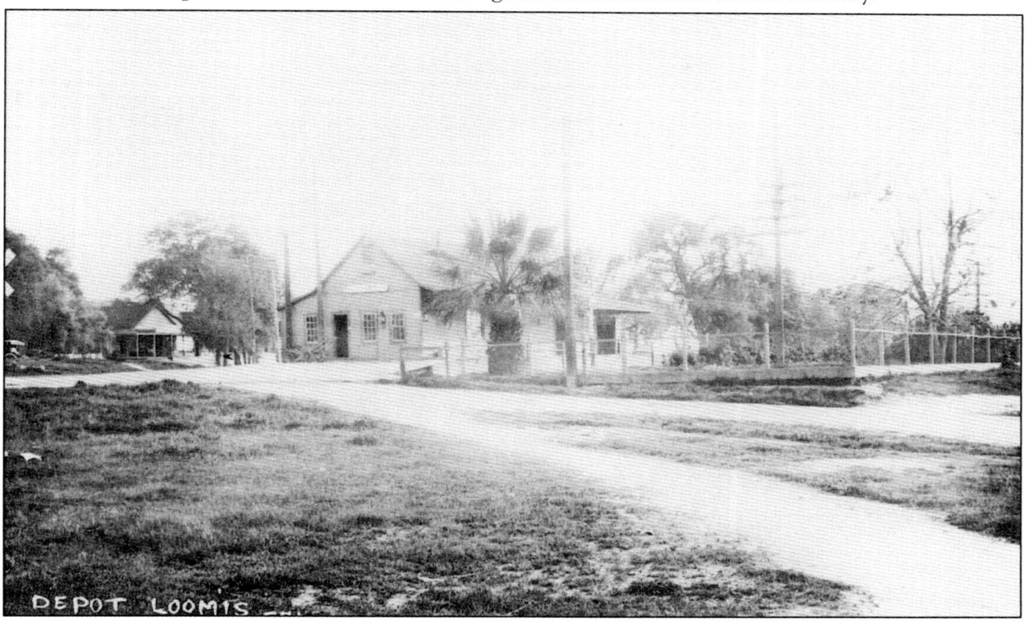

This is the Loomis railroad depot about 1908 in the town of Pino, prior to the name change. It was located on Webb Street near the north end of the Savings Corner Market lot. (This is now Jimboy's). The fenced area to the right of the depot was a park on the opposite side of the tracks from the depot.

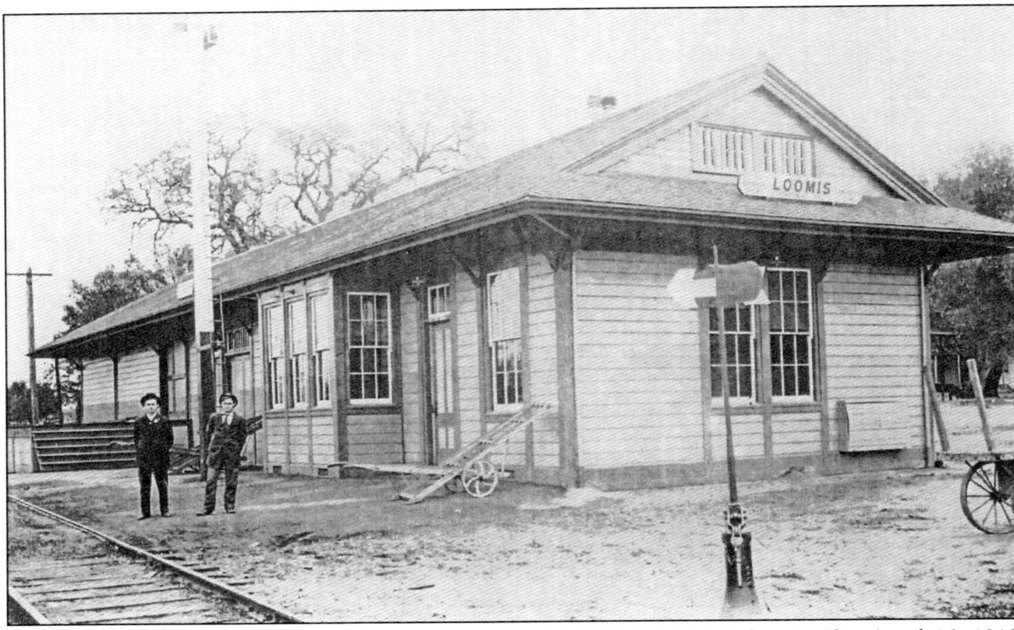

Two townsmen, unidentified, stand beside the tracks of the Loomis depot. The April 16, 1910, article of the *Placer Herald* stated, "Agent Aymer expects to take possession of the new depot in a few days. He had expected the S.P. Company would build so as to give him living quarters, but owing to a costly fire, having originated in the sheds from Agent Aymer's kitchen stove, housekeeping quarters were cut out and the depot is now a two story building."

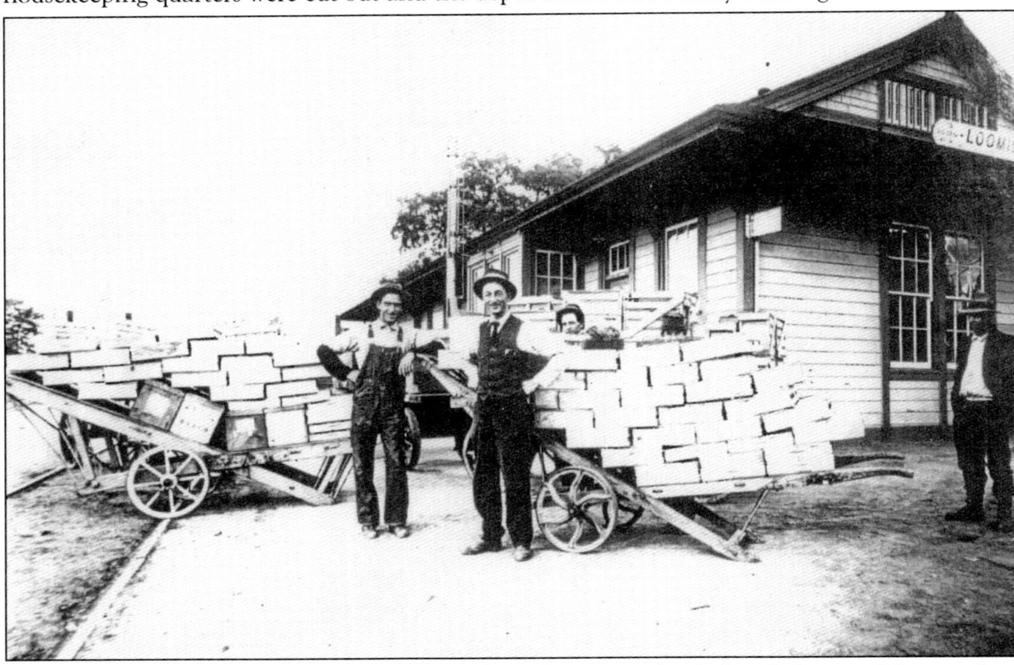

This photograph was taken in 1915. A number of carts are loaded with boxes of fruit such as peaches, cherries, and strawberries. The large boxes on the cart at the left are probably egg cases. The men are express agent Earl Howard (left) and depot agent Fred Martindale.

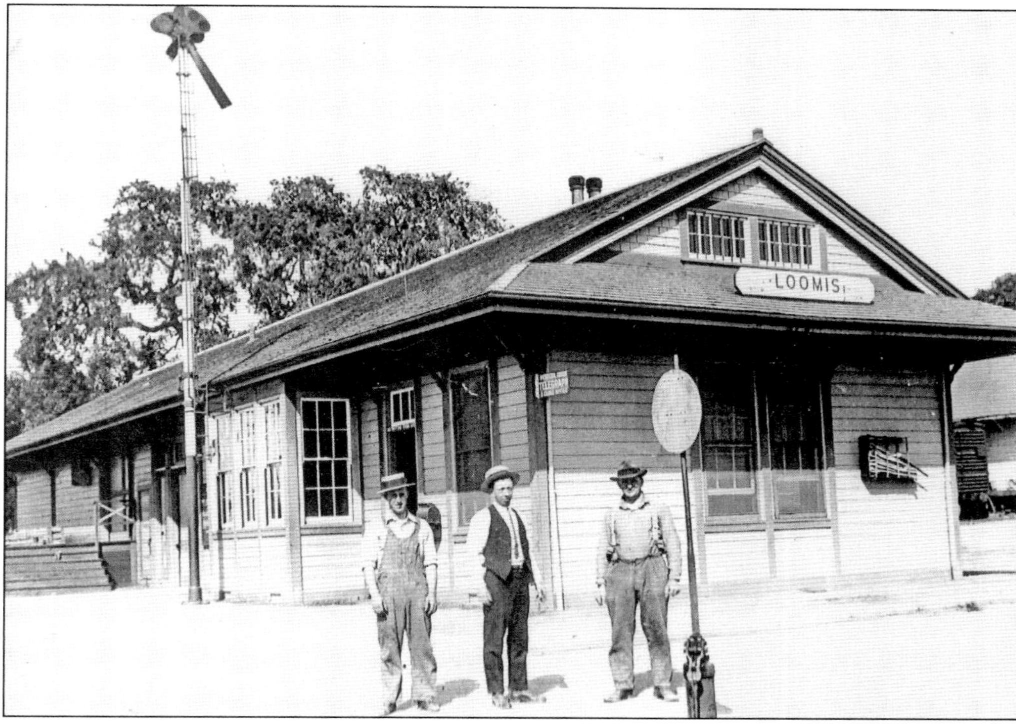

The Loomis depot is pictured in 1923. Ed Leavitt was station agent from 1918 until 1956.

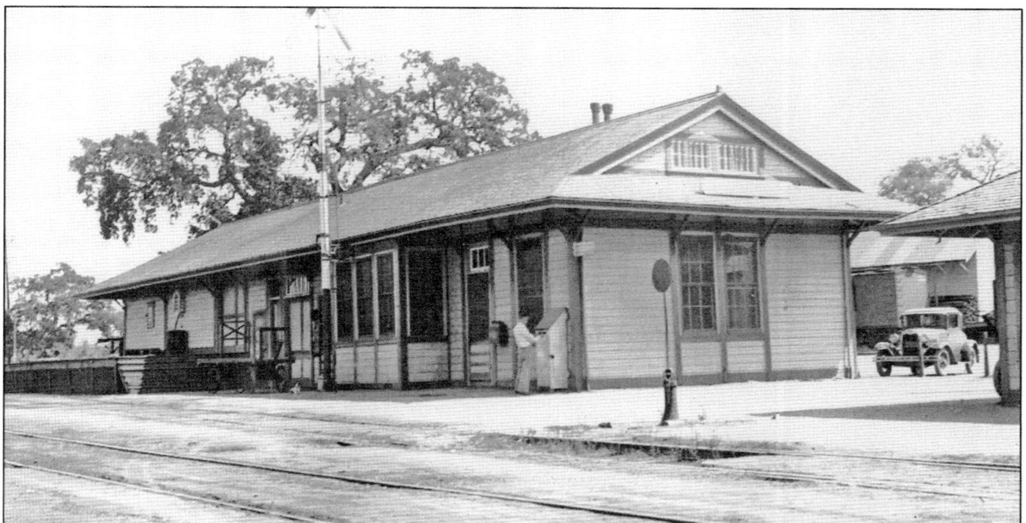

The Loomis depot—which in 1910 was rebuilt by the Southern Pacific Company, greatly due to the continuous urging of H. E. Whitaker, editor of the *Loomis Recorder*—still stands, in refurbished condition, as the focal point of the Loomis community. Many have memories of the train stopping to let soldiers disembark, so that they could return to their families during World War I and World War II. Now the depot has been refurbished to be a meeting place for the Town of Loomis and other community activities.

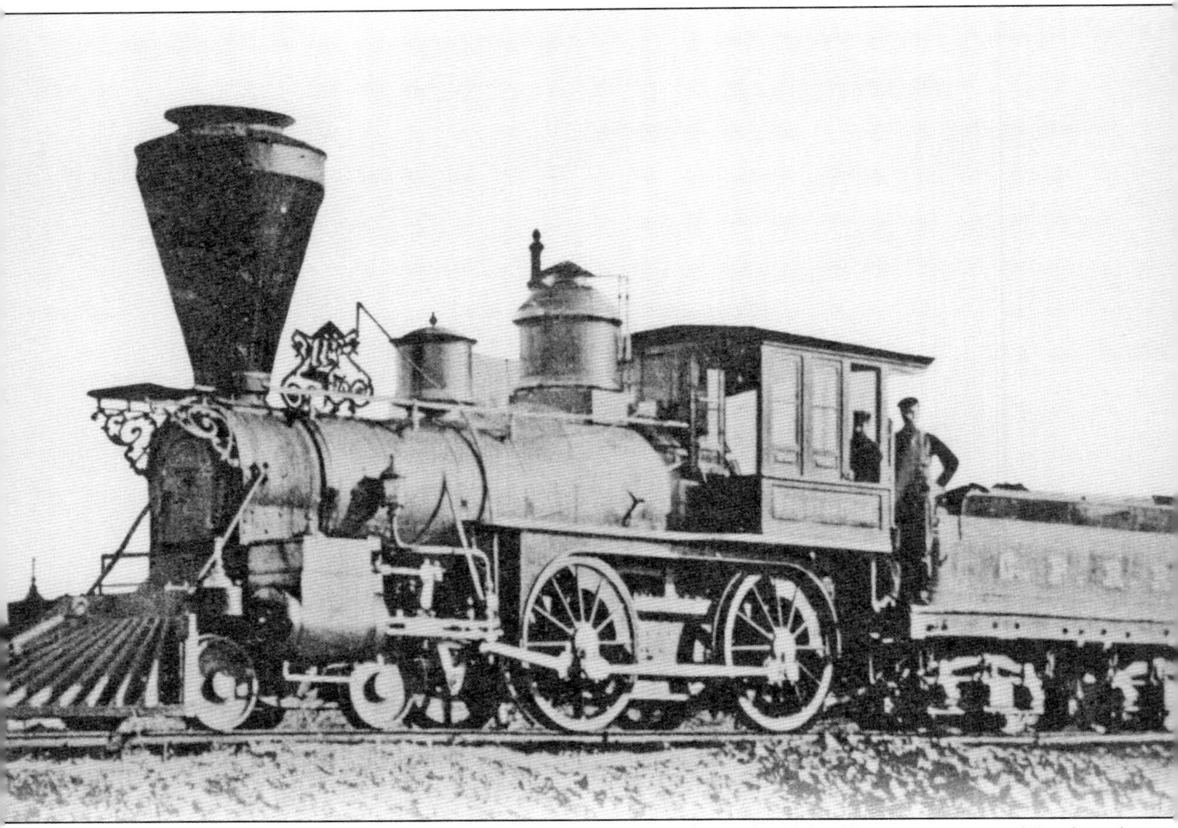

The Central Pacific Railroad, which built the western branch of the Transcontinental Railroad, laid track to what is now Loomis on May 21, 1864. These tracks carried carloads of Loomis fruit throughout the United States for nearly 100 years.

Two

AGRICULTURE

When gold mining waned in the area, fruit ranching became a stable economic foundation. The area became well known for its Mediterranean climate, which was ideal for growing a variety of fruit. Peaches, pears, plums, grapes, persimmons, strawberries, cherries, Asian pears, and olives thrived. Eventually kiwis were grown also. Most families either raised fruit or worked in the fruit industry. Most high school students spent summers working in the sheds. The fruit sheds were clustered near the train tracks so that train cars could be dropped off, filled with lugs of packed fruit, iced down, and prepared for the journey to the auction markets of the east coast. Fruit labels became well known. The sheds had their own labels, as did many of the individual ranches. Producers, Loomis Fruit Growers Association, American Fruit Growers, Pioneer Fruit, Earl, Rowell, Pacific Fruit Exchange, Law Brothers, Gerard, Nash De Camp, California Fruit Exchange, and Day and Company are some of the fruit packing sheds that were built in Loomis. The sheds were also known by the nicknames derived from their logos. The American was the Blue Goose. California Fruit Exchange was Blue Anchor. Loomis Fruit Growers was High Hand. All were readily recognizable from the labels. Even in the 1970s, Loomis fruit could be found in grocery stores back east.

The Loomis area was also well known for growing carnations and exotic plants. Bassett's Floral Company, California Carnation Company, and the Loomis Carnation Company were known throughout the United States and England for their flowers.

Fruit is still grown in the area on a much smaller scale. The industry slowly phased out when the costs became prohibitive. Driving down Taylor Road, it is obvious that the sheds were a proud mainstay of the area. On either end of town, an original shed has been kept as a landmark but modified for farmers markets, community events, nurseries, and restaurants.

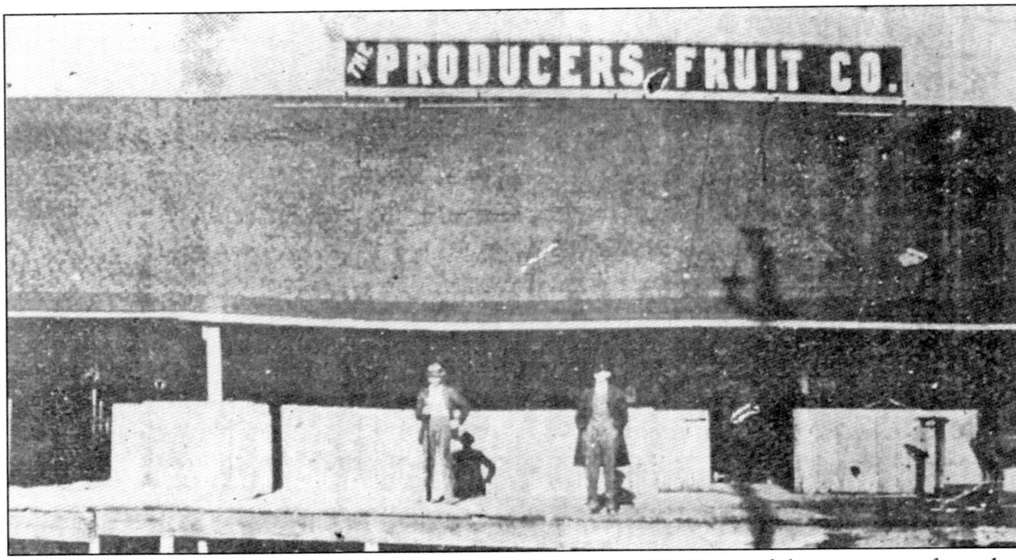

Producer's Fruit Company's fruit shed was in operation in 1903. Some of the varieties of peaches shipped were Crawford, Hale, Albright, Cling, Levi, and Phillips. Plum varieties included Tragedy, Burbank, Kelsey, Grand Duke, Diamond, Abundance, and Willard.

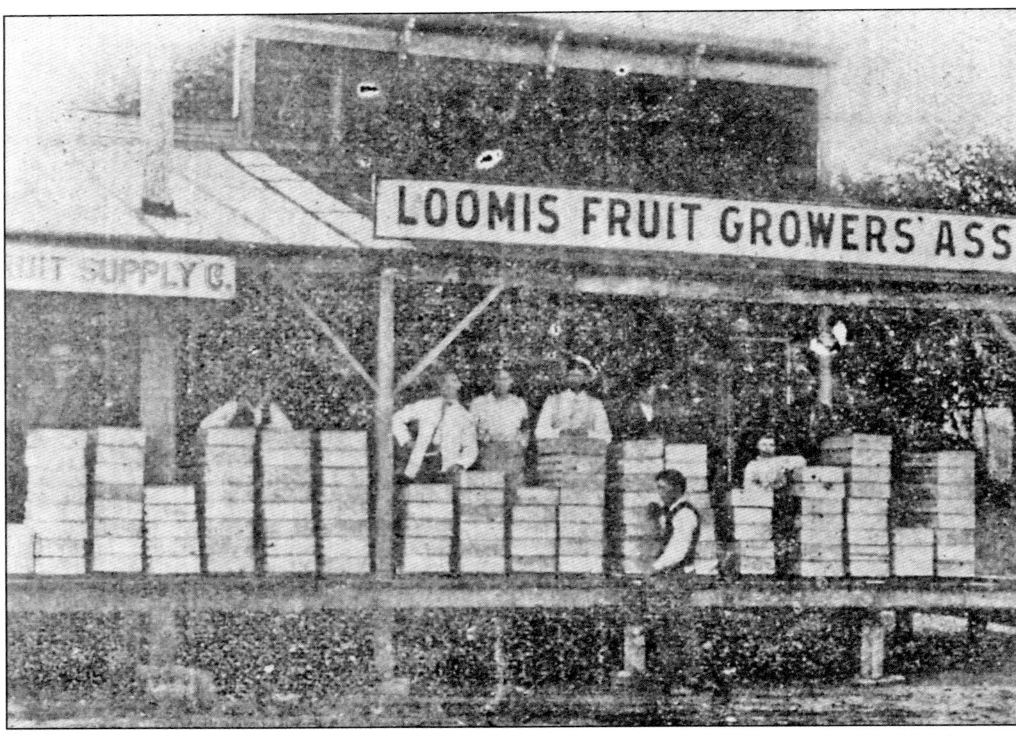

Six or seven unidentified workers stand on the Loomis Fruit Growers loading dock. This was taken from the January 27, 1911, *Loomis Record*. Lug boxes of fruit were trucked in from the ranches and stacked on the loading docks then emptied so the fruit could be sorted by size and packed prior to shipping.

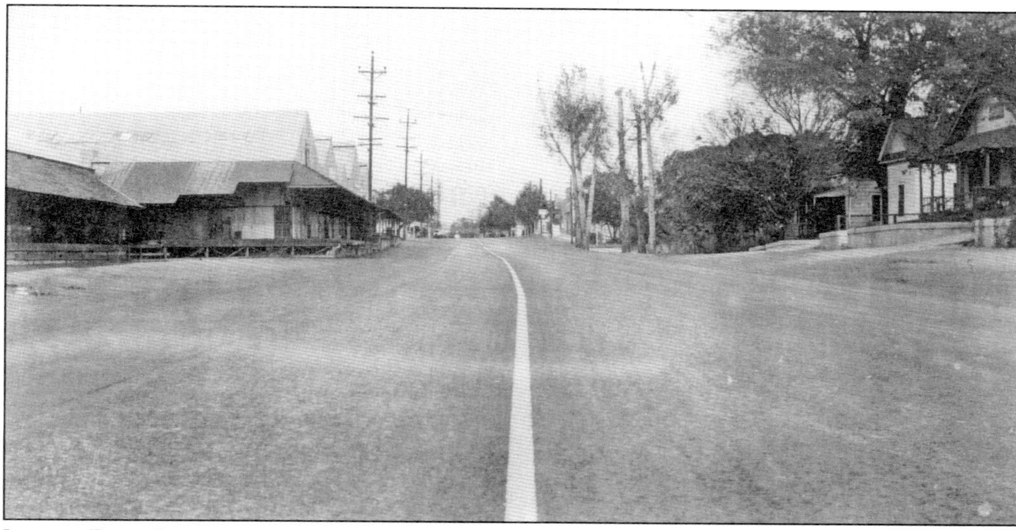

Loomis Fruit Growers Association (LFGA), pictured from Taylor Road, was chartered on April 29, 1901. In 1926, the LFGA built a modern and mechanized central packinghouse where farmers could bring their fruit to have it packed. Prior to this, they had to have it packed on their own ranches.

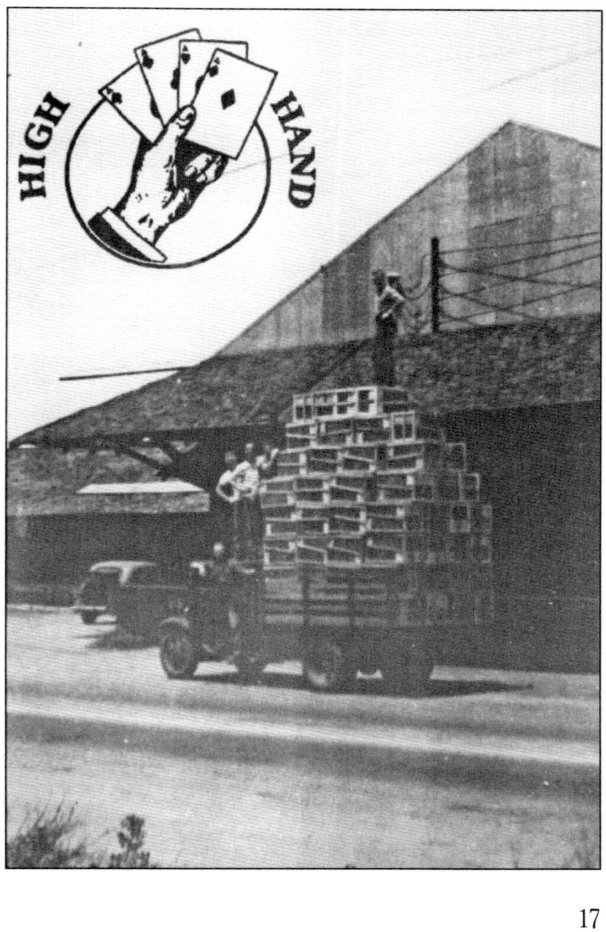

A truck delivers tin-top baskets for packing plums at the Loomis Fruit Growers Association's High Hand fruit shed in 1937. This is at Oak Street and Taylor Road. The "High Hand" label, depicting a hand holding four aces, is a registered trademark owned by the LFGA since 1926.

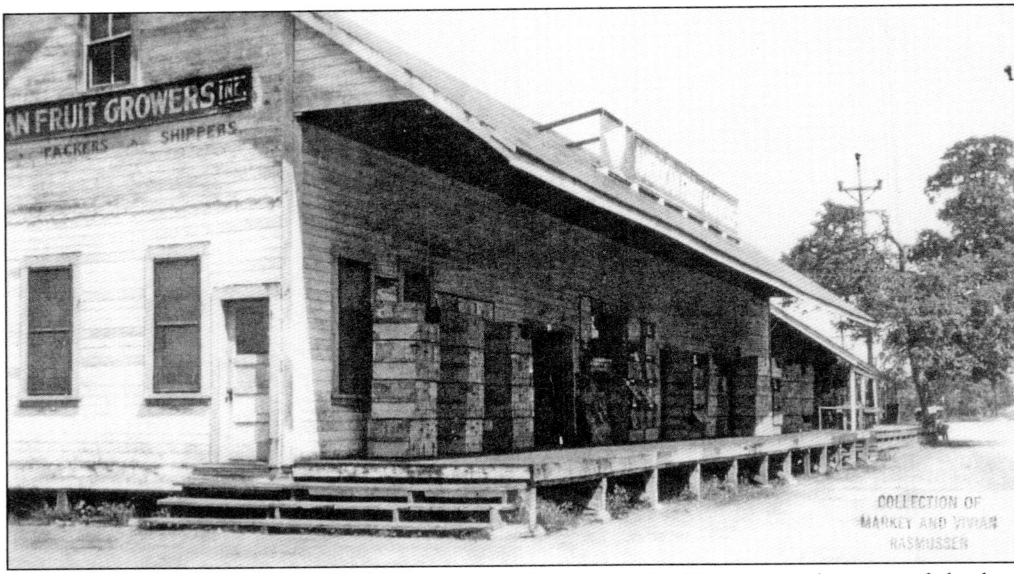

The American Fruit Growers building was also known as the Blue Goose because of the logo on the fruit labels. In 1920, the American Fruit Growers bought out a fruit company owned by H. M. Branstetter.

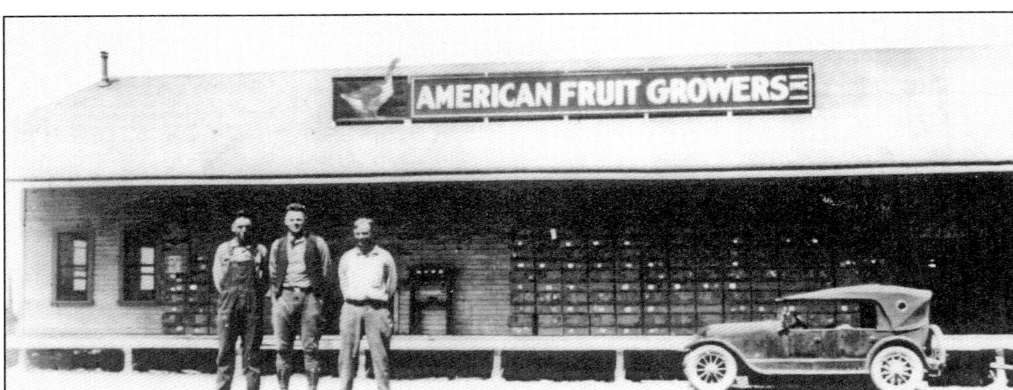

This 1923 picture of the American Fruit Growers, Inc., shows, from left to right, Bill Ramsey, manager Harold Leak, and Fenn Laird. From 1940 to his death in 1950, Porter Lee Taylor was manager of the American. (Courtesy of the Harold and Kate Leak collection.)

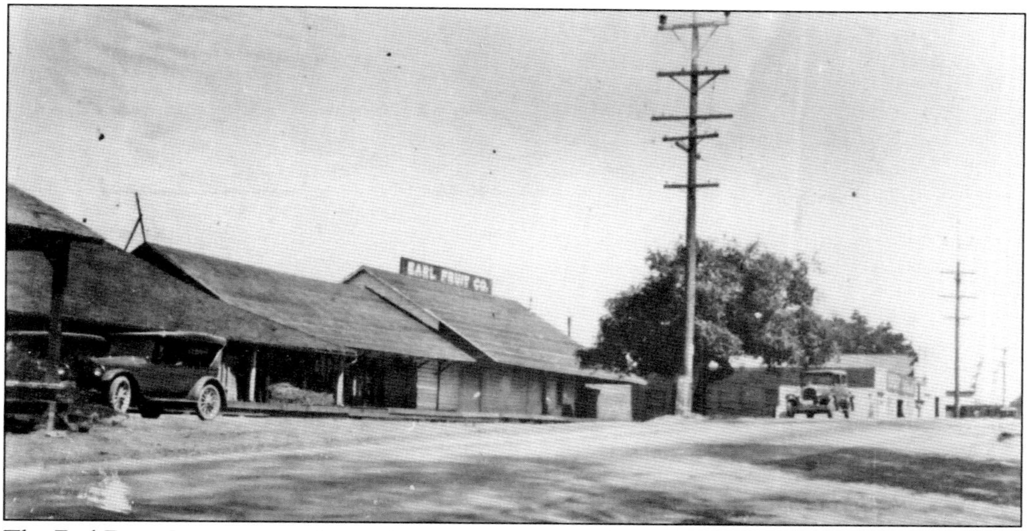

The Earl Fruit Company was located near Loomis Fruit Growers, closer to Walnut Street. A. D. Poggetto was manager. In 1934, Poggetto was named manager of California Peach Growers. The Earl Fruit Company, which had been shipping fruit out of Loomis since the 1890s, closed its doors for business as of January 1, 1957.

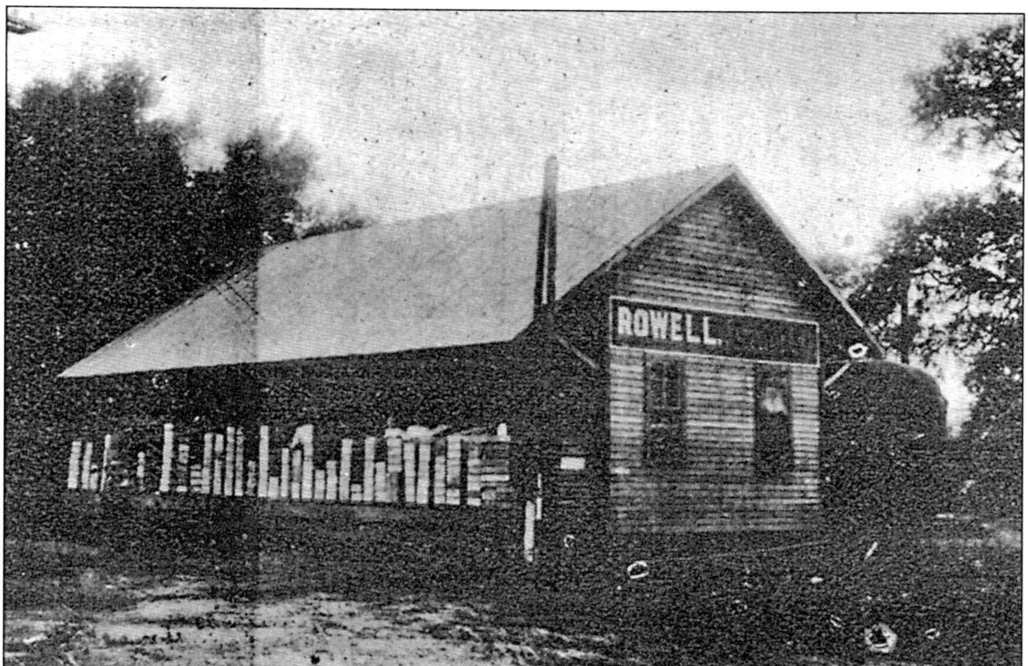

The Rowell Fruit Company was, according to the 1913 *Loomis Recorder*, formerly the Rowell and Day Fruit Company. H. M. Branstetter and his son purchased it in 1915. Lee Tudsbury, F. I. Otto, and C. G. Brainerd were on the board of directors. George F. Rowell was president and manager. The business was entirely express shipping. Rowell was an authority on the strawberry industry and shipped thousands of crates of the fruit each season. The shed was located at the north end of town.

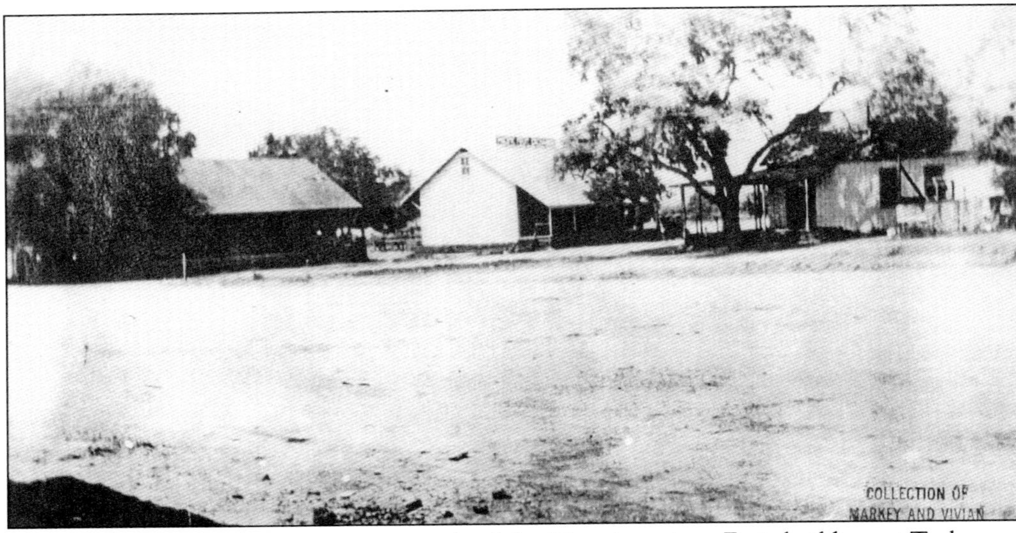

The Pacific Fruit Exchange was just north of the First American Fruit building at Taylor and Webb Streets in the early 1900s. The Gerard Company was the next owner of the building and used it to store the wood, called shook, that was used to make fruit boxes. In 1946, just after a huge shipment of wood had been delivered, the building burned to the ground. The shed was rebuilt and operated until the early 1960s.

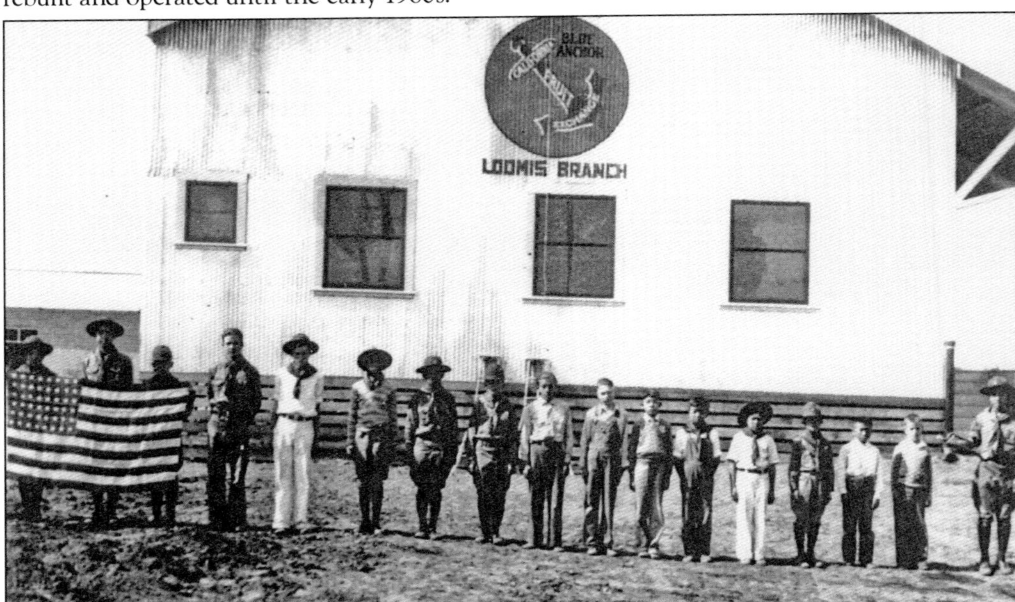

Blue Anchor Fruit Shed is pictured in the 1930s with Loomis Boys Scout Troop 12. This shed was near the intersection of Taylor Road and Horseshoe Bar Road, between Taylor and the railroad tracks. In 1960, Harold Struble was manager of the Loomis Blue Anchor Agency. The pear crop that year was the largest ever shipped. The April 1931 issue of the *Blue Anchor*, the California Fruit Exchange magazine, stated, "Construction work is well underway on a new Exchange packing house in Loomis. Beginning in July 1936, all Blue Anchor grade of fruit handled in the district will go out under the Blue Anchor X brand label, which was designed in 1935."

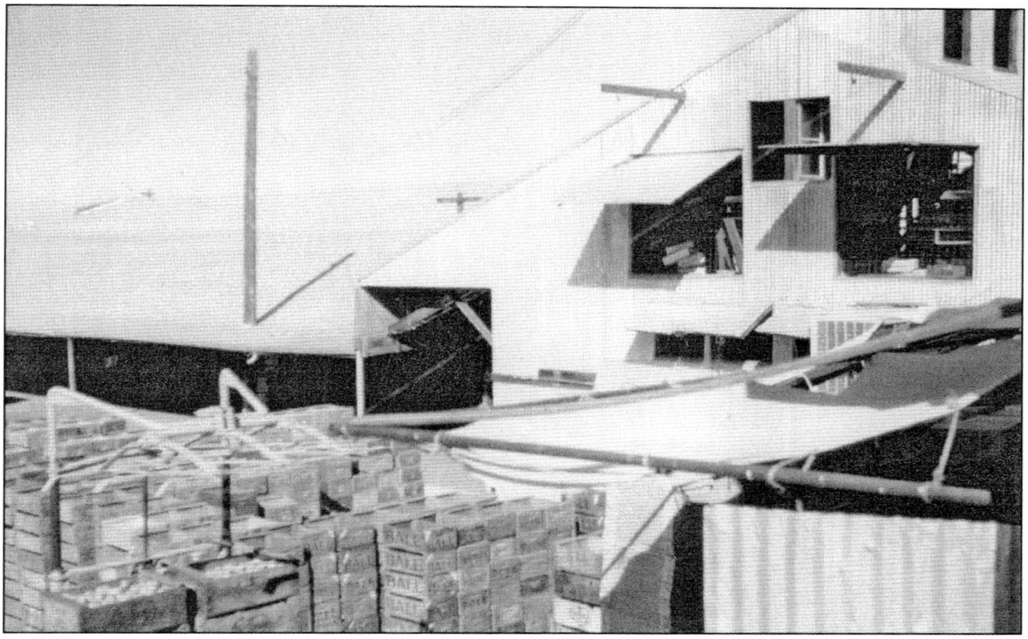

Lug boxes of pears are stacked at Blue Anchor Fruit Shed. The California Fruit Exchange, incorporated May 1, 1901, stated that this would be a cooperative nonprofit organization of growers of California deciduous fruits. It was the largest cooperative on the Pacific coast owned and operated by growers handling deciduous fruits. James J. Brennan was president and J. L. Nagle was general manager.

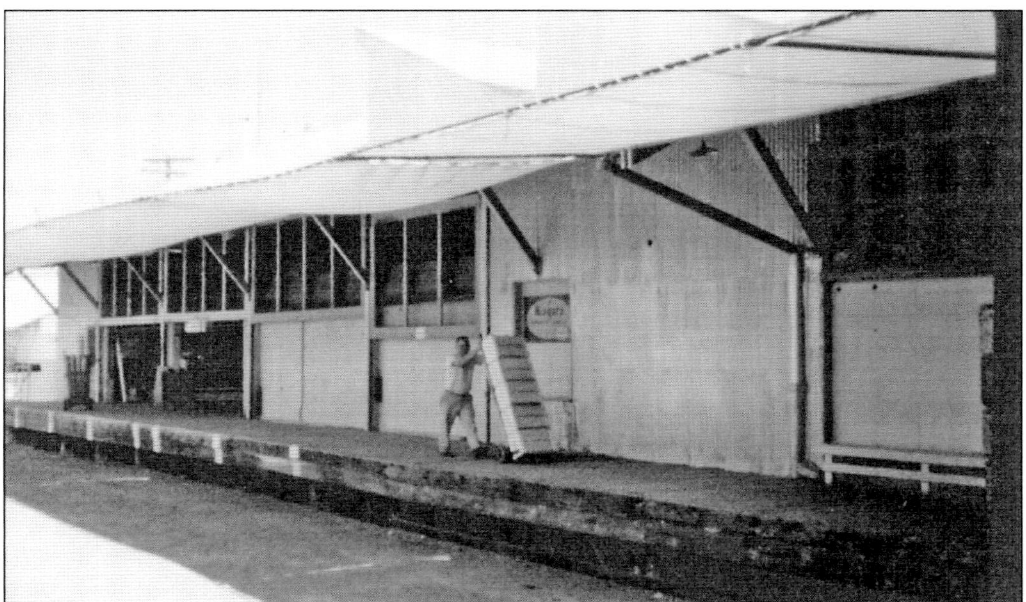

This worker is using a fruit truck, similar to a hand truck, to move stacks of packed pear boxes down the loading dock at the Blue Anchor Shed. This shed burned in September 2002.

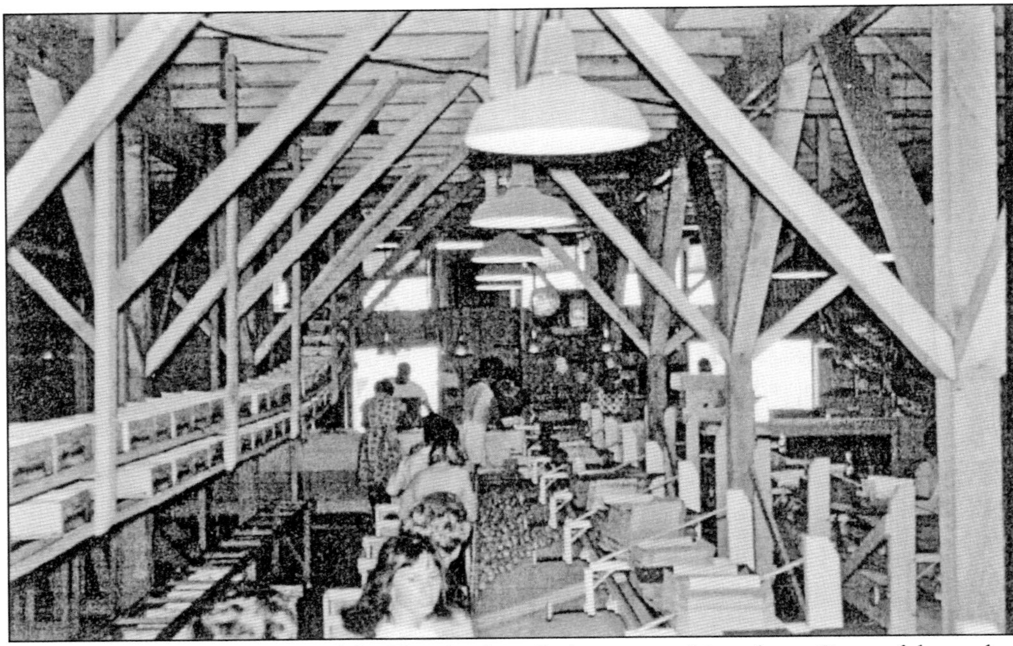

This is the crate packing area of the Blue Anchor. Packers are packing plums. Some of the packers that worked for Blue Anchor are Belle Ferguson, Marie Roads, Francis Boisa, Bertie Nevarez, Josie Ramos Gamboa, and Susy Uyeda. Forty to fifty packers would work to get the fruit ready for market.

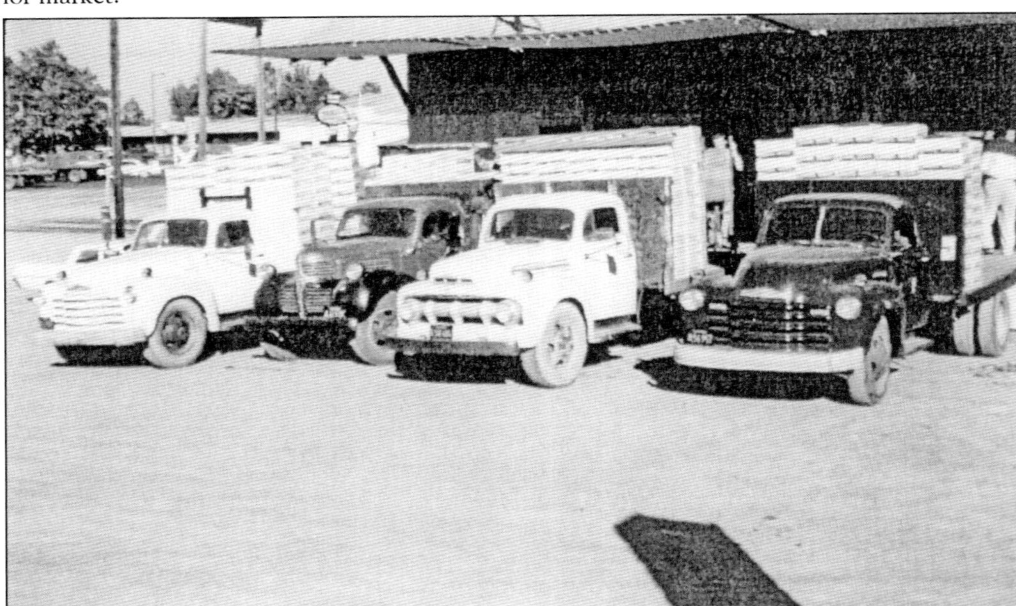

This was a typical nightly sight when the "ranch pack" trucks would deliver their packed crates to the shed. These crates were packed at sheds on the ranches and delivered to the main fruit shed for shipment to markets. Most of the fruit was ultimately loaded into railroad cars and shipped east. On a busy day, ranch pack trucks would have to wait in line for almost an hour until the trucks at the dock were unloaded. All these trucks were unloaded by hand.

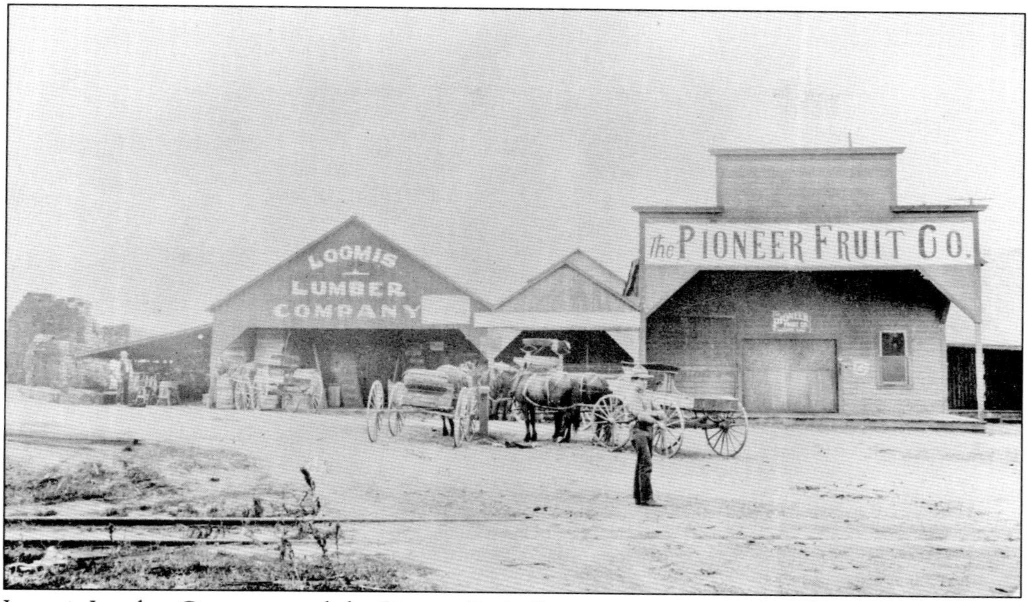

Loomis Lumber Company and the Pioneer Fruit Company are pictured in the early 1900s. The Pioneer was one of the oldest fruit buildings. It was operating in 1908. For a time, the American Fruit Company used the building. Later the California Fruit Exchange used it for storage and to pack plums. It has always been at the same site and was incorporated into the Blue Anchor building.

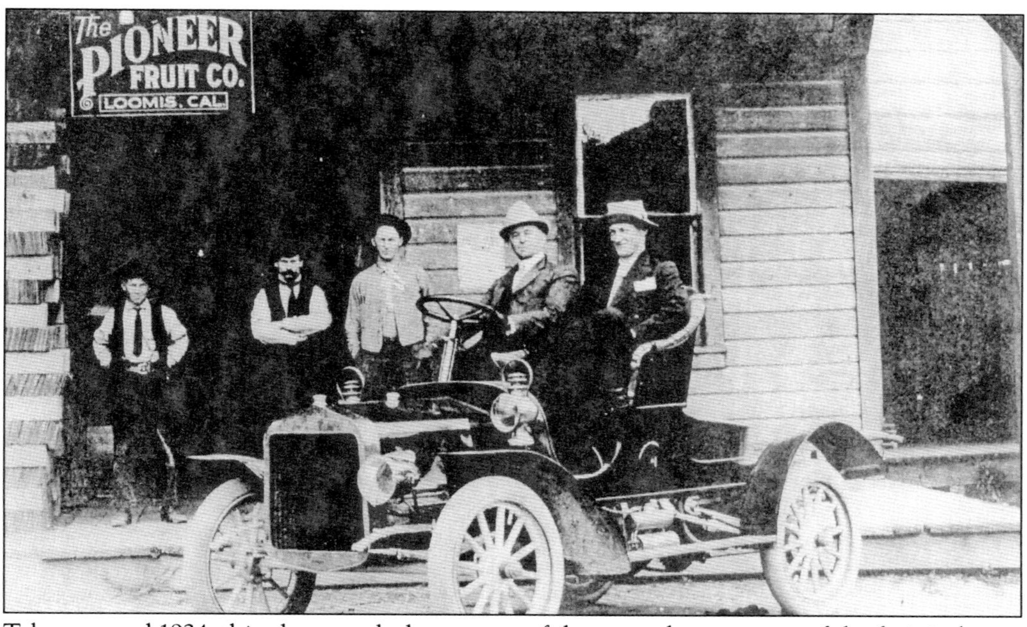

Taken around 1924, this photograph shows some of the men who were part of the fruit industry. William Holder Tudsbury is driving the car. The men on the left are standing next to stacks of shook. Shook was the name given to the lumber pieces used to make packing crates.

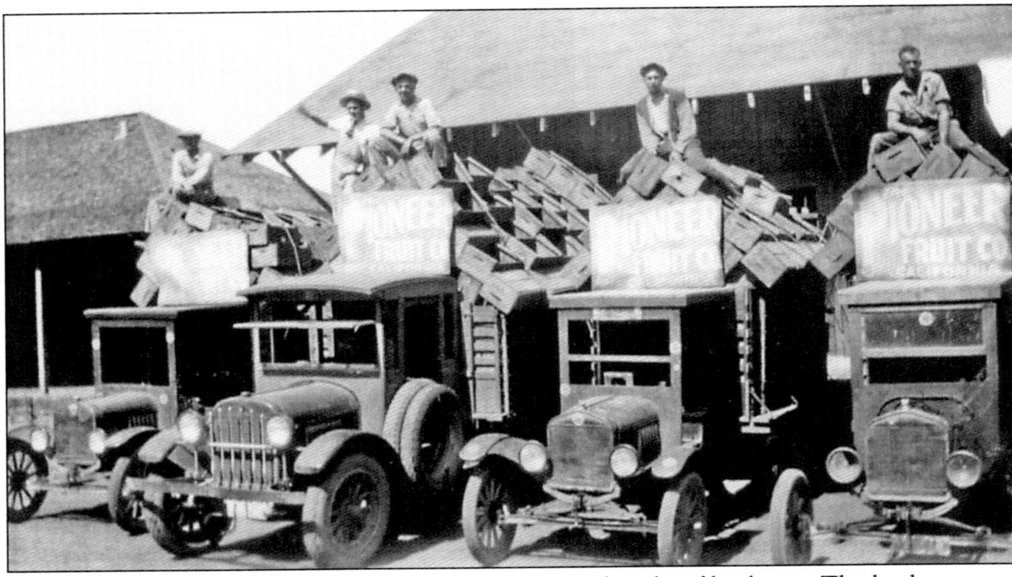

Workers for the Pioneer Fruit Company sitting on top of stacks of lug boxes. The lug boxes were used on the ranches to hold the fruit when it was picked off the trees. These boxes were brought to the sheds. Only empty boxes were stacked in this fashion.

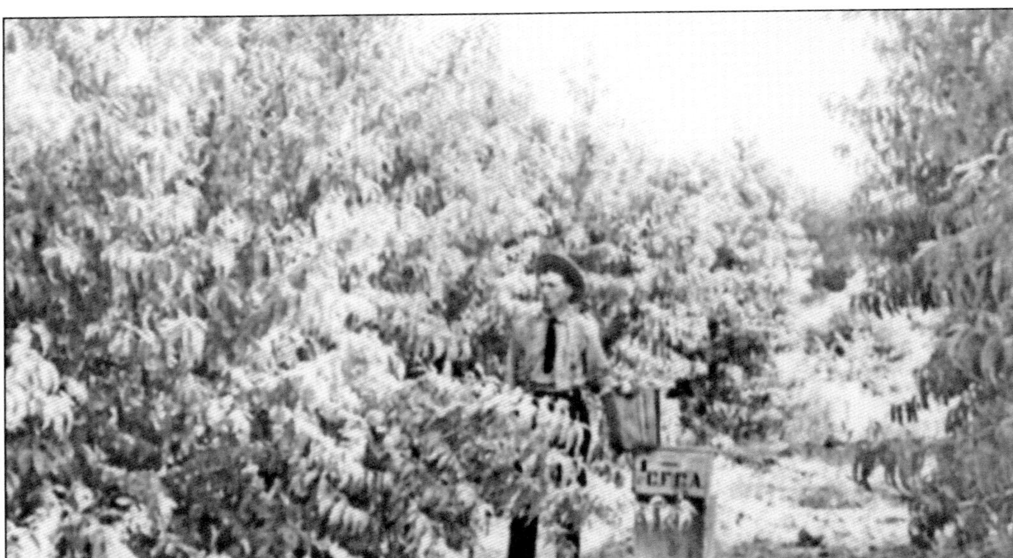

Porter Lee Taylor stands in one of his fruit orchards. He came to California from Slickrock, Kentucky, and was an active fruit grower. When he died in 1950, he had been the general manager of the American Fruit Growers, Inc. (Blue Goose), for 10 years. He owned Moonshine and Home ranches. He and his brothers owned many more ranches in the area.

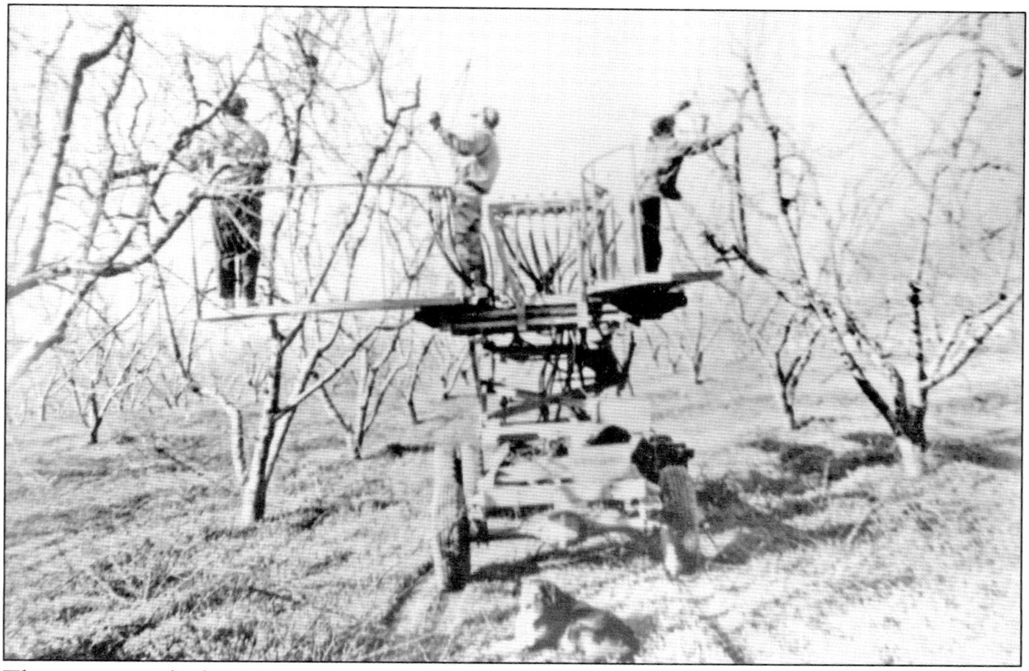

This pruning platform was hand-built by Frank Poirier to work among his peach trees. Frank Poirier owned Will-Glen orchard east of Loomis. He came to the area with his family in 1949. He planted 6 acres of Owari Satsuma mandarins. His trees produced about three-and-a-half 25-pound boxes each. Poirier also raised many varieties of peaches.

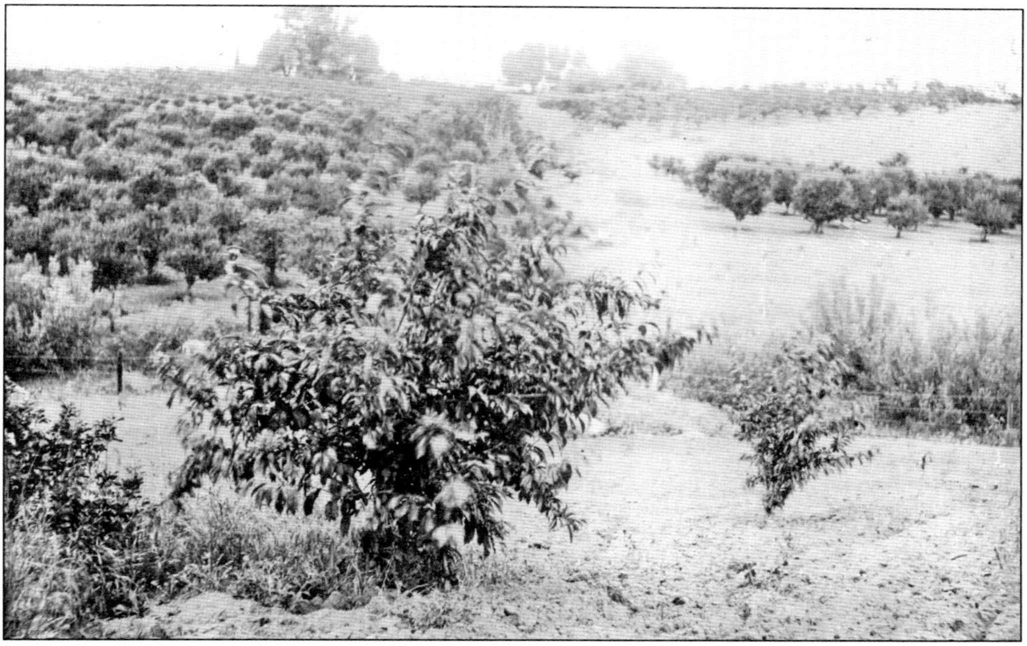

This fruit orchard is fairly typical of the method most widely used to plant. Trees were generally organized and planted by type of fruit, such as peach, pear, or plum, and then by specific variety.

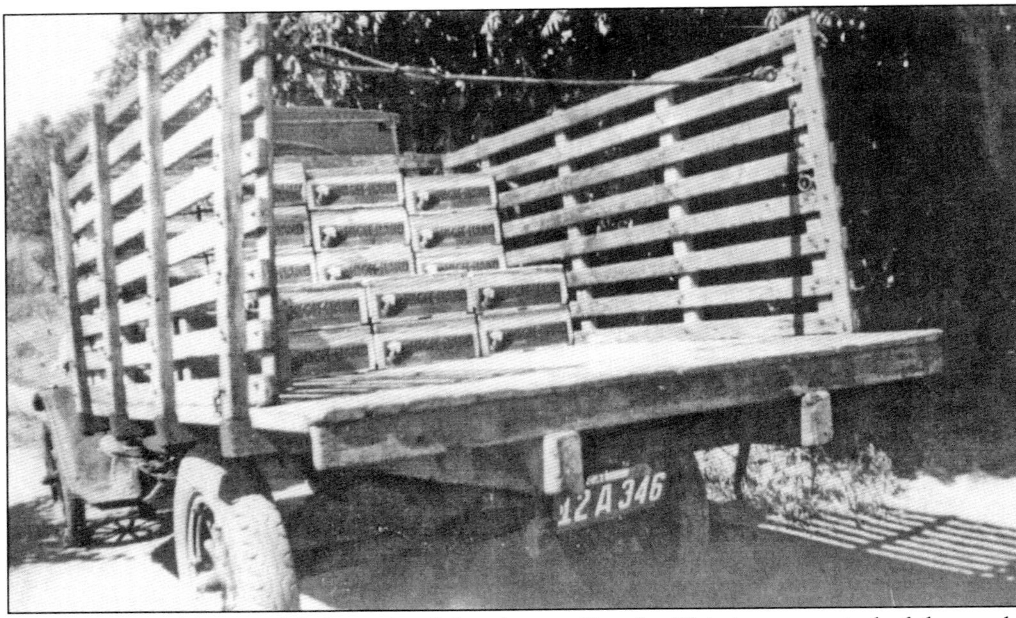

This 1920s Model T truck belonged to John August Sippola. This is very typical of the trucks that delivered "ranch packs" to the shed for shipment east.

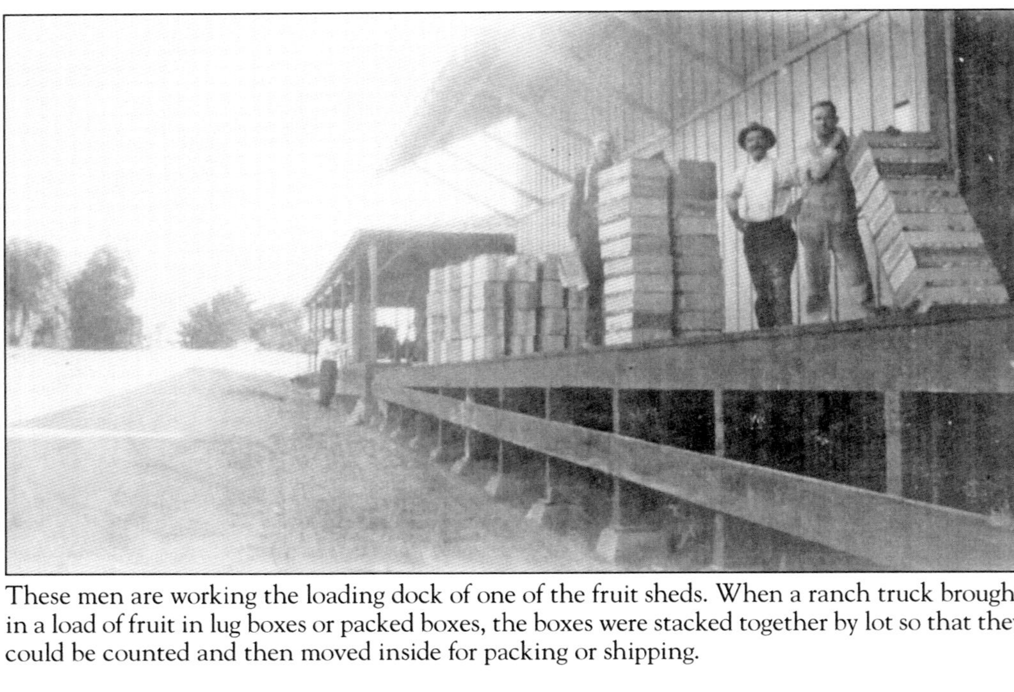

These men are working the loading dock of one of the fruit sheds. When a ranch truck brought in a load of fruit in lug boxes or packed boxes, the boxes were stacked together by lot so that they could be counted and then moved inside for packing or shipping.

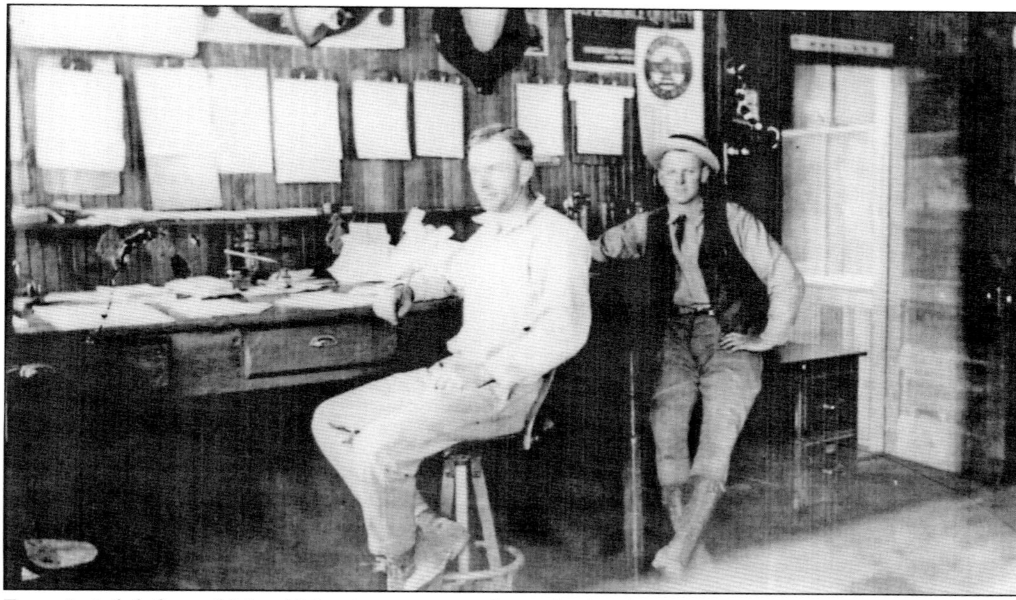

Fenn Laird, left, and Harold Leak are pictured inside the American Fruit Growers office in the early 1920s. The American Fruit Company was sometimes called the American National Growers Corporation, the American Fruit Growers, and the Blue Goose. Frank Nute was the manager of the shed in the late 1950s and early 1960s. This shed is still in existence as a community center, farmers market, and store.

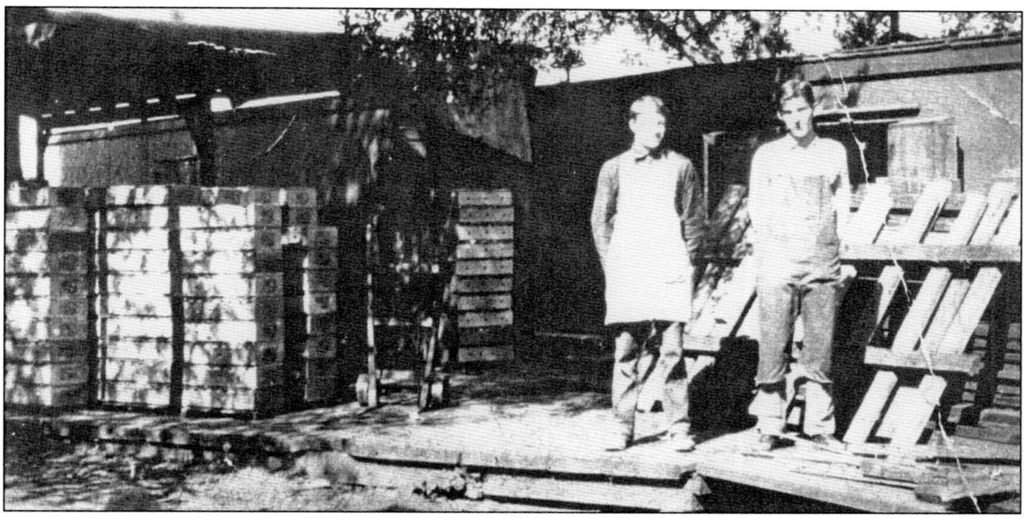

Earl Howard and Lee Tudsbury are pictured as what is probably the High Hand Fruit Shed. Lee Tudsbury, born October 16, 1888, became president of the Loomis Fruit Growers Association. He retired in 1957 and died in 1965. The association incorporated in 1901. E. L. Rippey was the manager of the shed. He was a rancher, and his extensive knowledge of the business helped build the organization. He successfully increased the number of fruit cars shipped every year. According to the January 27, 1911, *Loomis Recorder*, the officers of the exchange were president W. H. Tudsbury, vice president L. J. Kinney, secretary R. M. Nixon, and manager E. L. Rippey. The board of directors was W. H. Tudsbury, Neils Jensen, J. A. Ferguson, L. J. Kinney, and R. M. Nixon.

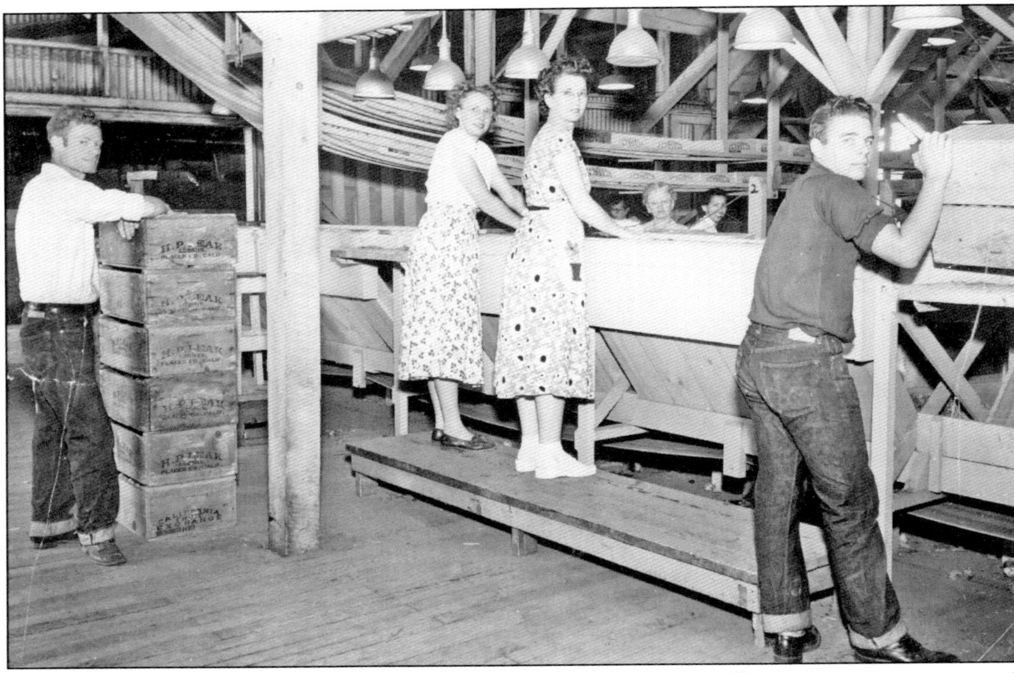

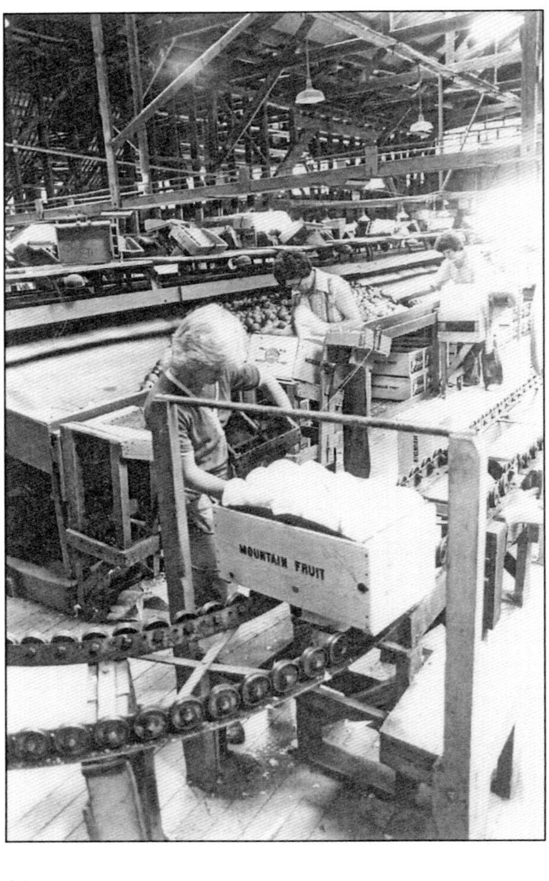

Generations of Loomis men, women, and teenagers were part of the work force that made the Loomis fruit shed run smoothly. This 1951 photograph was taken at the Blue Anchor Shed and shows George Coleman (left), an unidentified woman, Alma Wever, and Gerry Brashen. In the back are Belle Ferguson and Josie Brosia. Boxes of fruit are being brought to the sorting area prior to going to the packers.

Liz Montero packs pears at the Loomis Fruit Growers. The woman in front is stamping the packed pear box with the lot number (grower), type of fruit, and size of the pack.

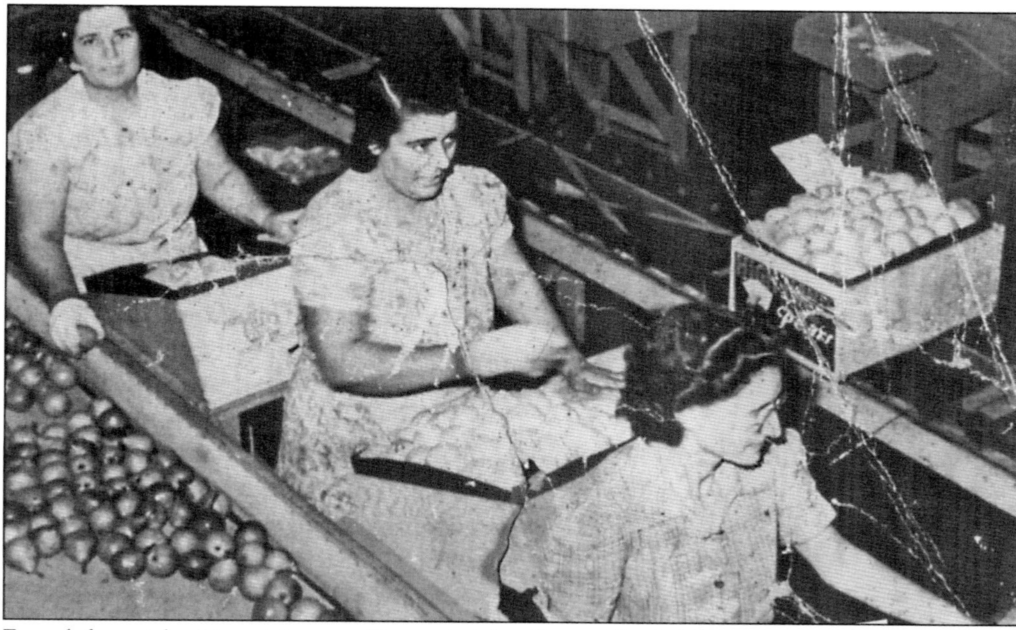

From left to right, Mary Montero, Presentia Morallis, and little Mary Montero pack pears at the High Hand (Loomis Fruit Growers).

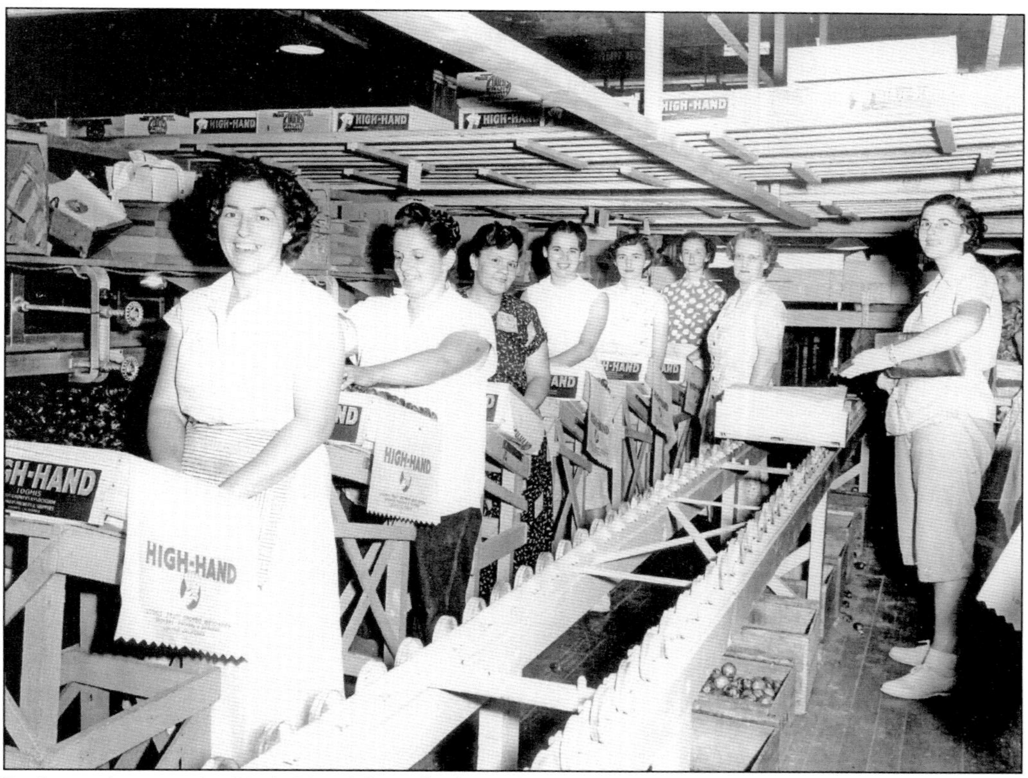

Packing plums at the High Hand fruit shed are, from front to back, Josie Sanchez Boisa, Delores ?, Mary ?, Bonnie Cliff, Alice Rippey, Janet Cook, and Dorothy Cook.

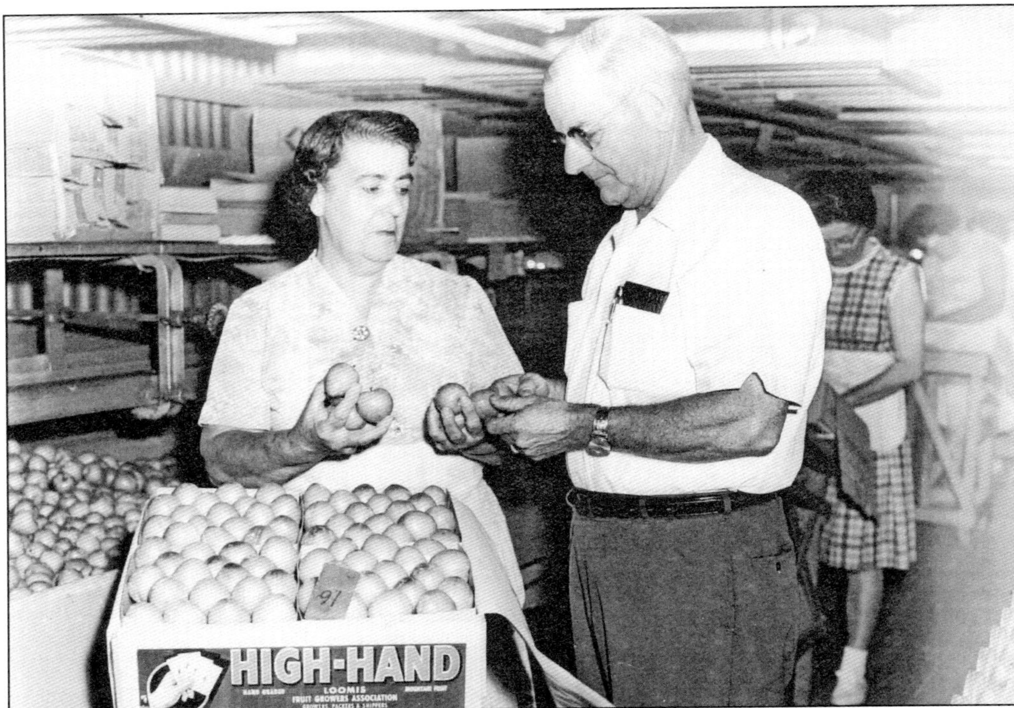

Packer Presentia Morillas and manager Harvey Carlisle check a finished four-by-five box of beauty plums. The four-by-five indicates the box contains five rows of four plums each. The small card over the second H in "High" indicates the packer number. The cards were used to keep track of the number of crates that packers finished so that they could be paid for their work. The photograph is from 1967.

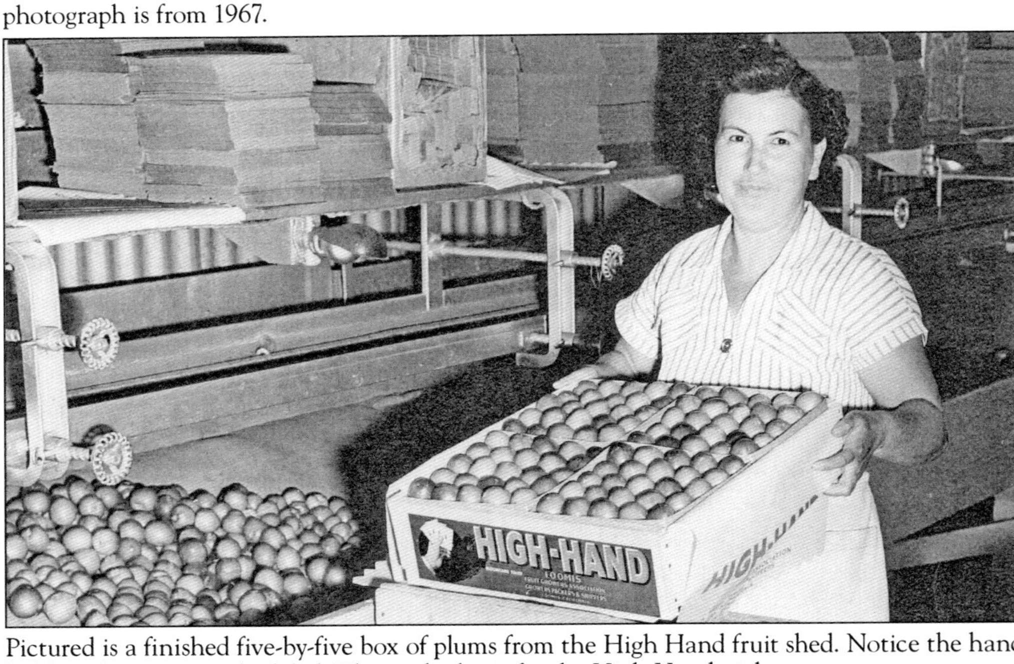

Pictured is a finished five-by-five box of plums from the High Hand fruit shed. Notice the hand holding four aces on the label. This is the basis for the High Hand nickname.

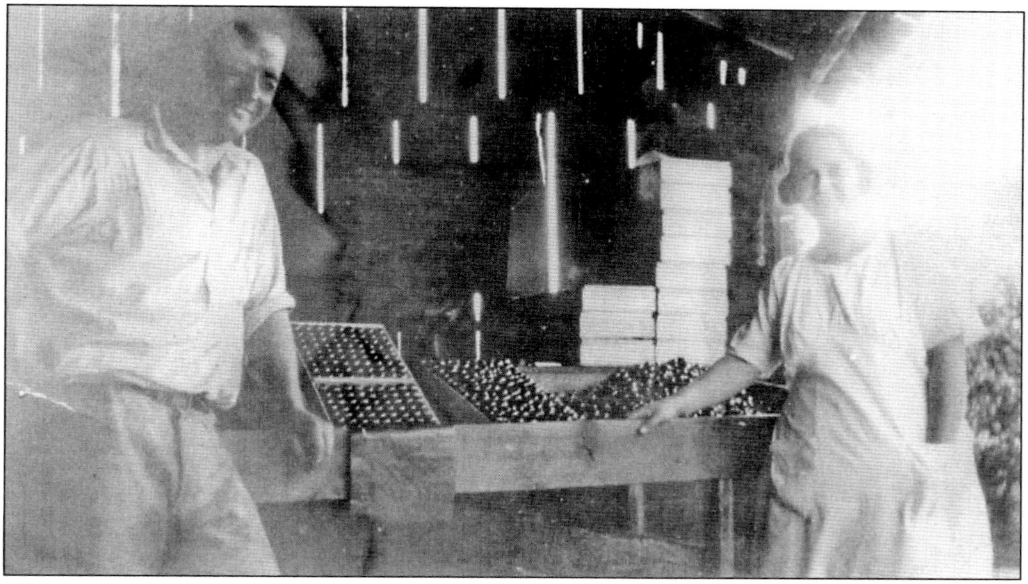

Al Larsen and Gladys Shelton check a packed box of cherries at the Loomis Fruit Growers.

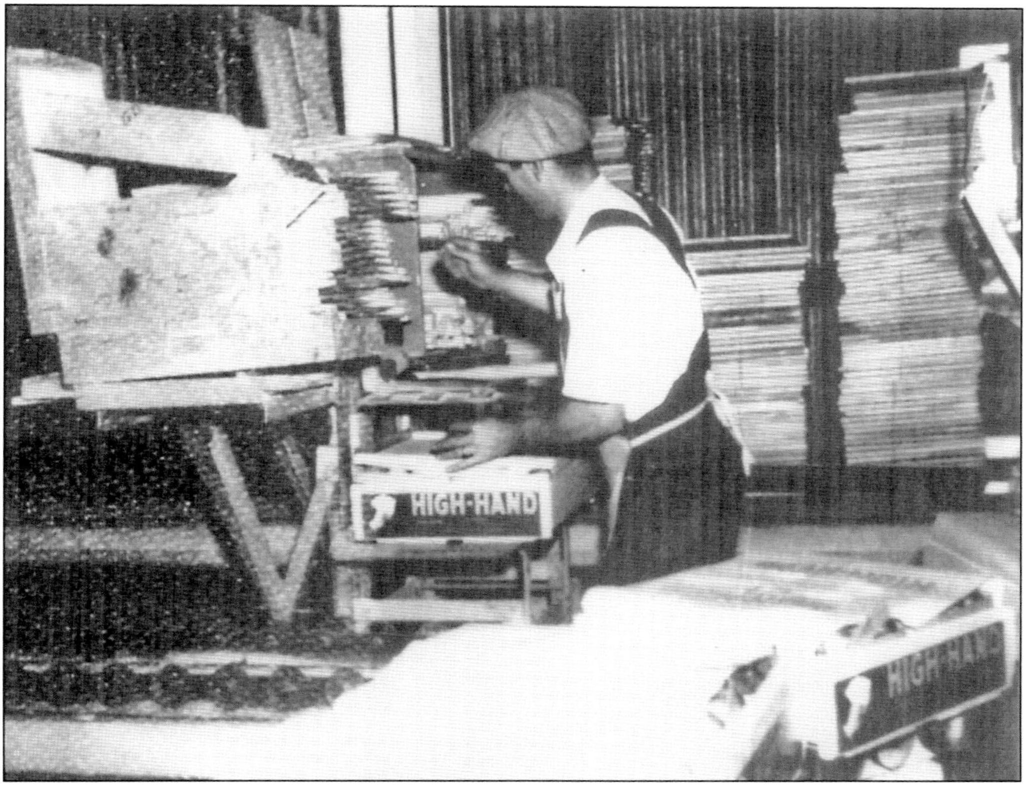

The worker is making a lid for the backed fruit box. In the foreground are many finished crates on the conveyor belt used to bring the boxes from the packers to the lidding area. The stacks of thin lumber in the back right are the lids. Each box had to be lidded and nailed closed. Each box or crate was made individually.

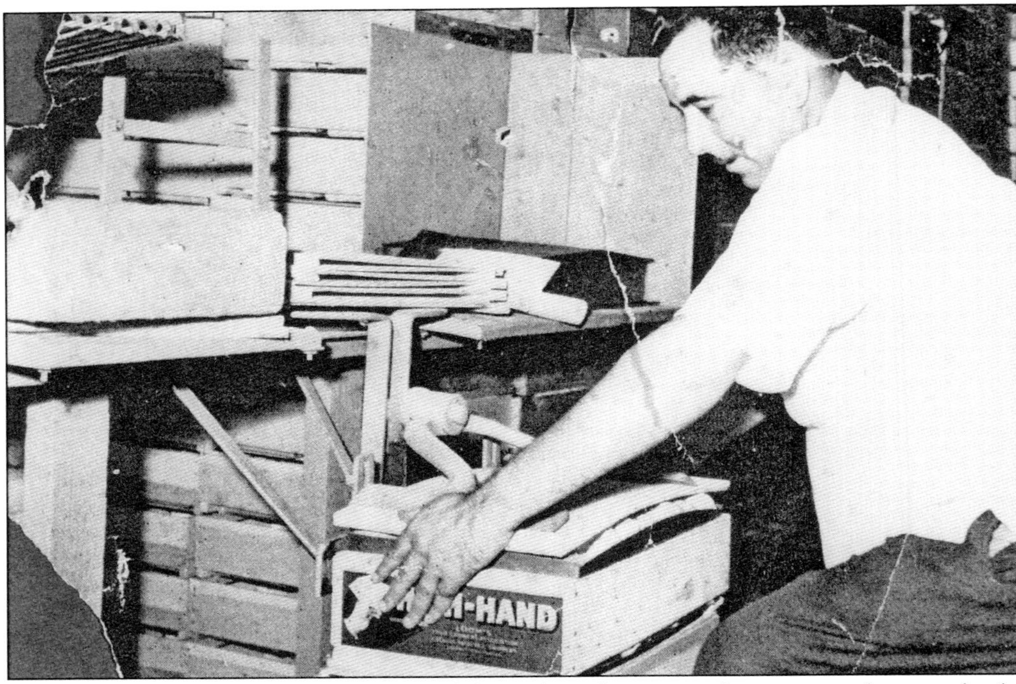

Although this is another generation much later than the one in the previous photograph, the method of lidding boxes is the same.

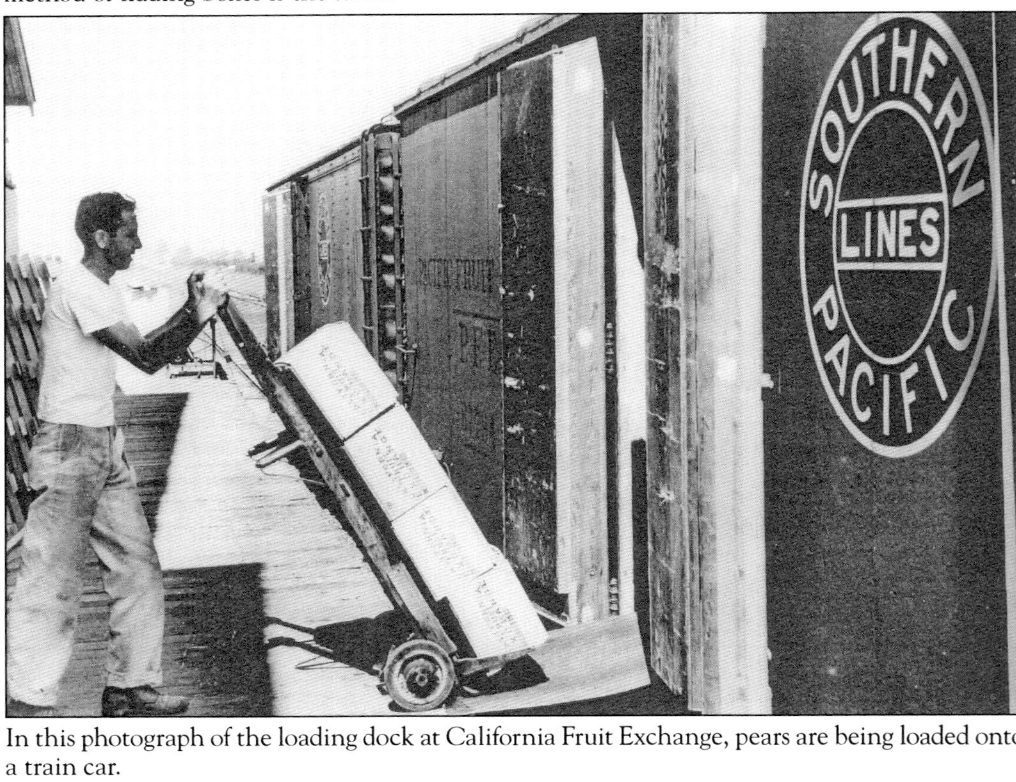

In this photograph of the loading dock at California Fruit Exchange, pears are being loaded onto a train car.

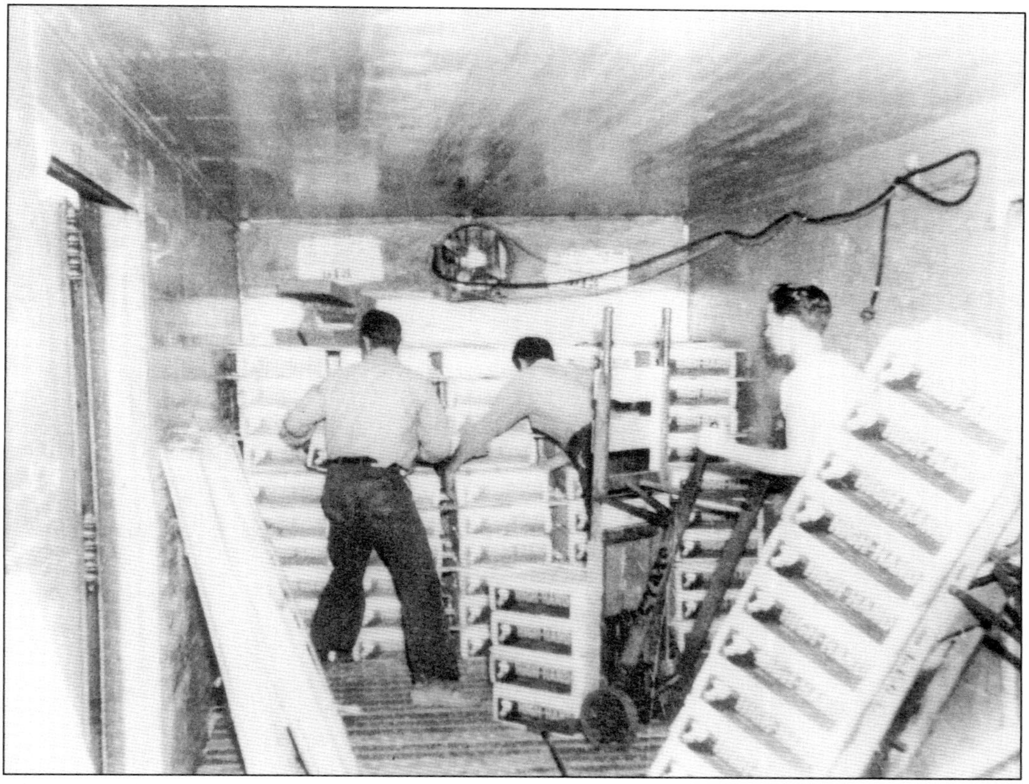

Three men from High Hand load a train car with packed boxes of plums prior to being shipped to eastern markets.

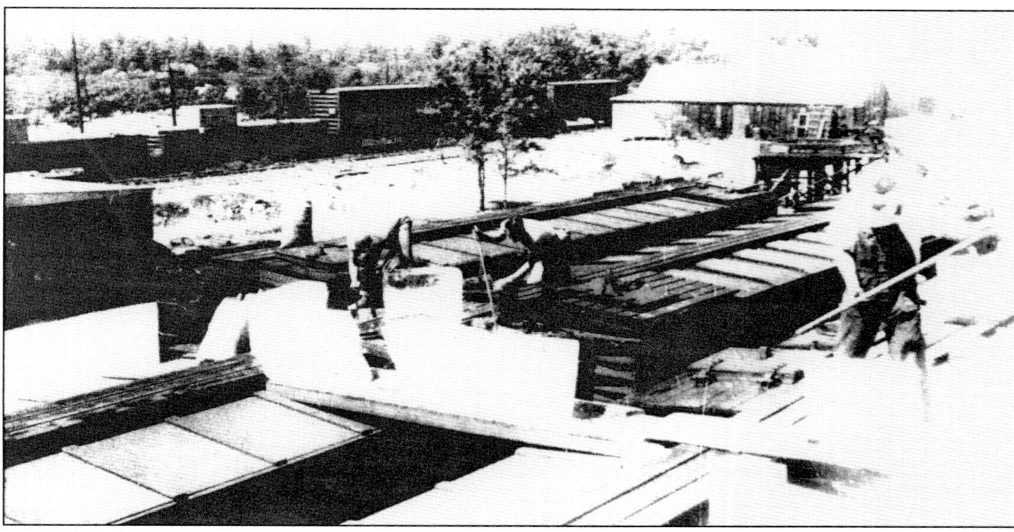

Large blocks of ice are loaded into train cars with special chutes and specially hooked poles so that the fruit will stay cool on the long journey to eastern markets. The main railroad line is in the background. Spur tracks ran behind most of the fruit sheds.

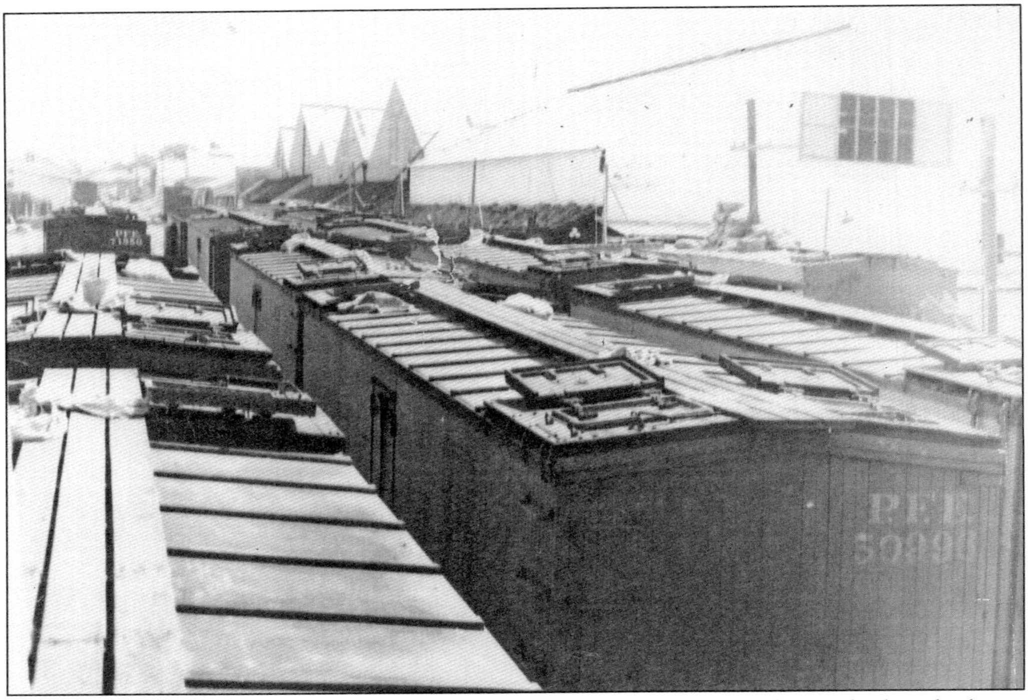

On this day in the early 1940s, thirteen railcars were loaded. The rooflines of other sheds are visible at the top of the picture. This is the typical view behind the sheds on a given workday.

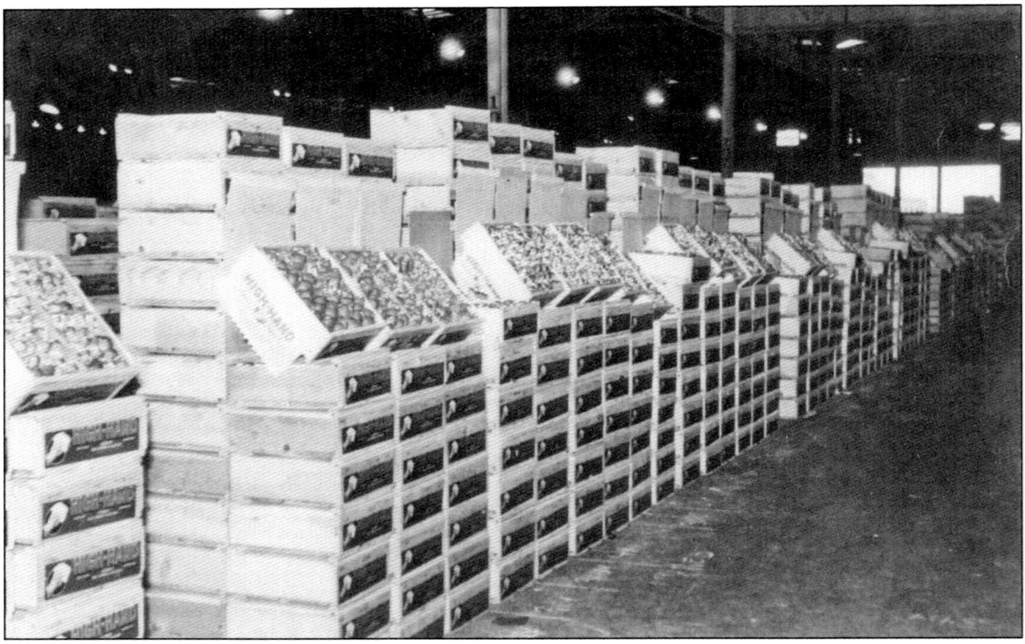

High Hand packed plum crates are pictured at the New York Fruit Auction in 1930. The prices received here are what helped to decide the fate of the sheds and the farmers. As the years progressed, the costs to get the fruit picked, packed, shipped, and to auction increased. Frequently the profit equated to only cents per box.

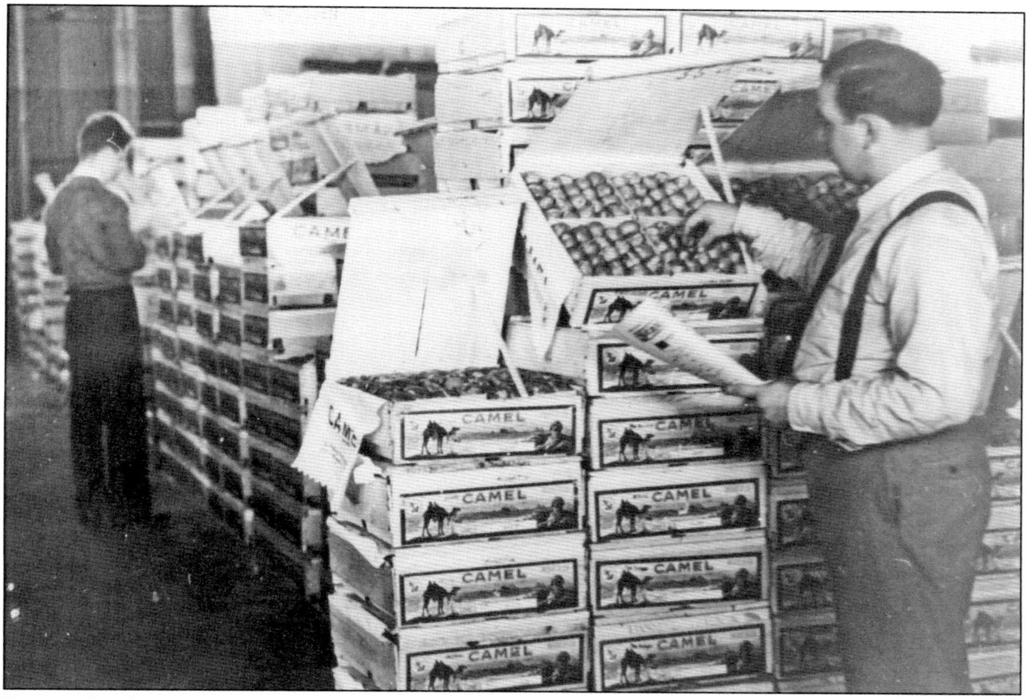

Buyers check Camel Brand plums from the California Fruit Exchange at the New York market.

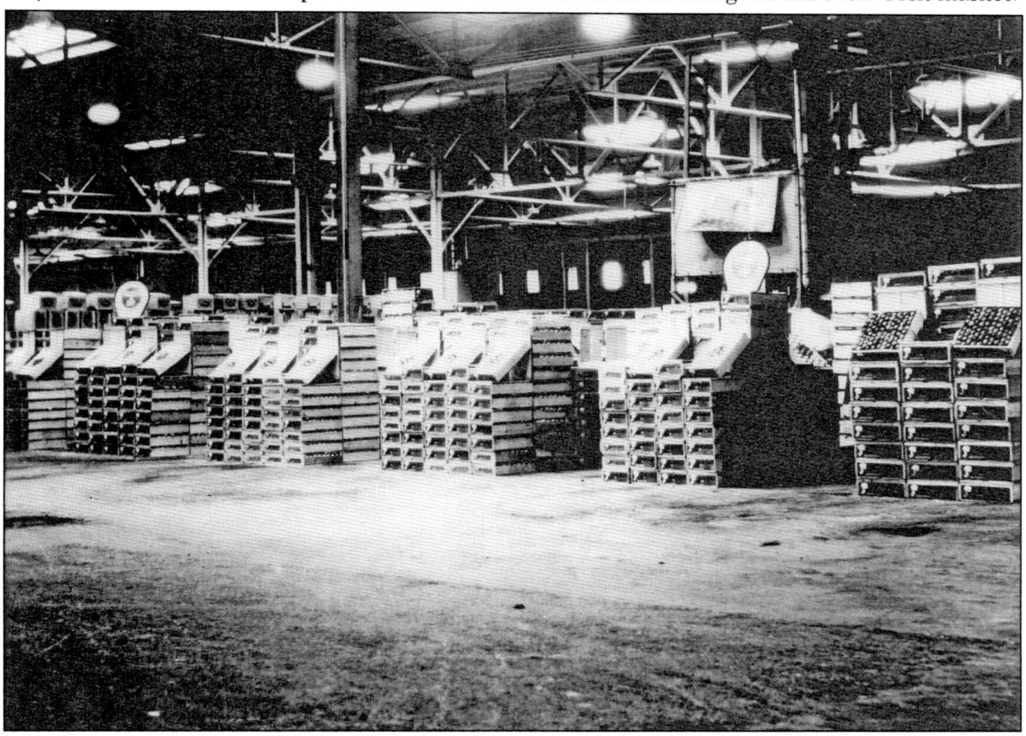
Another view shows High Hand fruit in the warehouse back east. These are probably peaches, as the fragile fruit is wrapped in very thin tissue paper to help protect it.

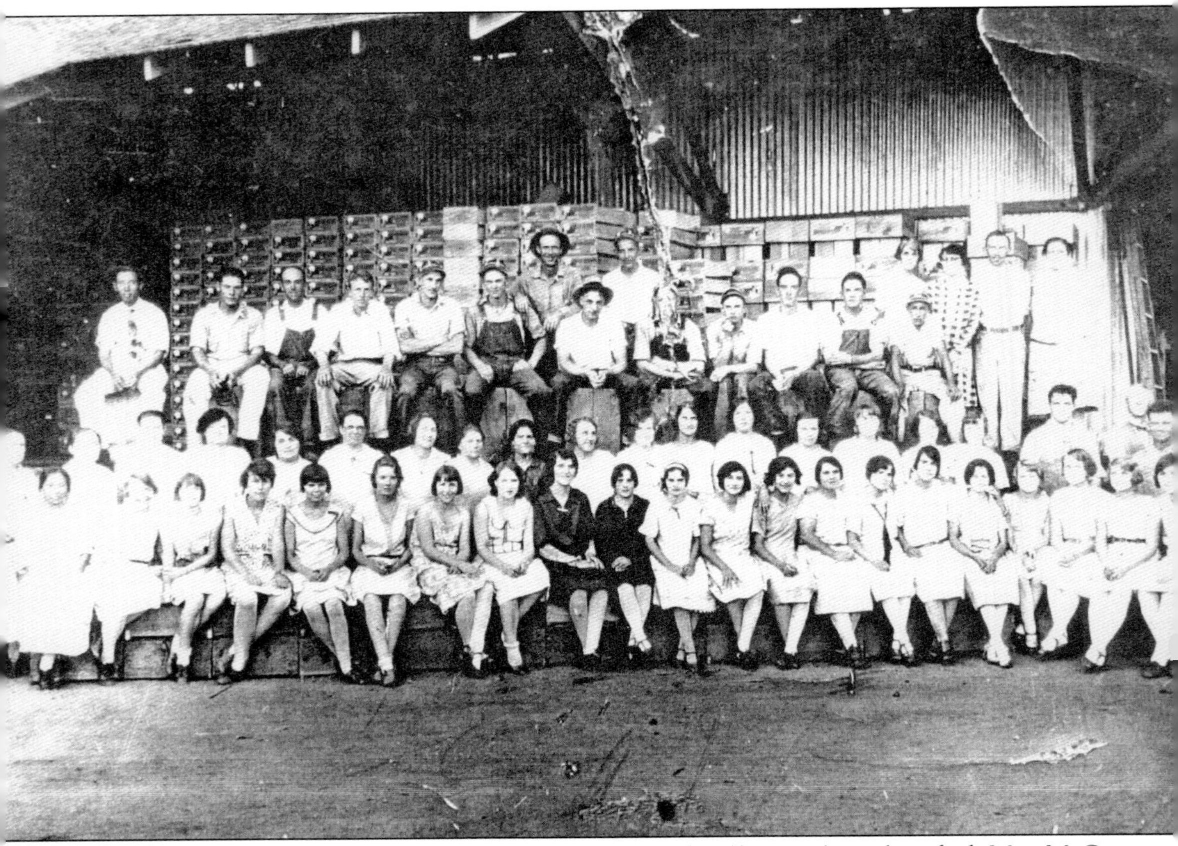

Employees of the LFGA in 1928 are, from left to right, (first row) unidentified, Mrs. McCoy, unidentified, Madeline Hones, Ethel McCann, Inona Taylor, two unidentified, Constance Rodrigues, Mamie Lozano, Josie Gill, Laura Morales Garcia, Annie Moon Basque, Mary Garcia Montero, Catherine Basque Montero, Presentia Basque Morillas, Mary Montero Lankford, Elsa Hartikka, Sima Hartikka, Mamie Hartikka Cook and Flora Woodworth Eastman; (second row) Remedios Munoz Arias, Nellie Boller, Ina Vance, an unidentified Roseville woman, Effie Barnes, Mrs. Gale, unidentified, Annie Moon, Tini Wallen, Esther ?, Helen Taylor, Ollie (Mrs. Frank) Johnson, Evelyn Jensen Mehl, Margaret Leak Rasmussen, Doris Day Barkhaus, Dorse Hite, an unidentified school teacher from out of town, and Frank Johnson; (third row) unidentified, Joe DeFuentes, Charles Woodworth, Barton Smyth, an unidentified Roseville boy, Owen ?, unidentified, Albert Pilliard, Park Wilson, Jack Brainerd, Tony Garcia (in overalls), and Donald Dunton Jr.; (fourth row) (starting in middle) Clarence Mehl, Edmond Rippey, Mamie Silva, Mable Dunton, Howard Lusk and floor lady Mrs. Allen.

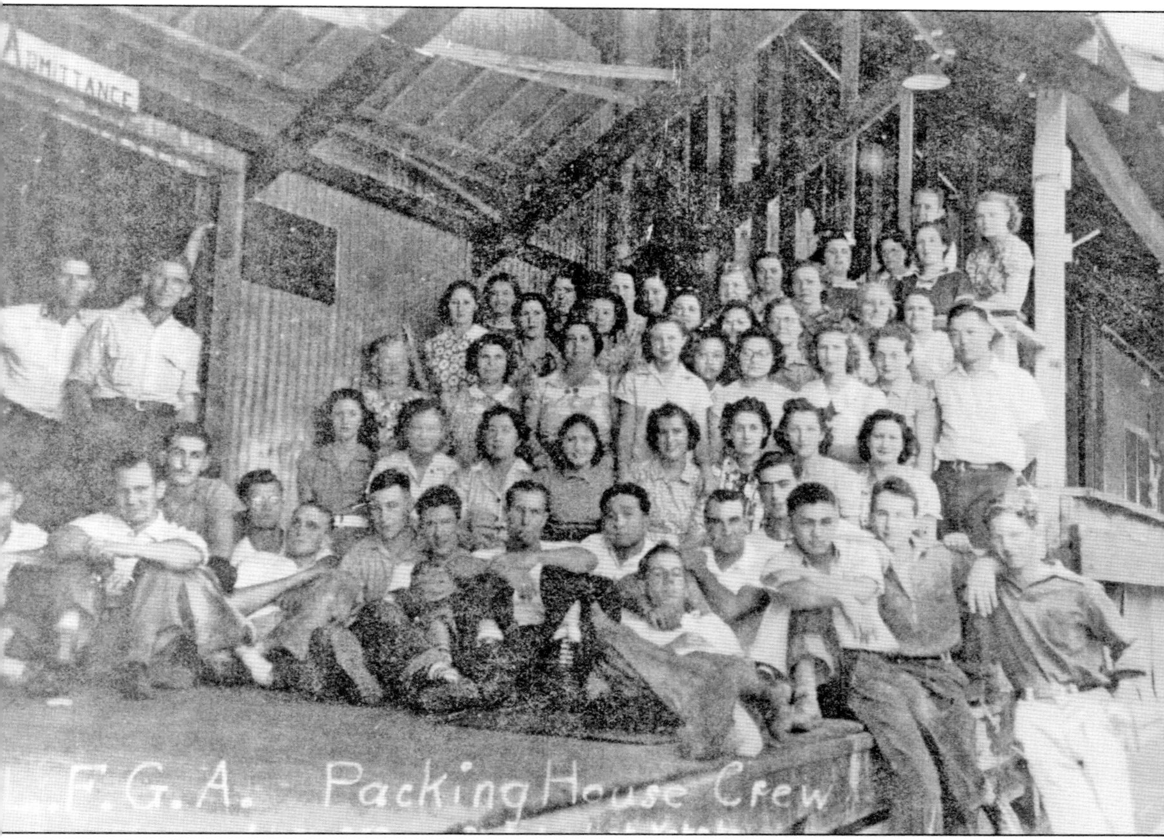

Pictured is the 1939 work crew at the LFGA. The men in the doorway are Tony Morales, left, and Earl Howard. The others are, from left to right, (first row) Jack Ogden, Ed Arndt, Sal Garcia (with moustache), Frank Vail (with glasses), Bill Vail, unidentified, Jim Howard, John Montero, Joaquin Gaylado, Shigeo Yokote, Jack Stacker, Frank Montero (toward the front), Manuel Blanco, Aster Kondo, Frank Ogden and Morgan Marsh; (second row) Ann Morales Garcia, Flora Terada Takahashi, Mitsuye Uyeda, Rose Morales Day, Arliss Dolce, Carman Perez, Delores Morillas Wagner, and Josie Montero Viegos; (third row) Belle Ferguson, Carnation Lopez Montero, Mary Garcia Montero, Ann Aguilar, Elsie Kondo, Helen Nitta Horii, Connie Gaylado Accuri, Alice Wallen Park, and Hajime Mitsui; (fourth row) Isabel Morales Basque, Mary Perez Morales, Singer Terada Kuratomi, Katherine Basque Montero, Mary Nitta, Mina Dolce, Mrs. Tini Wallen, and Calendyne Ogden; (fifth row) Mary Aguilar Munoz, Presentia Basque Morillas, Fannie Stevens, unidentified, Carmen Rhodas, Elise Pilliard, Ollie Johnson, and Nora Willis Castro Martin; (sixth row) Tillie Basque Wilson, Mary (Little Mary) Montero Lankford, and Frances Lozano Gaylado; (seventh row) shook foreman Edmund Rippey and ticket and payroll collector Lois Hansen. The information is courtesy of Flora Takahashi, Rose Morales Day, Laura Morales Garcia, Dolores Navas, Harvey Carlisle, Edmund Rippey, and others. The photograph was taken by Jack Yokote for the *Loomis News*.

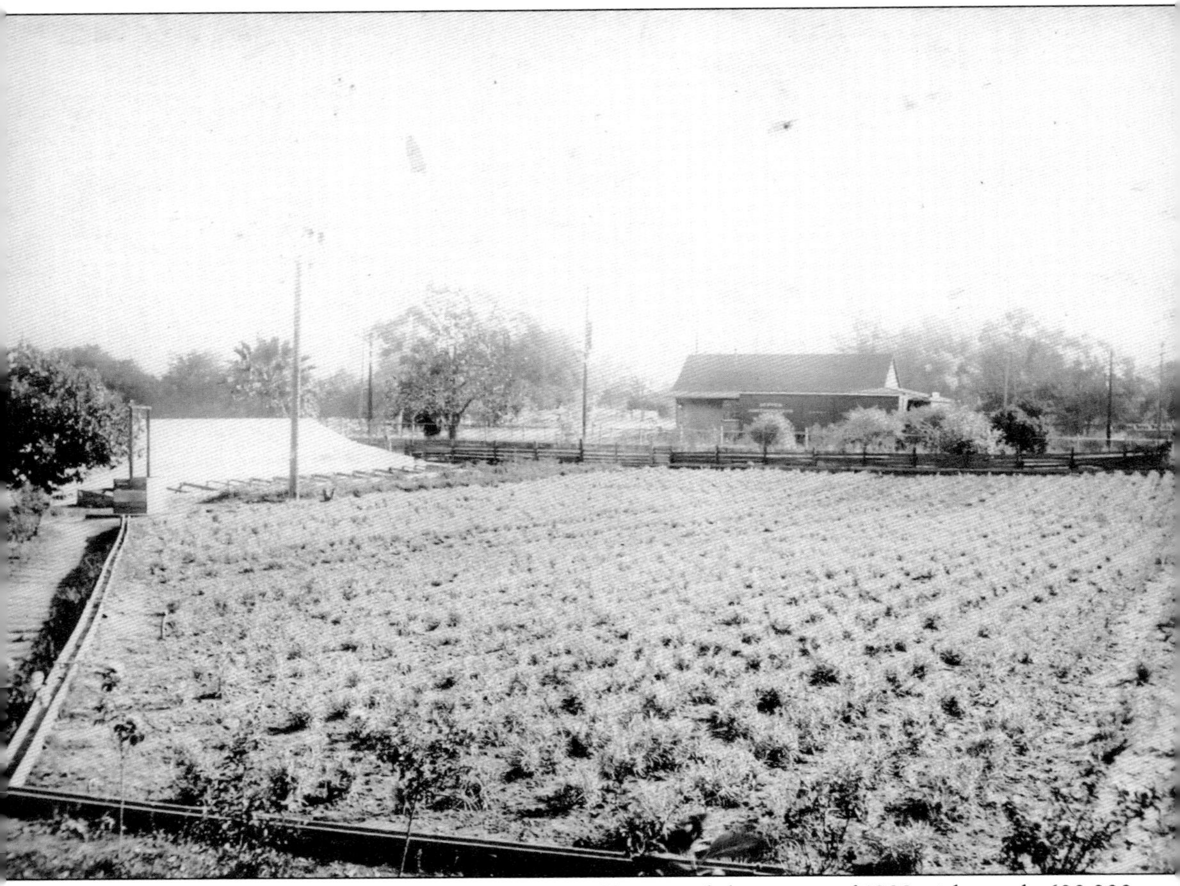

D. F. Roddan was a pioneer carnation grower. He started the winter of 1908 with nearly 600,000 carnation cuttings. About 10,000 of these were rooted for his individual retail trade. The remainder was shipped to florists in wholesale quantities. Roddan also had 5,000 to 6,000 roses in all the choice varieties and a fine collection of houseplants. His growing fields are directly across from the train depot, in the back of the photograph.

Three

Street Scenes and Businesses

The main streets of Loomis were near the railroad lines. Olive Street, which was later renamed Taylor Road, was the main street for businesses in the community. Horseshoe Bar Road, originally Pine Street, led into town from the ranches, homes, and Folsom Lake. Many of the buildings constructed after the fire are still in use today. The buildings have changed little from the time they rebuilt after the fire to today. They are still landmarks from generations past. The streets were originally named after trees—olive, pine, oak, walnut, and magnolia—Olive and Pine Streets changed, but the others are still there, as are many of the original homes. Now more of the roads and streets are named after families that settled the area. These include Laird, Taylor, Rippey, Rasmussen, Barnes, Callison, Bankhead, Swetzer, Hansen, Leak, Tudsbury, Suzuki, Brennan, King, and others. The photographs in this chapter show the change in the town as the years wore on. There is even evidence of one of the few years the area experienced snow. This is not a common sight at this elevation!

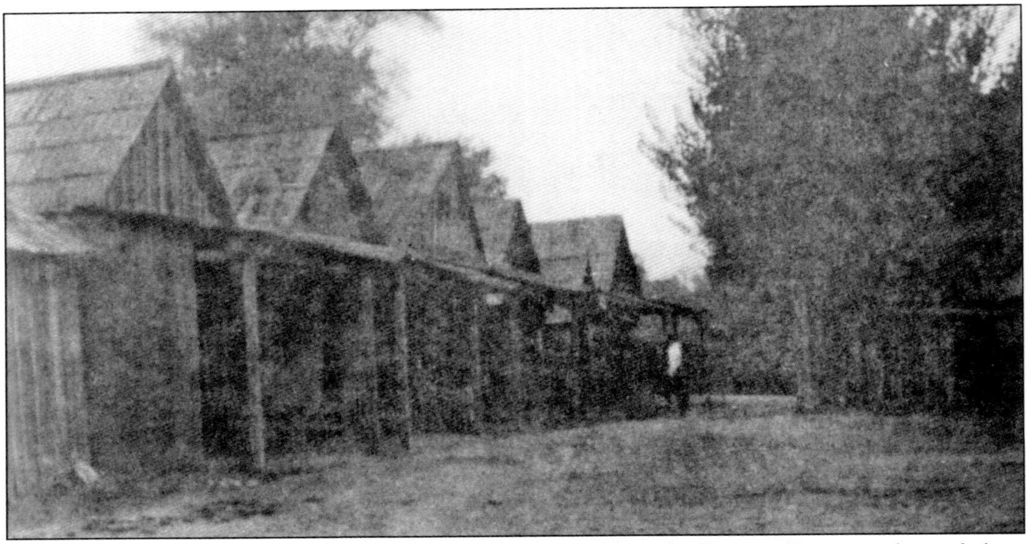

The Chinese came to the Pino area to work in the Gold Rush. Eventually, many formed their own settlement along Secret Ravine on King Road. This was located on property belonging to Pearl Howard Webb and the Boyington family. One store in the settlement was the Wo Chung Lung Company Store. Another store was owned by "Big Jim" Quan Chong Kee and his partner Kee Slip. Ho Wo Yeun, owner of the Wo Chung Lung Company Store, went home to China and returned with a bride named Ong Shee. They had nine children, including Wing, Moon, Kim, Earl, Mae, Suey, and Ming. The boys all took the surname Quong. Suey was the only child to stay in the area.

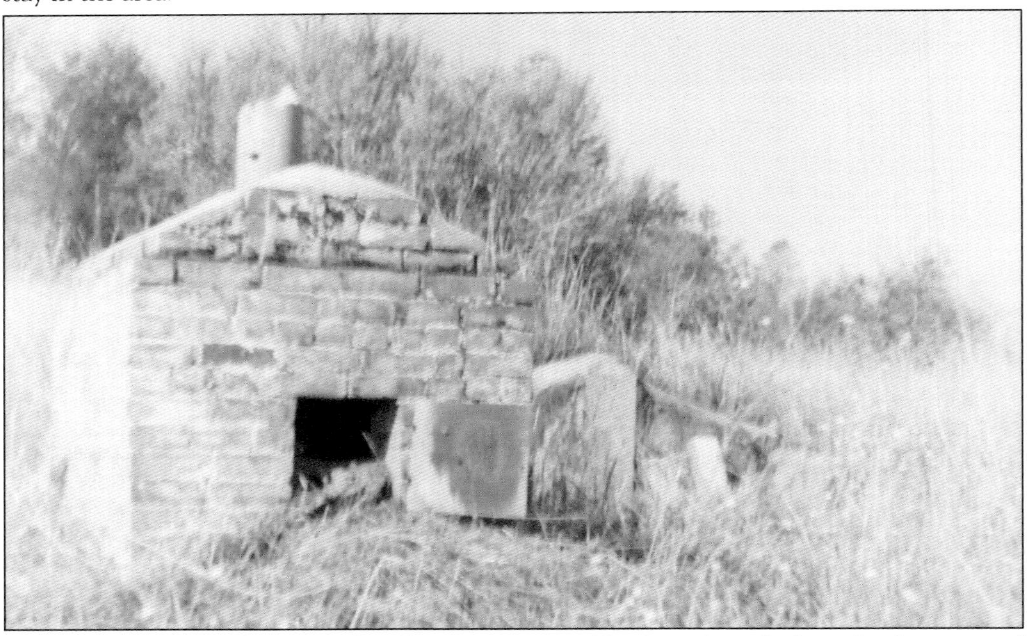

This was a ceremonial oven at the Chinese cemetery. Food was brought here for the spirits of family members who had passed away. There is very little left of this landmark. The historical society dedicated a plaque in the King Road Park to honor the Old Loomis Chinatown and the Hoo-Quong family in 2001.

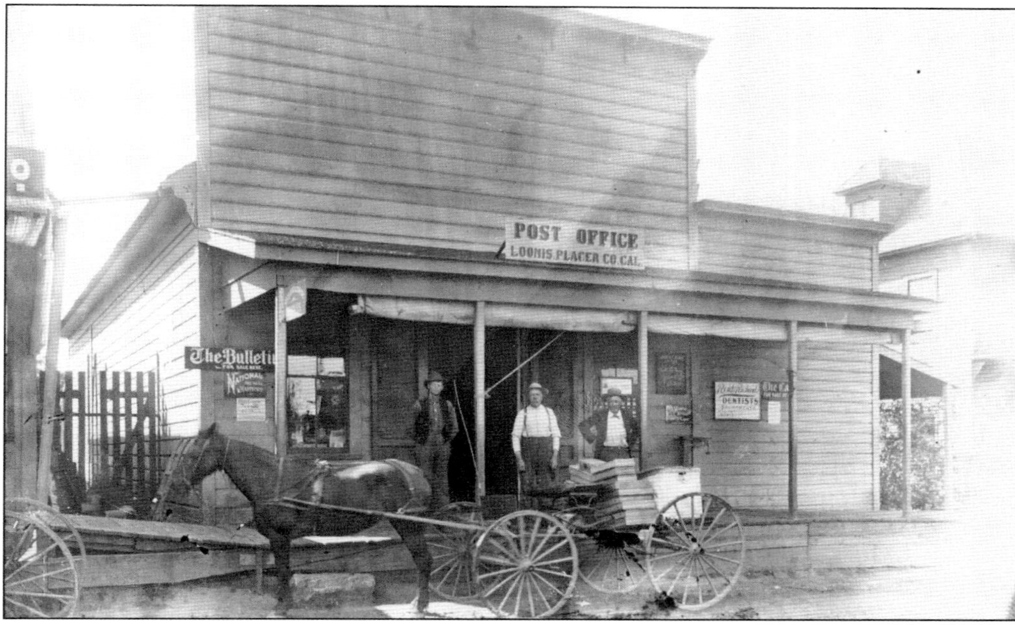

This building is Frederick Turner's store and post office. The sign on the front clearly states, "Post Office, Loomis, Placer Co., Cal." The gentleman in the center with the white shirt and suspenders is Turner. The picture was taken between 1895 and 1915. The hotel can be seen on the right, and the drugstore is on the left. The faithful horse Bell is ready to deliver the load of packed cherry boxes and full strawberry crates in the spring wagon.

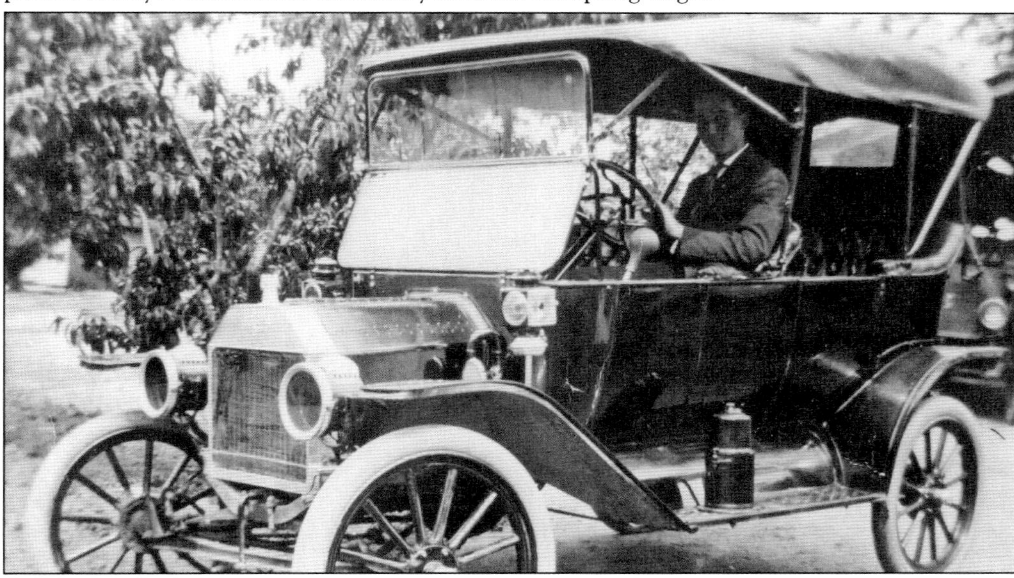

The first touring car used to deliver mail was owned and operated by Veggo Jenson. He delivered mail from 1912 to 1916. Fred Turner was the first postmaster from July 16, 1889, until Jenson took over. On March 19, 1914, Charles Francis took over as postmaster. Art Flynt took over about seven months later. The post office was in the Poggetto building at this date. In 1935, William S. Williams served until retirement in 1940. Irwin Mehl then served as postmaster from September 1940 until April 16, 1941. Katherine Coe and Wes Barnes were also postmasters.

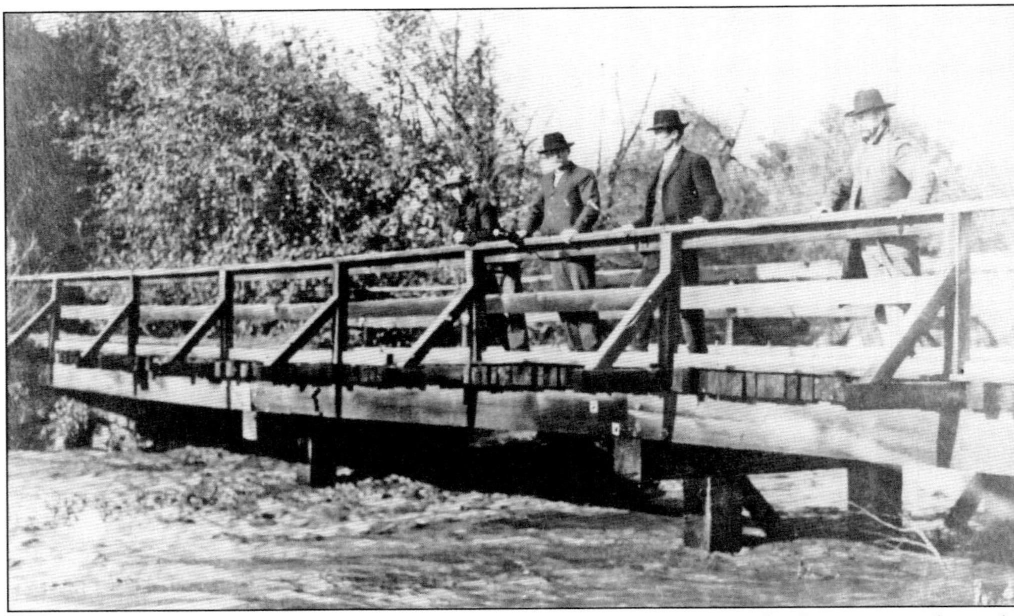

Secret Ravine Bridge is pictured in 1910 or 1911 on Horseshoe Bar Road. The men watching the high water rising are, from left to right, Carrol Roddan, clerk in the Rochdale Store for many years; James Day, who had been in the area since 1900 and was fruit house manager at both the Earl and Producers Fruit Companies and was fruit inspector for many years; Harry Swetzer; and George Turner, farmer and quarryman. He lived in the area of the original Pine Grove.

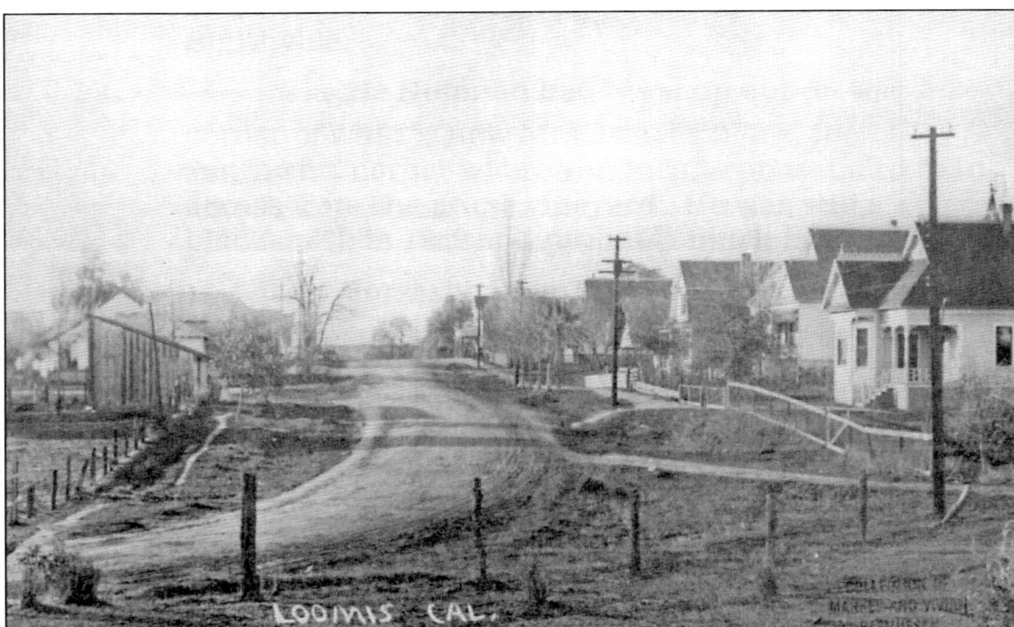

These cottages are on Pine Street (now Horseshoe Bar Road). The first house on the right is still standing. This is near the curve in front of the Loomis Veteran's Memorial Hall and Library Drive.

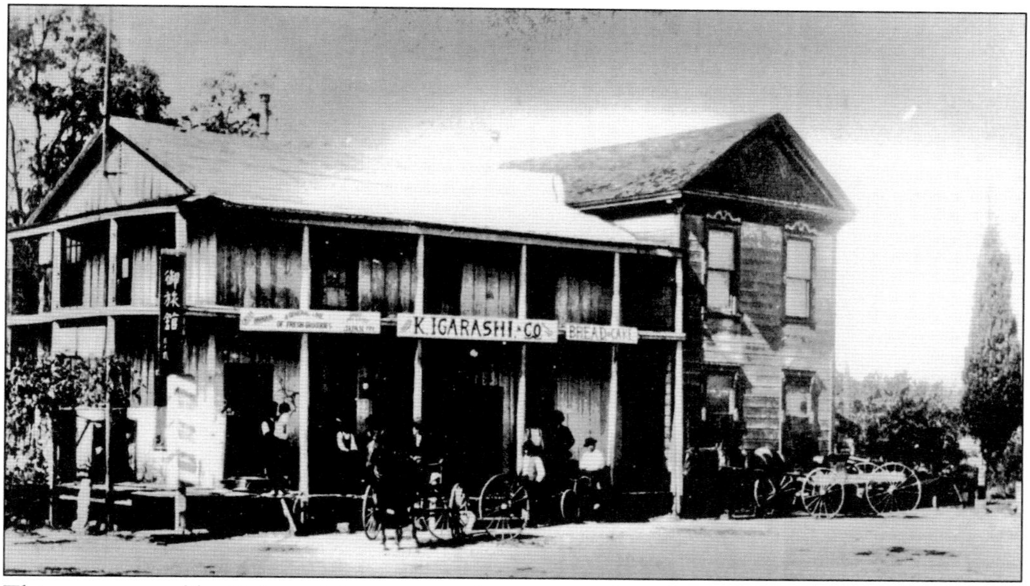

This store owned by K. Igarashi stood near the train tracks at Laird Street. The Japanese had a custom that if a wife's family line was to die out because there were no males to carry the family name or her name was of a high class, then the husband took the wife's name. This is what Sanjiro Igarashi did, and members of the community knew him as Sanjiro Mayeda. He lived to a ripe old age in Loomis. Sanjiro is on the left in this picture with his brother, Kanematsu Igarashi. The long sign in Japanese on the left side of the store states, "Rooms for Rent."

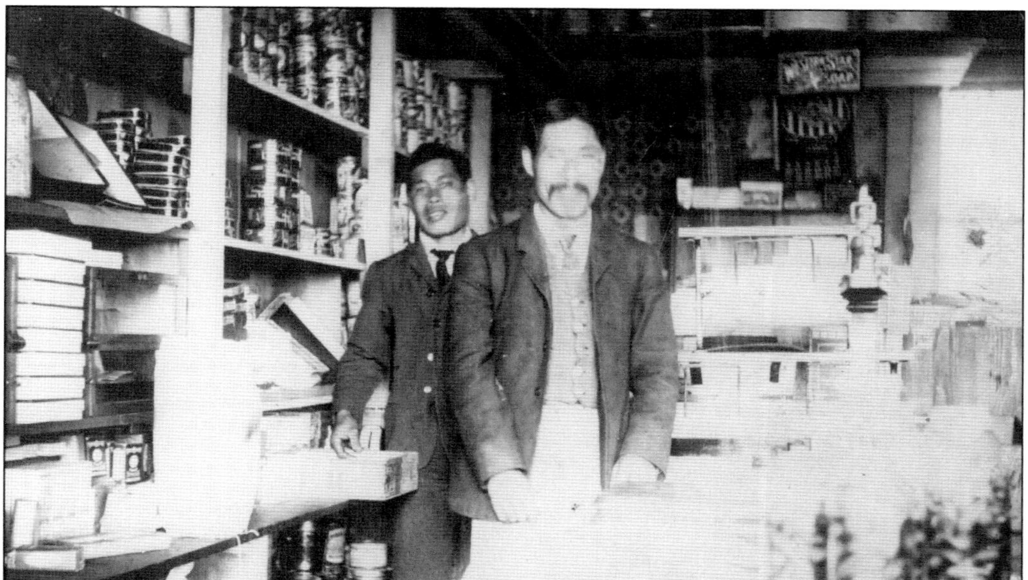

These two gentlemen are the Igarashi brothers, owners of the store. This large two-story building had living quarters upstairs. Ferdinand Bock and his wife, Dorothea, built and opened the store in the 1880s, after Ferdinand had become a U.S. citizen on August 31, 1875. After Ferdinand died in 1885, Dorothea and their son, John, ran the store. When John died in 1910, his mother sold the store to Shinzo Makabe, who shortly afterward sold it to the Igarashi family.

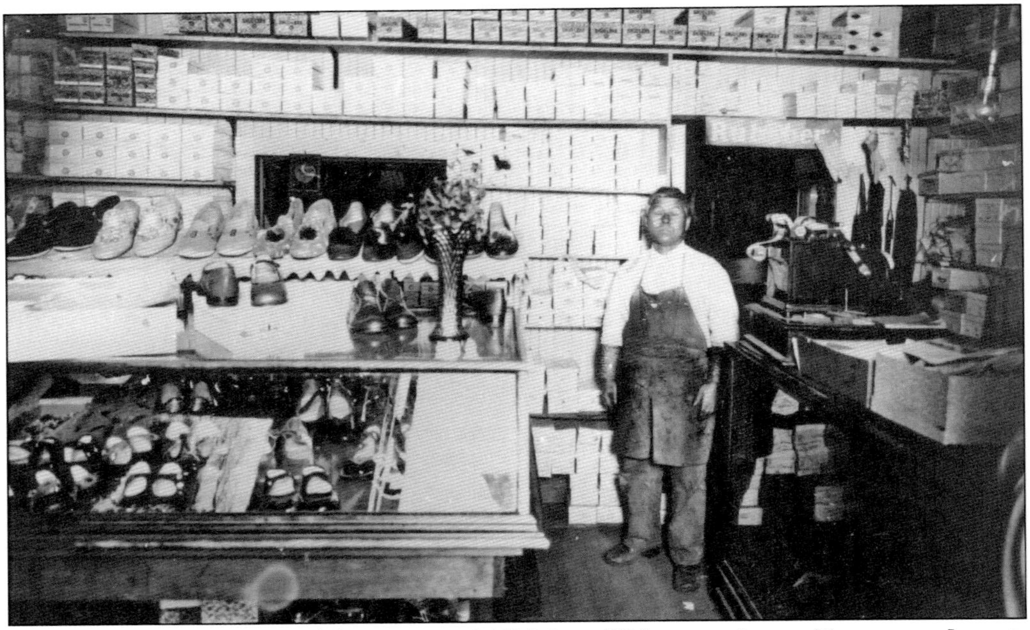

Frank Takagishi came to California around 1900 from Wakayama, Japan. He came to Loomis in 1902. He worked in the fruit orchard to learn management skills. In 1910, he and Mr. Otani became partners in renting the Pendleton ranch. After working the Pendleton orchards and having the crop survive the hard frost that was wiping out other orchards, Frank bought shares in the Mutual Supply Company. He was in partnership with Tamejiro Takahashi for many years. In 1918, he decided to open a shoe store. He learned the cobbler trade from Napoleon Rivard. The shoe repair shop was next door to the present Loomis Fire Station.

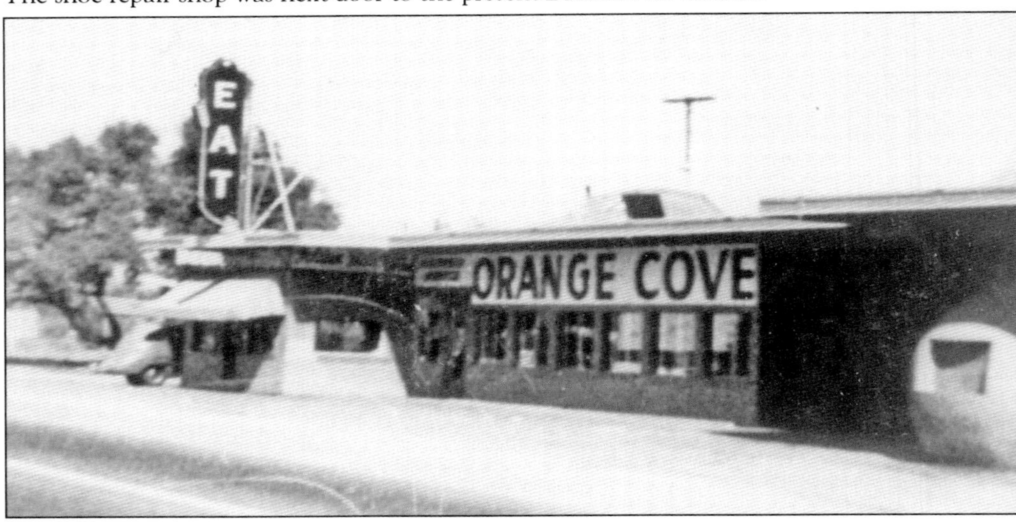

The Orange Cove Café faced Taylor Road at Webb Street. It was a very visible landmark, as it was painted bright orange and in the shape of a flat-bottomed orange. It was built after 1937, when the road was straightened. It was still in existence in 1941 and was owned by a family named Parks. The building burned, and it was rebuilt with a new, more standardized shape and went on to be home to a pool hall, a variety store, and a doctor's office. From 1976 to 2008, it was the Loomis Hardware Emporium.

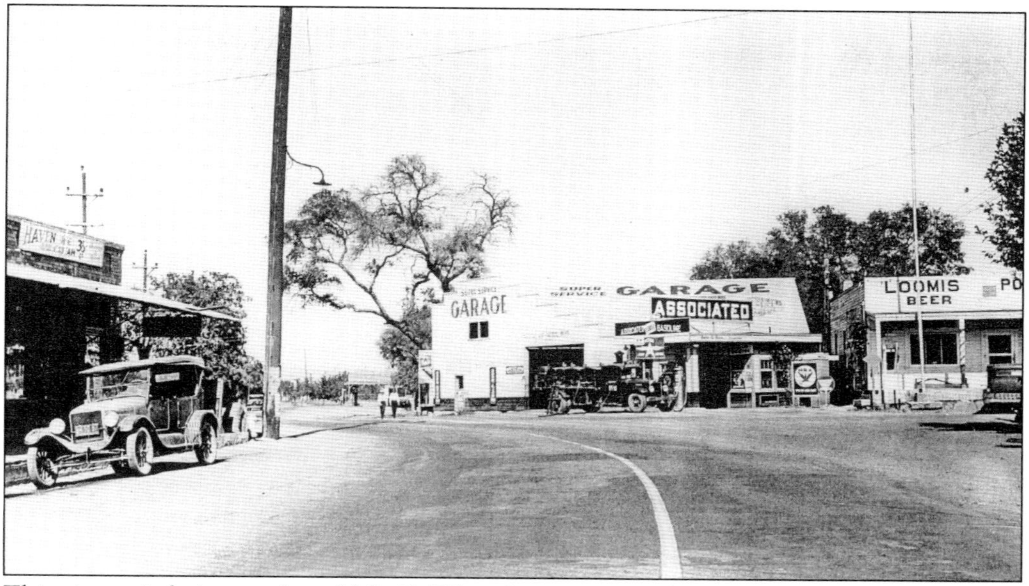

This picture is facing north on U.S. 40 (Olive Street, now Taylor Road) and Pine Street, which became Horseshoe Bar Road. This was taken in the early 1930s, before U.S. 40 was straightened out and the Super Service Garage Building was removed. The Haven Ice Cream Store is on the left. The garage was managed by Jim Friedley in the 1920s. Friedley had a root beer stand adjoining the building. The Associated station was operated in the early 1920s by Edsil Gordon. Before 1929, Friedley left the area, and John Vierra and Walter Young continued with the station.

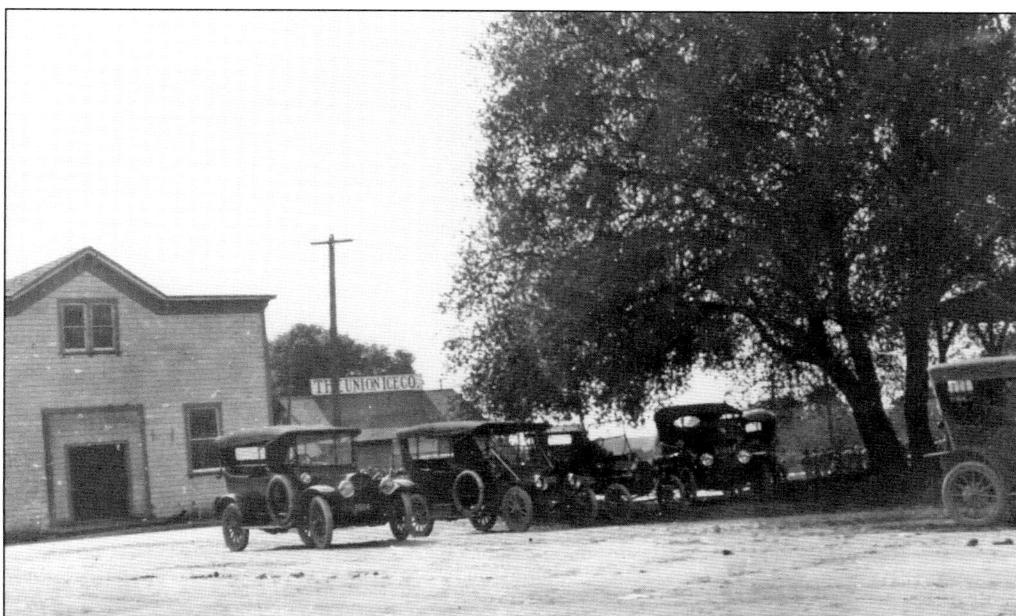

The Union Ice Company and Misley's Hall were located at Taylor Road and Horseshoe Bar Road toward the train tracks. This is now the area of the renovated depot.

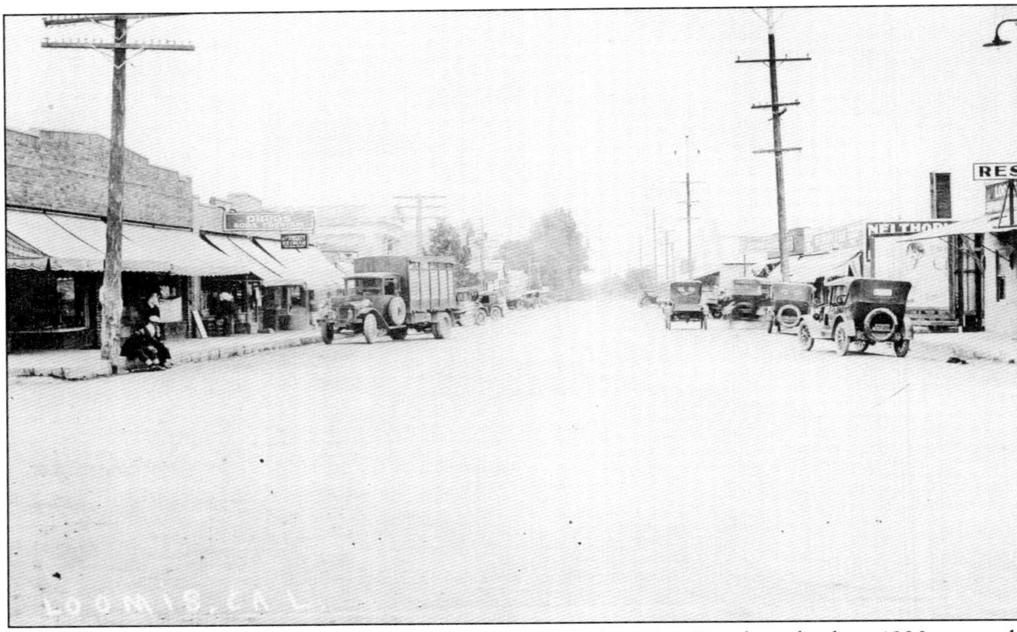

This is another photograph of Taylor Road and Horseshoe Bar Road in the late 1920s or early 1930s. Nelthorpe and Sons is visible. On the left side of the street, Loomis Drug and Soda Fountain sold Liberty Ice Cream. The rebuilt Loomis Bank building is on the left. Parking places evidently did not exist.

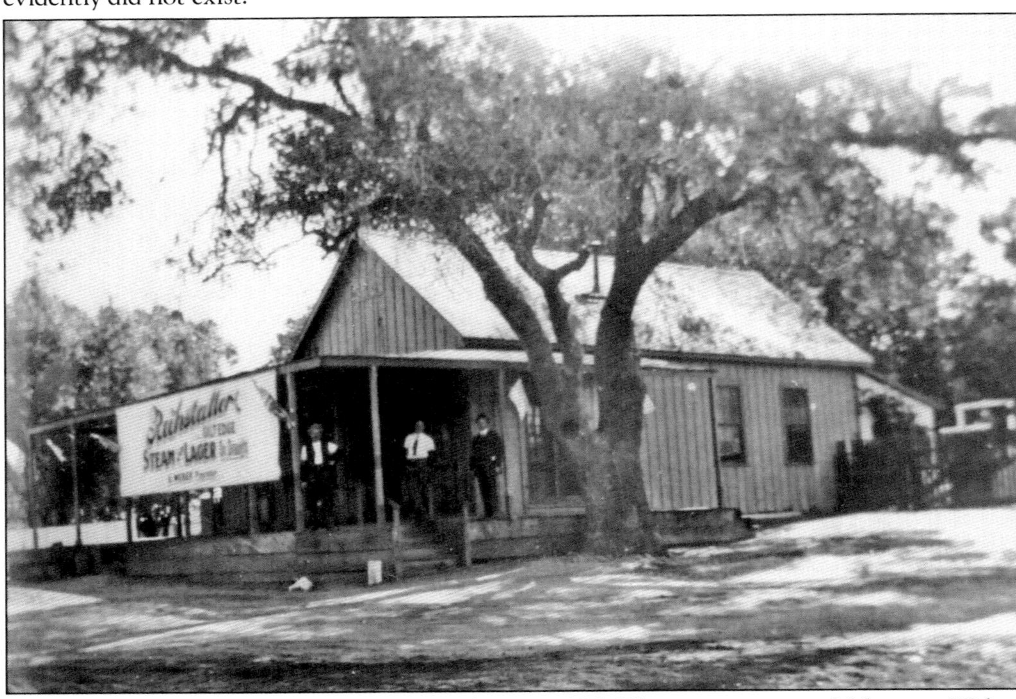

This photograph of Weber's Saloon was taken in 1906. The proprietor was Valentine Weber. The establishment sold Ruhstaller's Lager. This was located about where the Saving's Corner Market parking lot was.

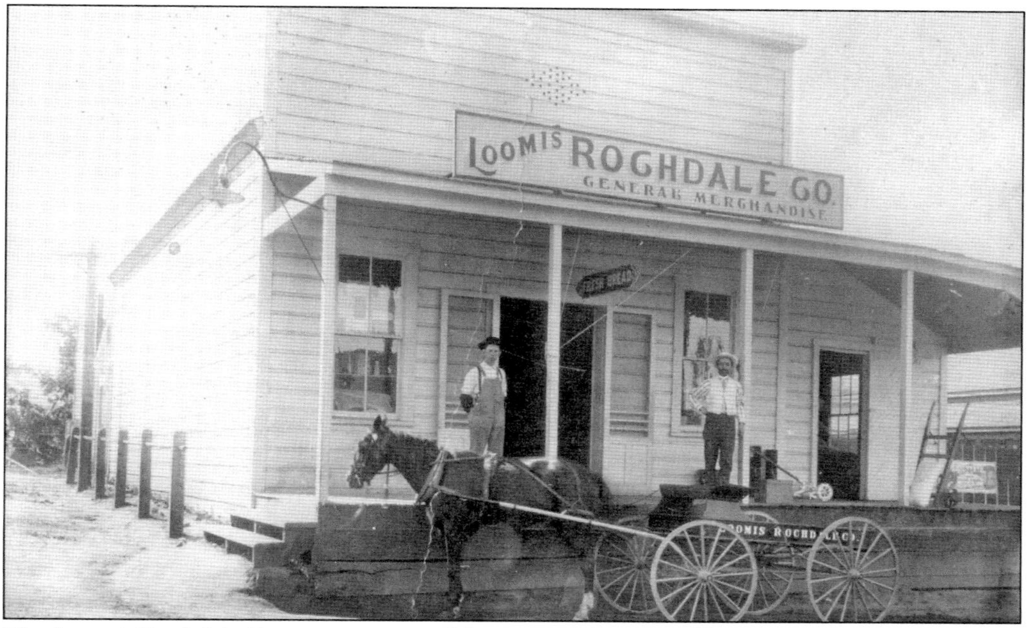

The Loomis Rochdale Store was so named because of the type of business system it used. It was based on a system used in Rochdale, England, instituted in 1844. The system met the demand for a less expensive means of exchange between the producer and the consumer. The system promoted the principles that all memberships were equal; that one person can hold only one membership and has only one vote; and that no voting could be by proxy. Employers got a fixed salary and had to be bonded. Profits were returned to members in proportion to their purchases. Pure goods were handled and full weight and measure given.

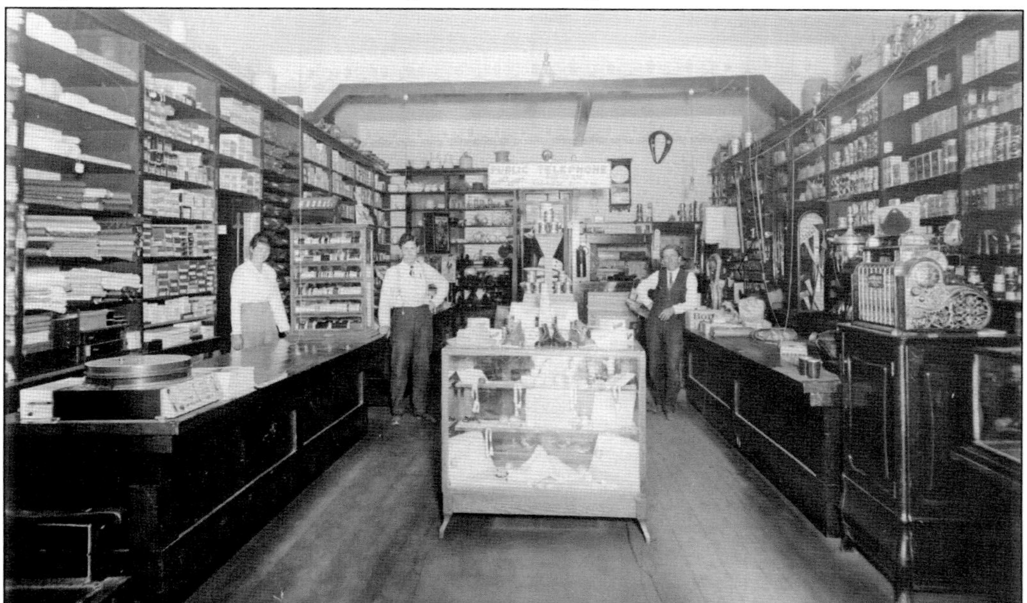

Pictured is the interior of the Rochdale Store. The store was located near the intersection of Pine Street and Olive Street.

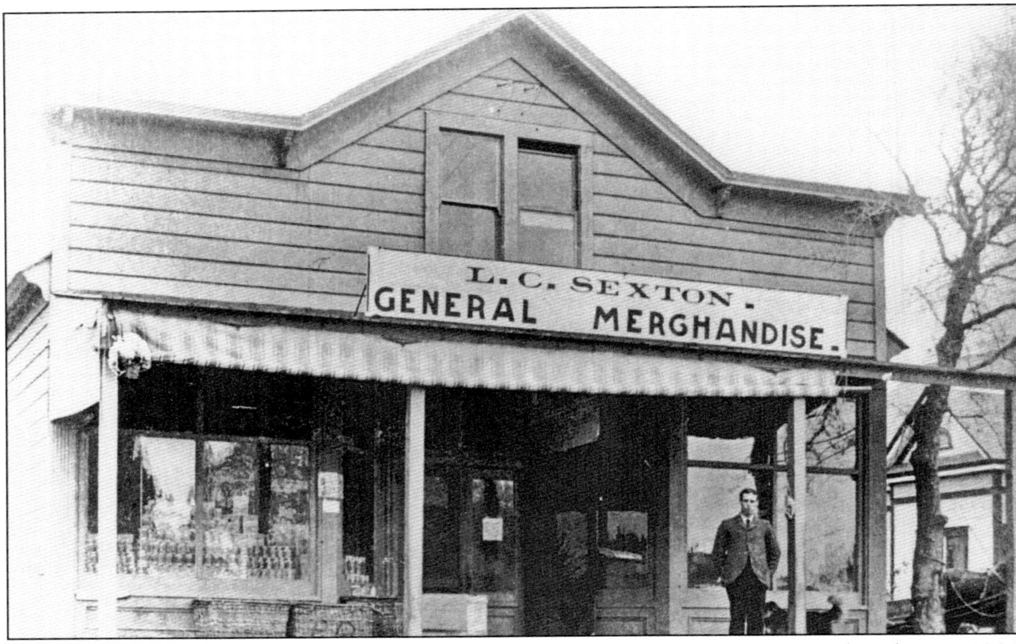

Sexton Store was at the intersection of Pine and Olive Streets. This photograph, taken in 1906, shows Elmer Worth, the clerk for the store, standing on the front porch. There are wicker bread baskets on the porch. The bread was delivered on the Colfax local train from Sacramento at 8:30 each morning. The bread carried well and was still warm when it was delivered. This building is now where the store room for the Loomis Mutual Store was. In 2009, it is the G'Day Donut Shop. The Misely home is visible on the right.

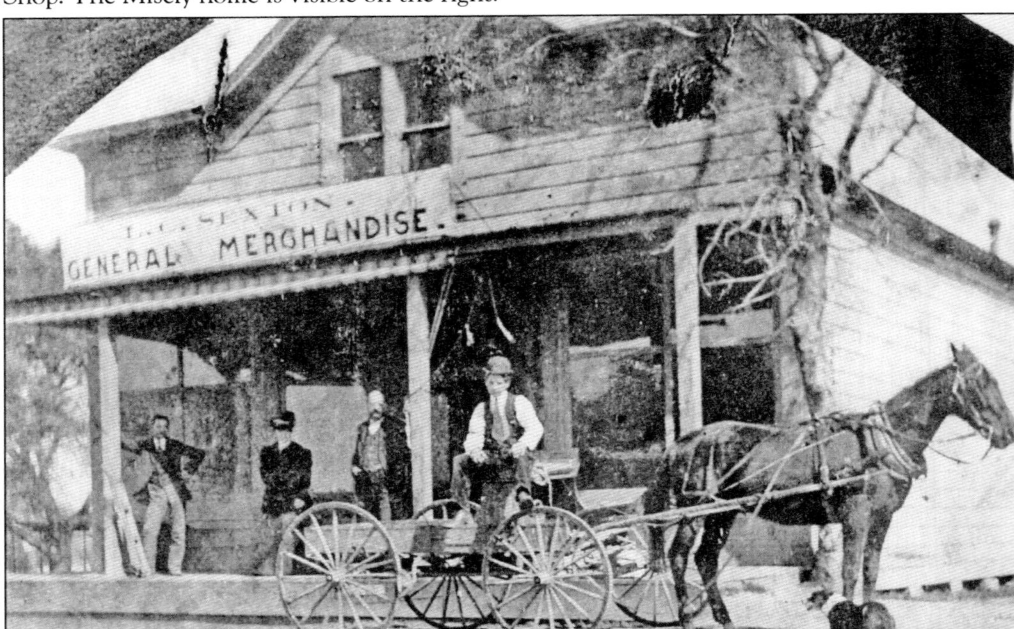

This is a view of the Sexton Store taken in 1900. Charles Cook is probably the man in the buggy.

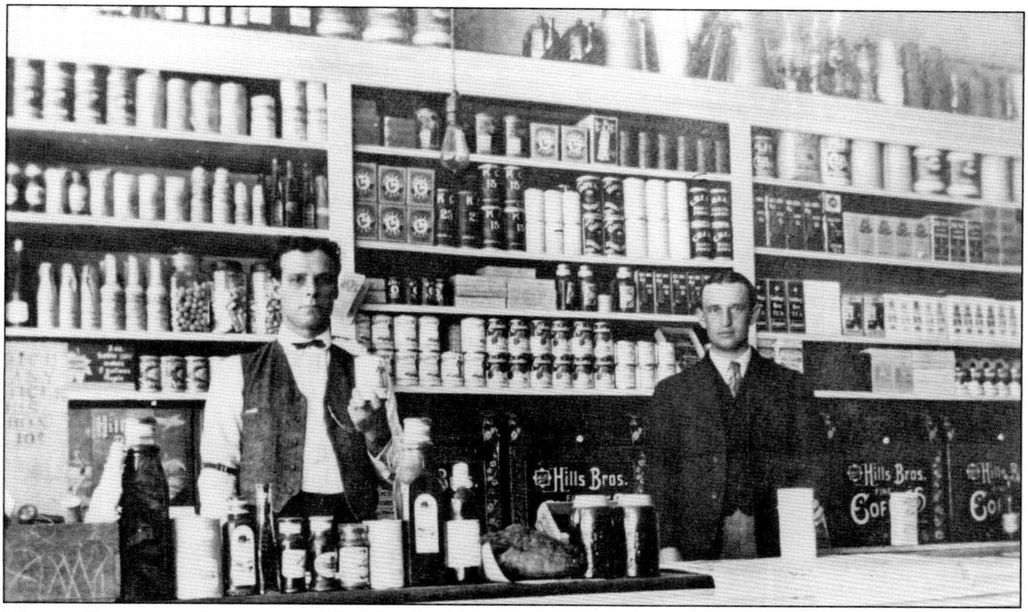

The well-organized interior of the Sexton Store is seen in 1906. Elmer Worth (left) and George Ainsworth are behind the counter.

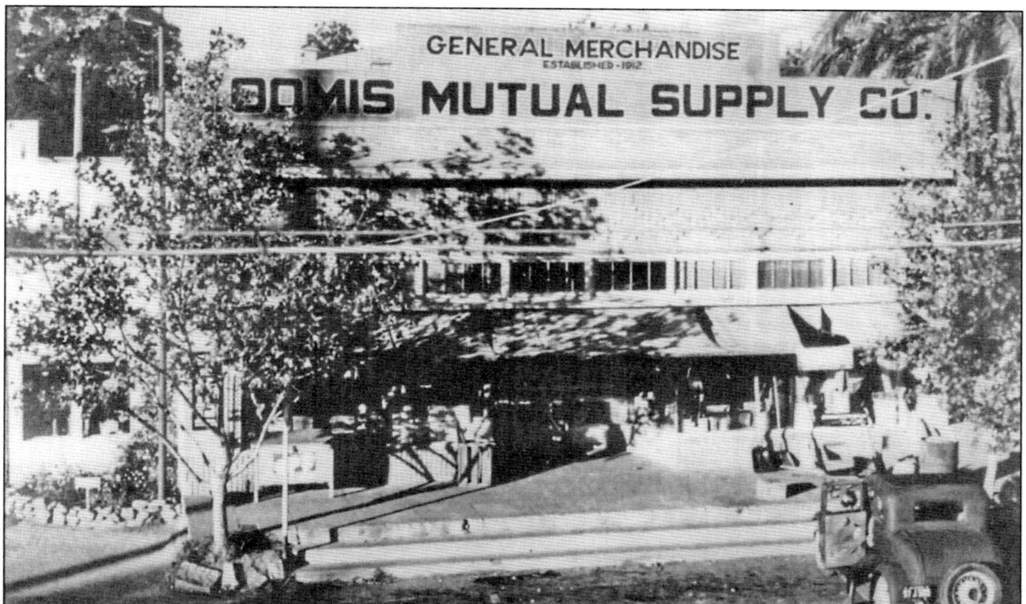

In 1912, Tamejiro Takahashi and Frank Takagishi took over the Igarashi brothers' store, and they operated it in the same location until 1918. During that time, the store burned and was rebuilt. They moved into town in 1918, buying an old building from Charlie Francis that had been the post office, a second-hand furniture store, and a funeral parlor. Shortly after this, the partnership split up, and Frank started his shoe store across the street. A new store was built on the site in 1923 and used until 1962, when a modern market was built and the original store was used for a supply room. The market continued for many more years.

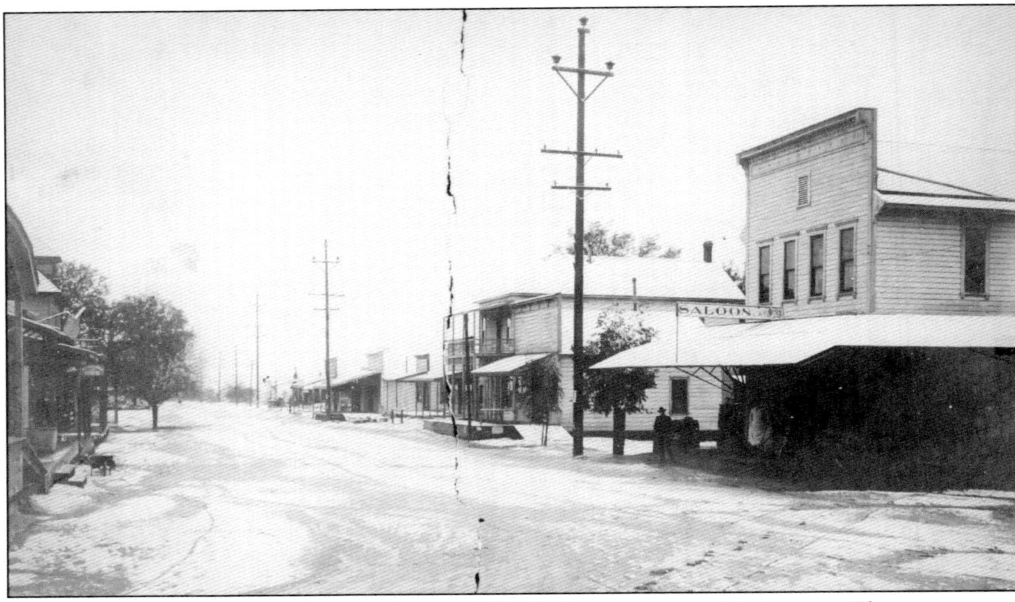

It is not a common sight in this area, but in 1911–1912, a snowstorm hit Loomis. This street scene shows the Dick Cook Saloon and the Ryder building.

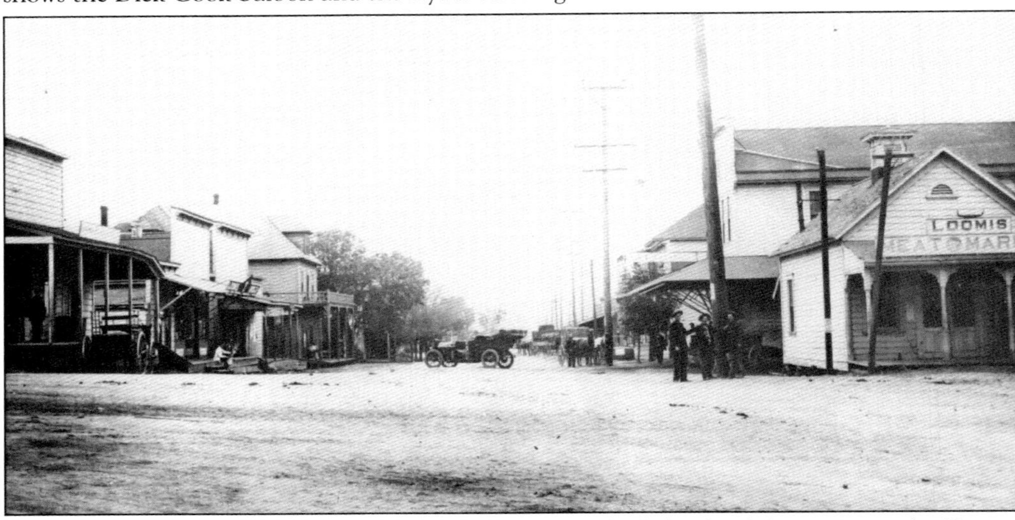

This photograph of Main Street was taken in 1906. On the left side of the street are the Kramer Grocery Store, a drugstore, the Wells Fargo office, the post office, Turner grocery store, a barbershop, a boardinghouse, and the shed for horses from the livery stable. Walnut Street separated these shops from the Frank Cook Saloon and the first newspaper office, with H. E. Whitaker as the publisher. On the right side of the street are T. B. Misley's Ice House and Butcher Shop and R. T. Cook Saloon. The second story of this building was used as a lodge hall and for dances. The Andrew Ryder building was next door with a shoe repair shop and living rooms upstairs. The Ford residence was next, with the L. L. Crocker Ripe Fruit House beyond that. This later became Law Brothers. George Moskovitch operated a grocery store. Across Walnut Street was the George Boller blacksmith shop, the Earl Fruit Company Shed, and the Producers Fruit Company. The last building in this area was the George Gilmore home. The car in the street is Al Pendleton's Thomas Flyer.

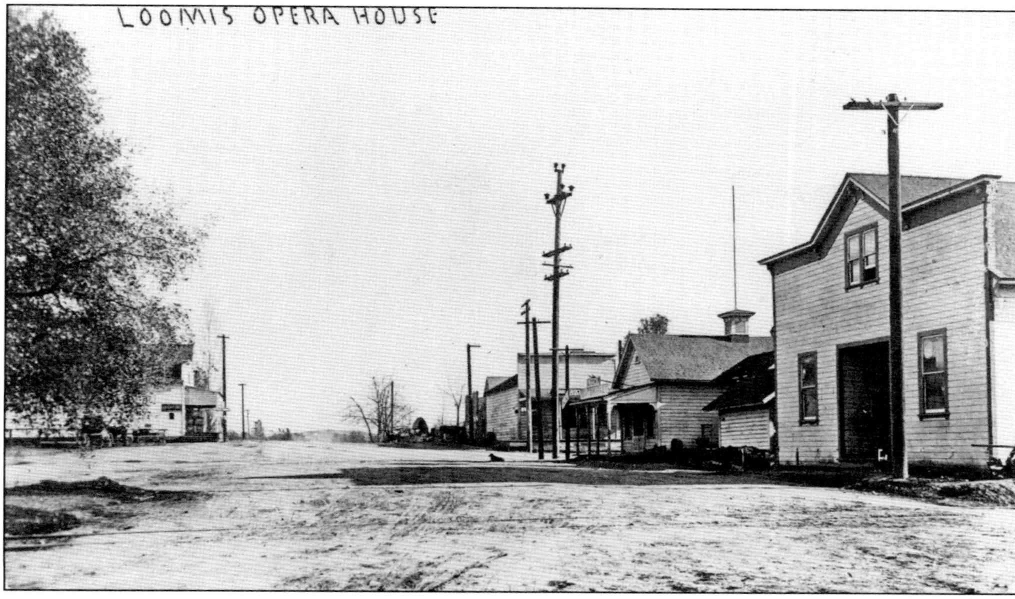

This photograph, taken before 1915, shows the Loomis Opera House. It was taken looking southeast from Webb Street to Horsehoe Bar Road, looking from the depot toward the opera house.

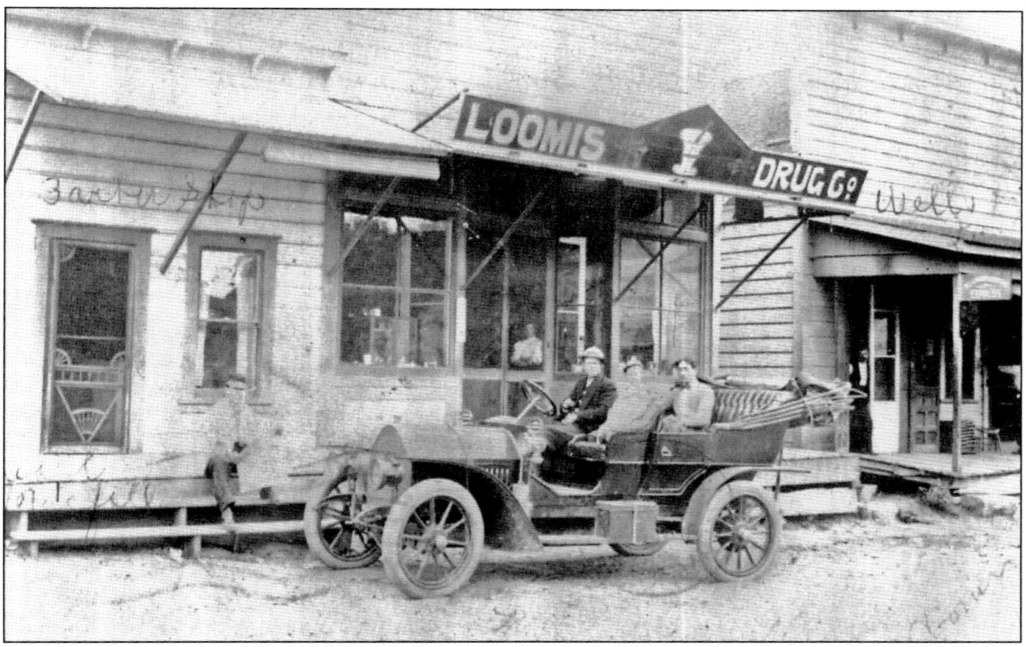

Loomis Drug was on Main Street, next door to the barbershop run by Carl McFall and the Wells Fargo office run by Frederick Turner. Mrs. Hughes, the wife of druggist Bill Hughes, is standing in the doorway. Al Pendleton's car, a Thomas Flyer, is in front of the store. The car was purchased in 1905 or 1906 for $5,000. Hughes is in the backseat. Pendleton is the driver, and his son Norman is the passenger.

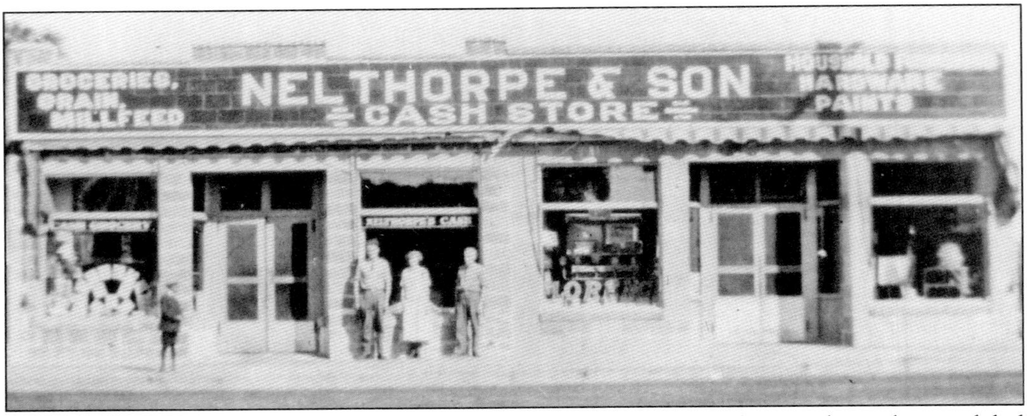

The Nelthorpe and Son Cash Store can still be seen on Taylor Road. Now the cash store label is no longer on the building. Edgar, Mary, and Lindsley Nelthorpe are in front of the window. Edgar was a carpenter, and since he was always busy building in the area, he decided to start a store in town after the disastrous fire of 1915.

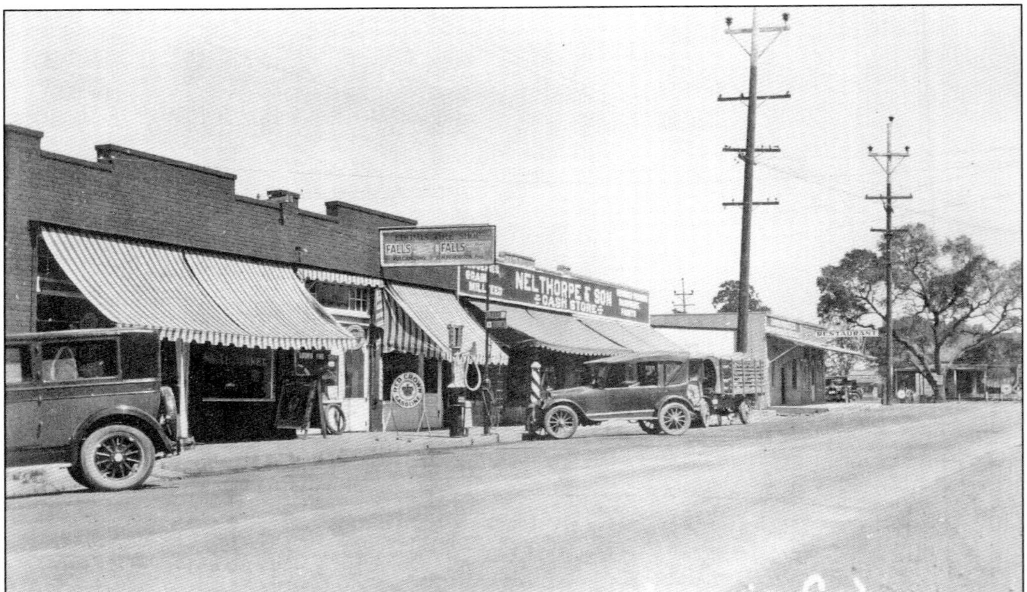

The Nelthorpe store had changed little by the late 1920s and early 1930s. Edgar Nelthorpe was a native of Essex, England. He was born in 1865, and in 1895, his family immigrated to Janesville, Wisconsin. In 1902, the family came to California to visit his wife Martha's sister Grace Kirk Tupper. They liked the area well enough to buy land and settle in Loomis.

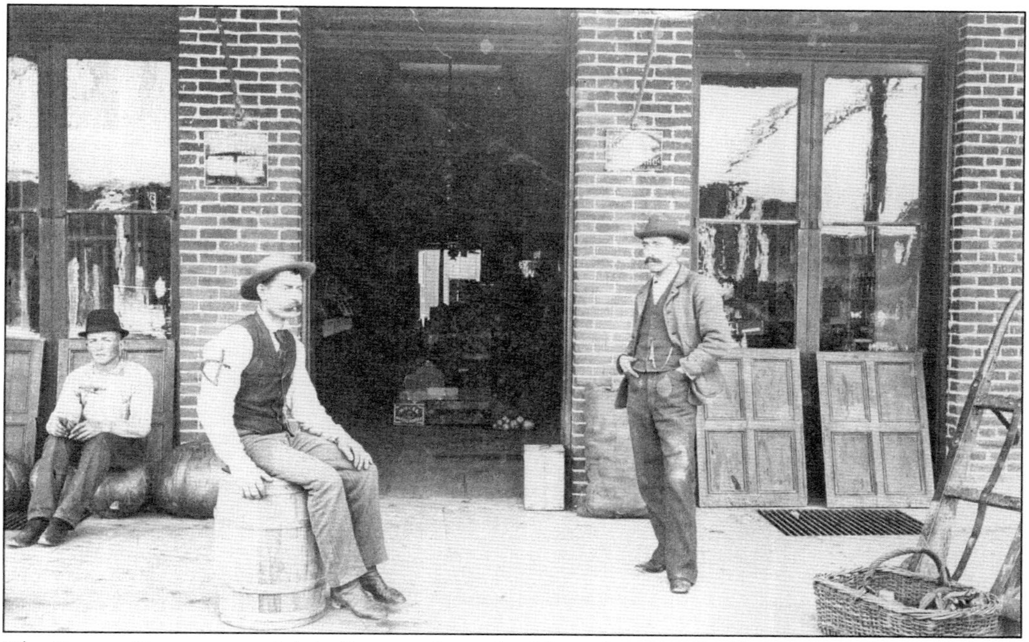

The Fassett Store was on Main Street, where the Horseshoe Bar Grill is today. The man on the right is W. P. Fassett.

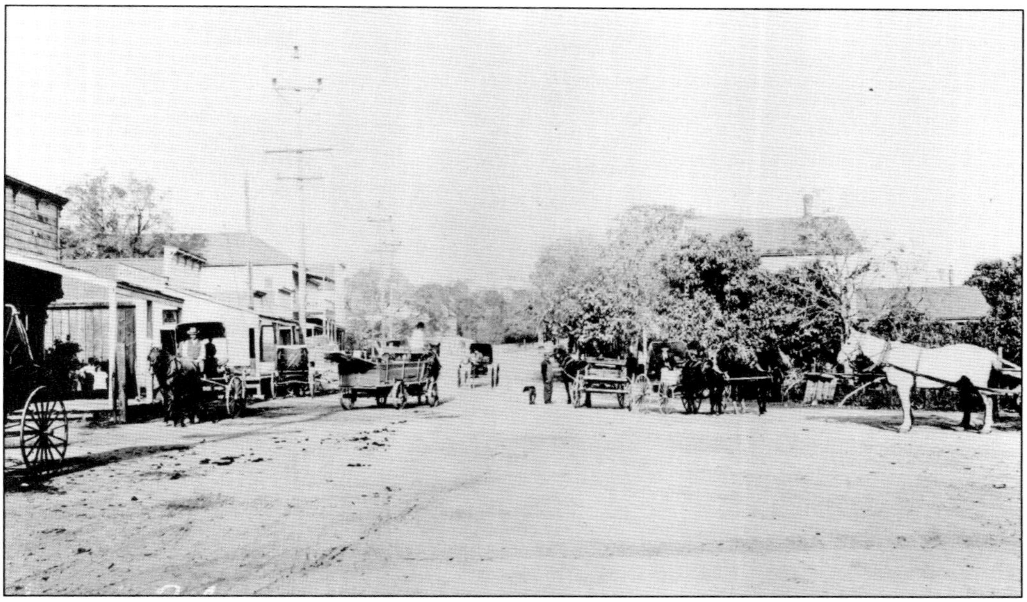

This Loomis street scene was taken before 1915. The main means of transportation was horse and buggy or horse and wagon.

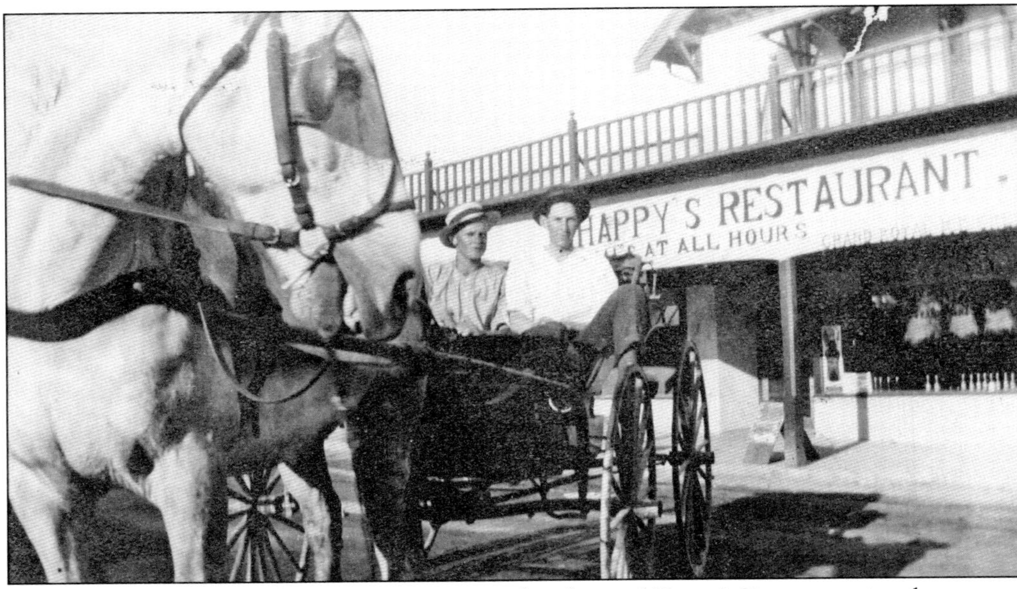

Eddie Larsen, left, and Albert Fieser are pictured in front of Happy's Restaurant in a horse cart. It can be noted that Grand Royal Ice Cream was available.

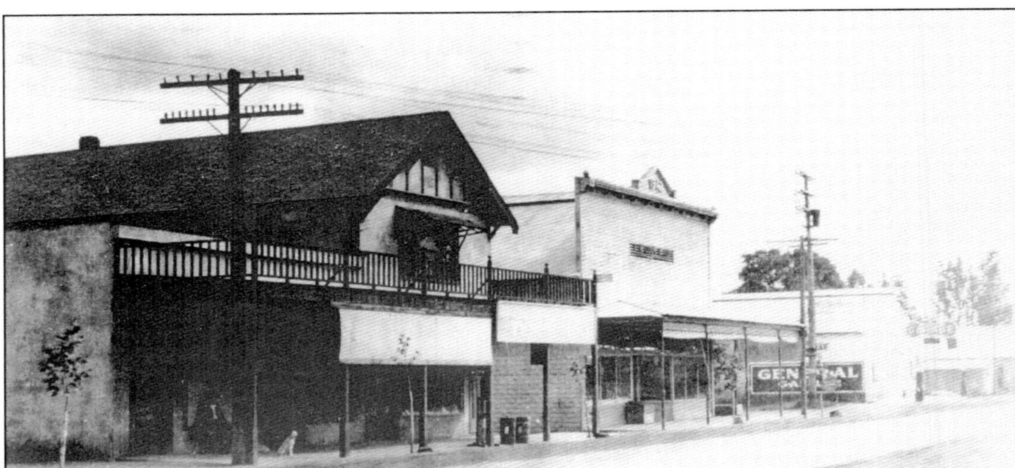

This 1927 photograph looks south on Taylor Road. The two-story building with the balcony housed the post office and the office of Judge John Randolph, who was justice of the peace. In his earlier years, he was editor for the *Loomis Recorder*. The sign indicates Mrs. Pearl Blemmer's Bluebird Tea Room. Only lunch was served. Pearl Blemmer loaned her collection of books to customers for a fee. When Judge Randolph died after five terms of office, Pearl Blemmer became the judge. The other two-story building is Cook's Store, now the Main Drug Store. Across Walnut Street is the General Garage. In 1919, Bernard Mehl built a garage on the site of the Peach Tree Inn as well as where the grandstand used to be at the beginning of the 20th century. In the beginning, the garage was managed by Larry Dunn. The last building in the picture is the Loomis Veterinary Hospital, owned by Seth Law.

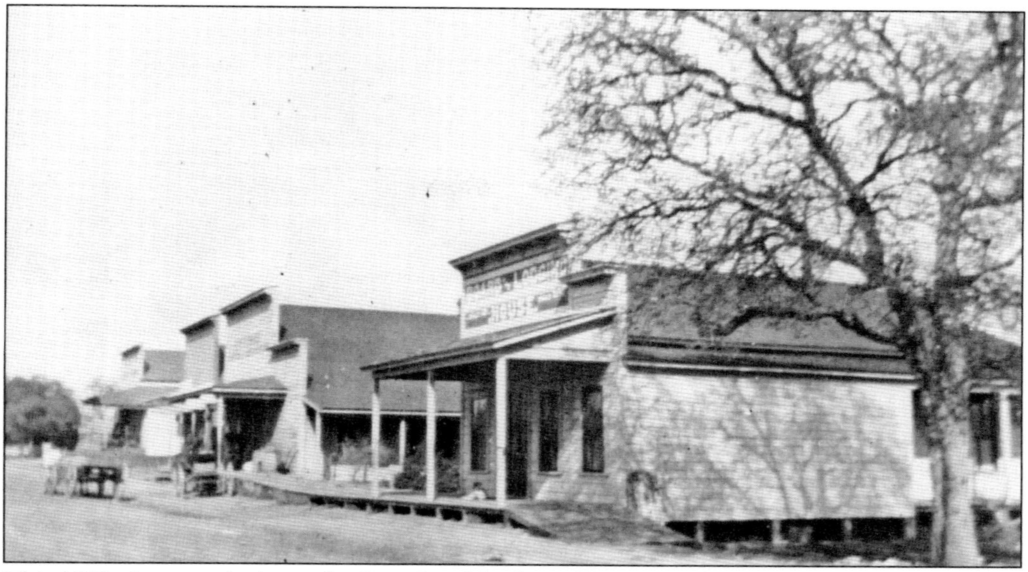

This 1890 photograph shows the Board and Lodging House, run by Joseph Turner. The Turner store, the post office, the drugstore, Crammer's shoe store, and Laver's grocery store were in the same building. Note the wooden sidewalks in front of the stores. In 1895, a second story was added to the building.

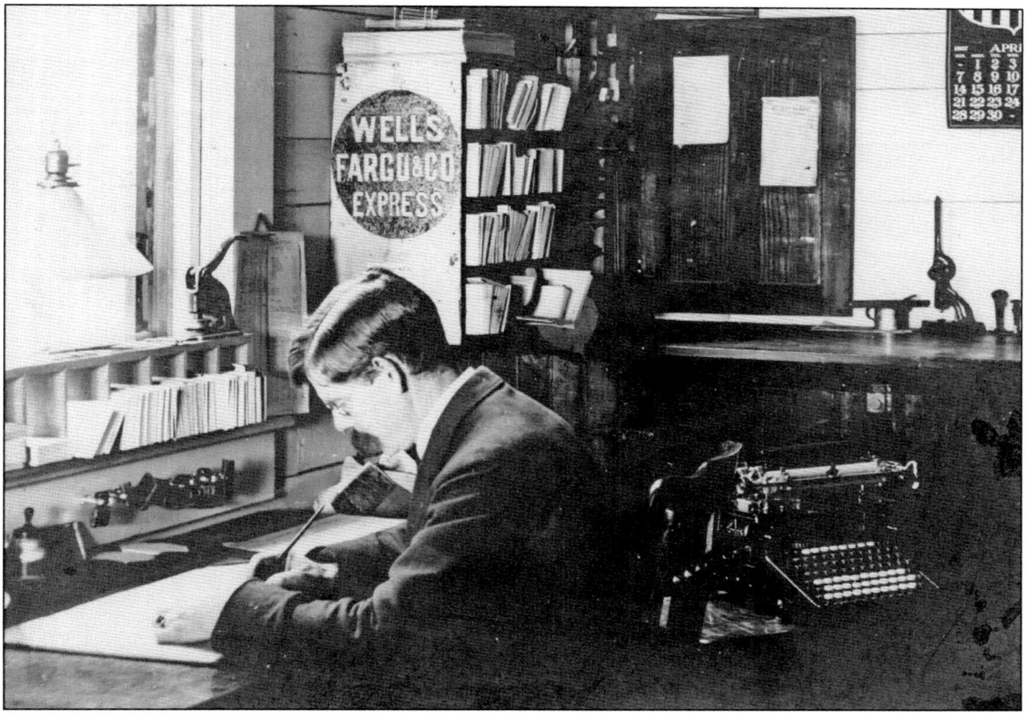

Frederick W. "Will" Turner was appointed postmaster of Loomis by President Harrison in 1889. He also served as agent for the Wells Fargo Company for 25 years. During World War I, he volunteered his services and served as a private in the M. T. C. Detachment No. 1. He was also a company clerk and did commendable work in the U.S. Intelligence Bureau.

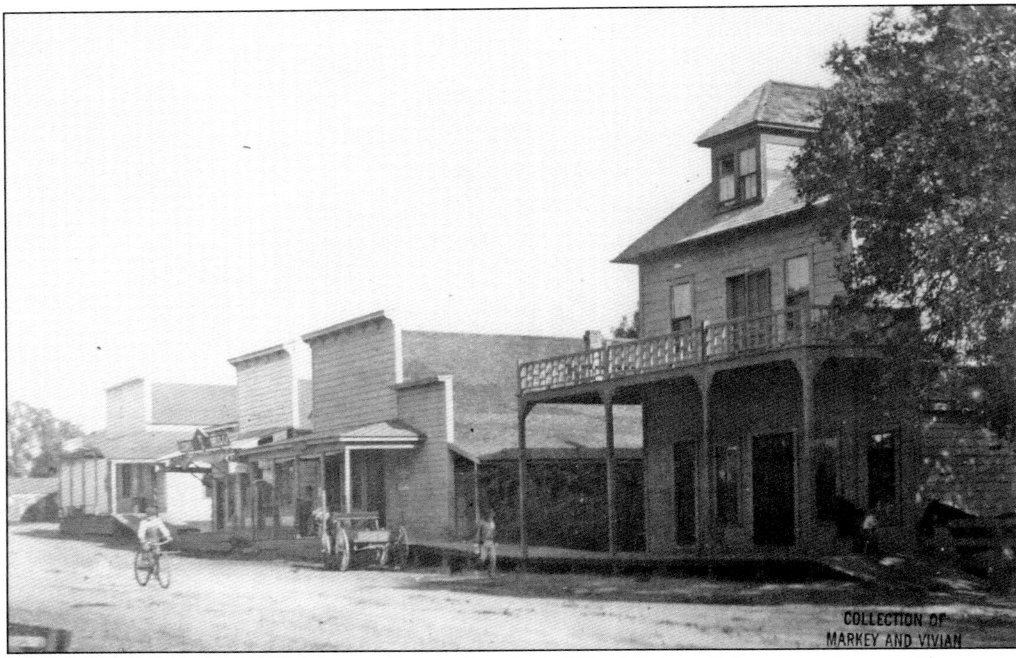

This photograph shows the Turner Hotel after the 1895 addition of the second story. The rest of the street did not change, and the wooden sidewalks are still in use.

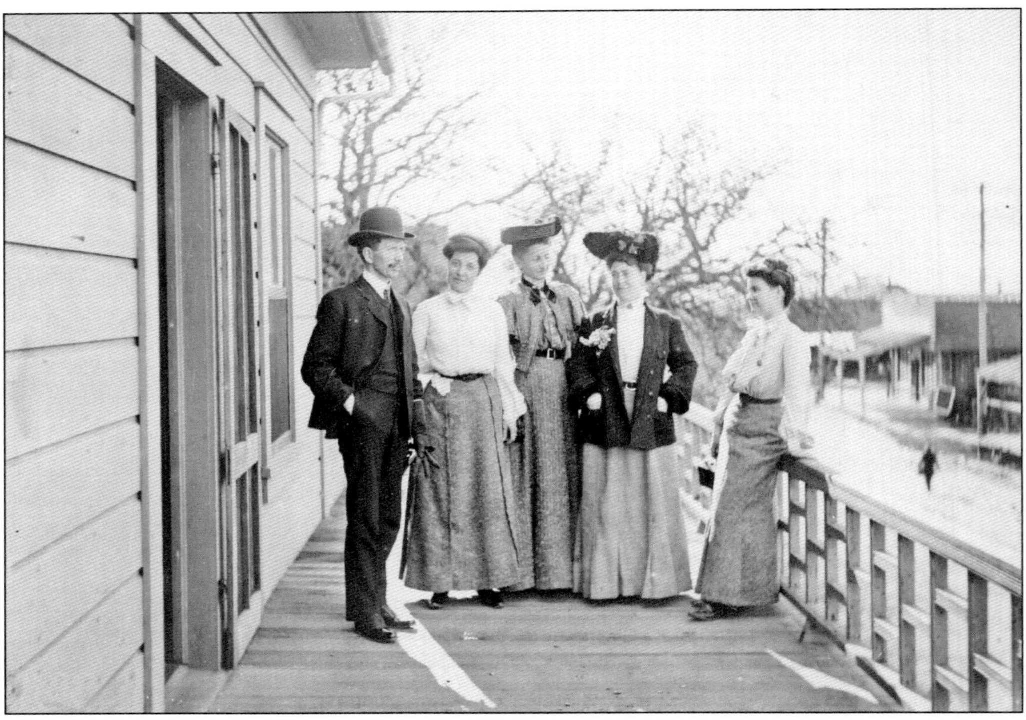

On the second story of the Turner Hotel, Will Turner and his wife, Carrie, who is leaning on the railing, chat with three unidentified women.

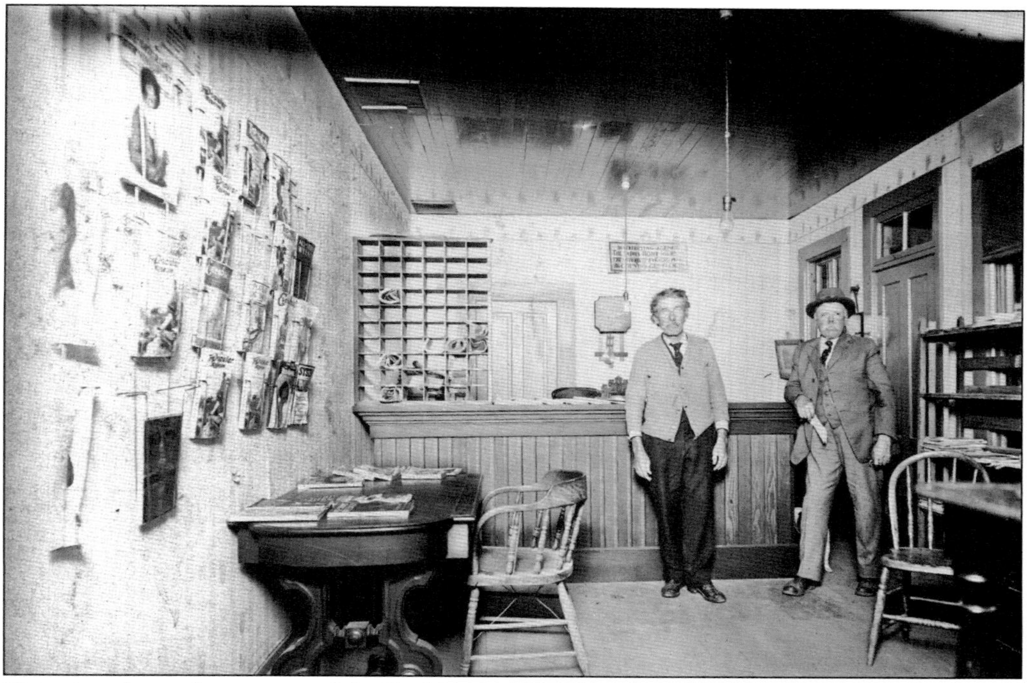

This view shows the interior of the Fred Turner's Reading Room. Fred Turner is the man in the hat leaning against the counter. The other man's identity is unknown.

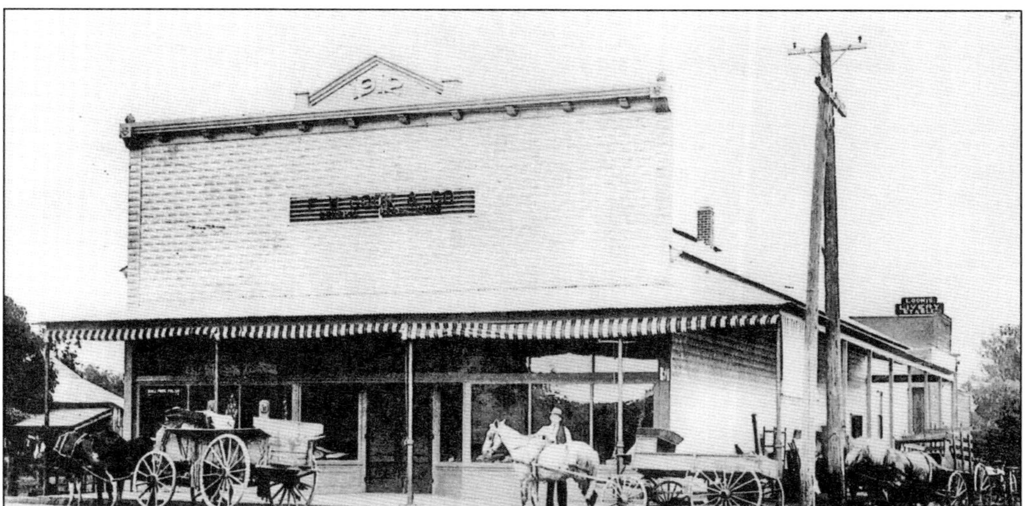

Cook's Store was located at Taylor Road and Walnut Street. Cook's delivery wagon is in front of the store. Fred Keeley is standing near the horse. Brahm's wagon is in front, and Celestine Cordell's wagon is on the side street. The Turner stable is behind the store on the right side, and May's Loomis Livery Stable is behind the store. A sick horse in May's stable is blamed for kicking over a lantern that started the fire on July 12, 1915.

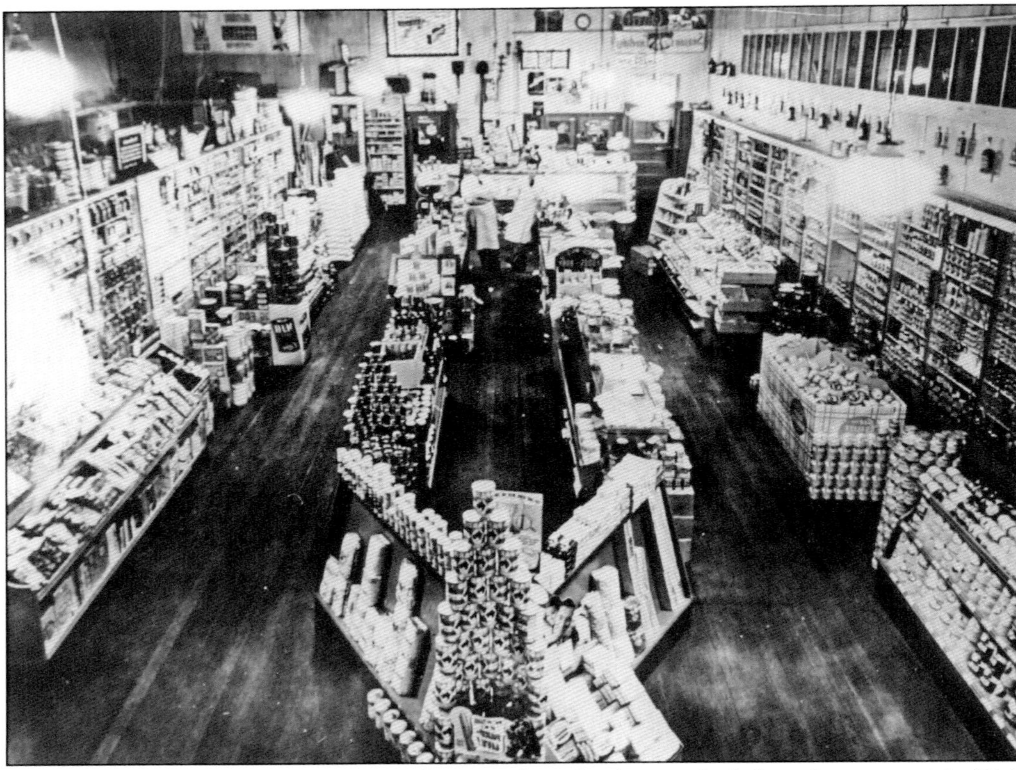

This is the interior of Cook's Store. William Nathan Cook is on the left in the center aisle. This store was built in 1912 by Charles Dolce for Frank Warren Cook.

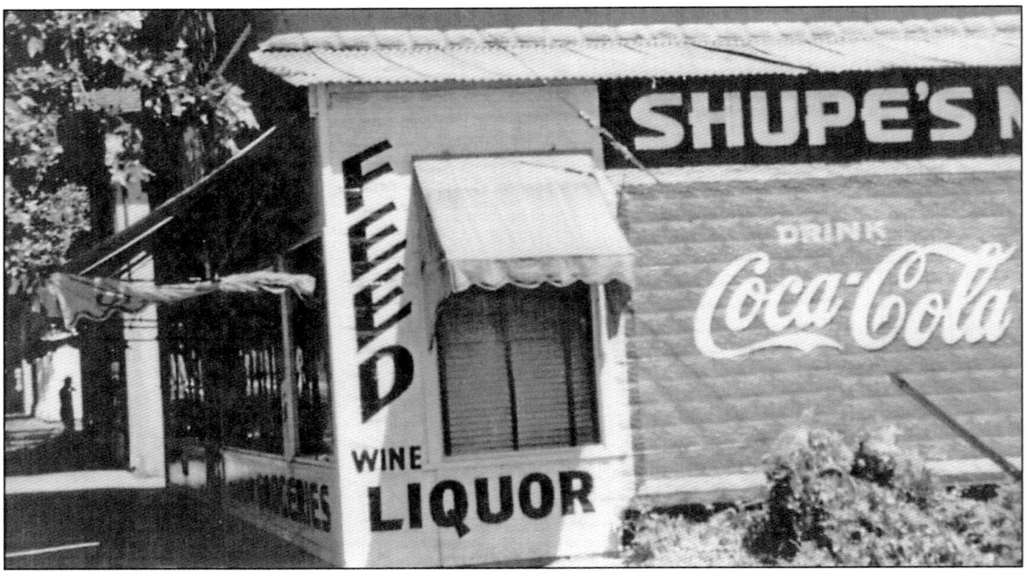

This building, Shupe's Market, was built by George Boller. Boller was a blacksmith but also built several of the business buildings, including the first packing and shipping shed (variously named Producer's, Pioneer, and Earl Fruit Shed) and 60–70 homes. He also patented a "pear-lidding machine." In 1947, at age 93, George Boller was one of California's oldest-living native sons.

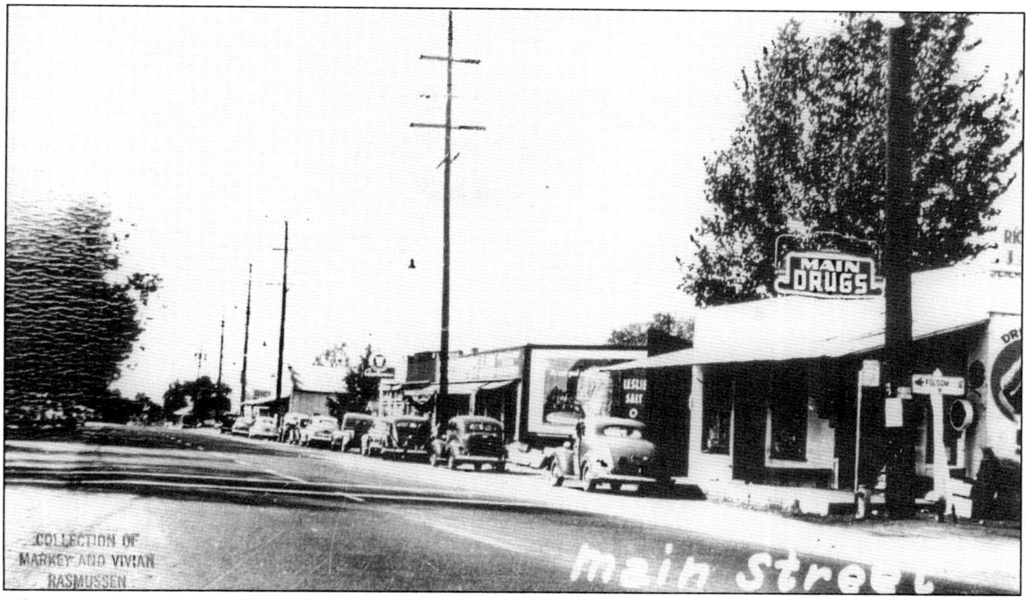

This was the original Main Drug Store, owned by Hiroshi and Rose Takemoto at Taylor and Horseshoe Bar Roads, up the street from Nelthorpe's, which has added an appliance sign to their storefront. The city of Folsom is 12 miles from Loomis, according to the sign.

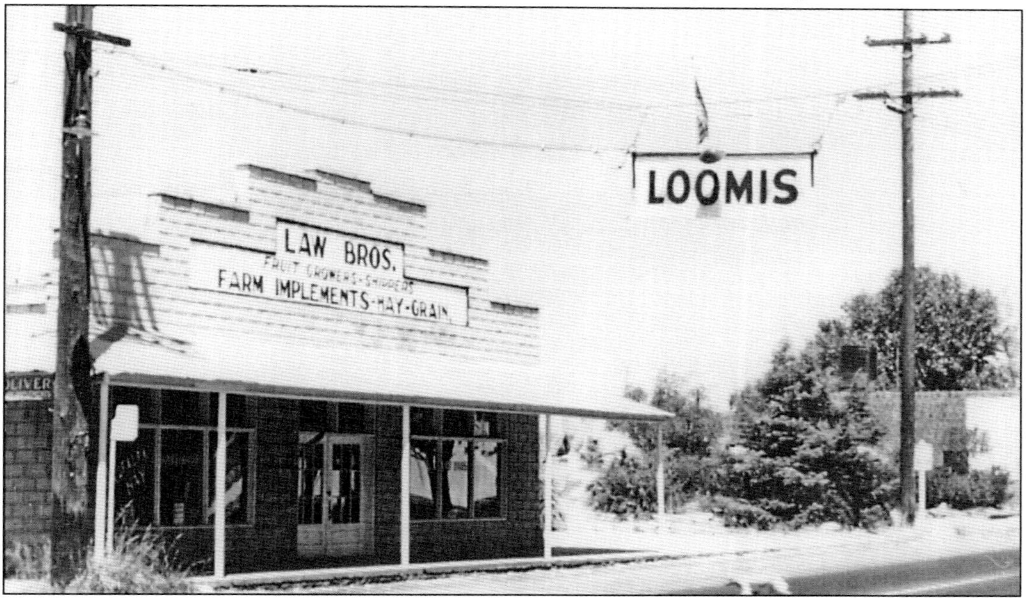

Law Brothers Farm Implements, Hay, and Grain Store is at the corner of Taylor Road and Walnut Street. Law Brothers were also successful fruit shippers. Albert Law came to Loomis from England in November 1892 and started fruit ranching. His brother, Seth, followed in 1885. The January 4, 1911, *Loomis Recorder* states that "in 1908 they embarked in the fruit shipping business on the firm name of Law Brothers. During the shipping season there is hardly a train leaving Loomis that does not carry a shipment of fruit from Law Brothers. Their customers cover the territory from Montana to Washington on the North to Colorado and Arizona on the East and South. They ship only the best quality of fruit—'Quality' being their motto."

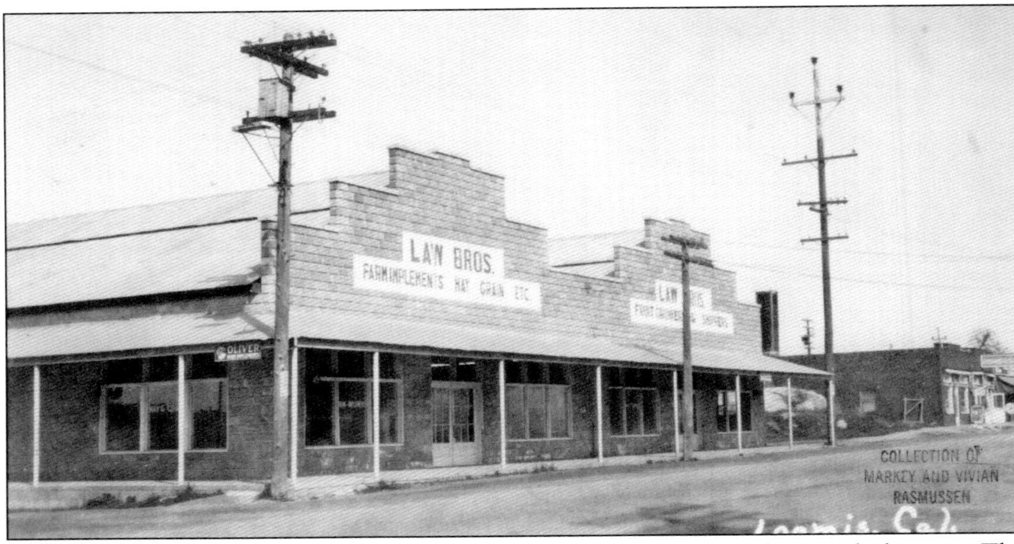

This shows the Law Brothers store prior to September 24, 1939, before fire struck the store. The right-hand section of the rebuilt store eventually became the building that housed the Bank of America. Law Brothers eventually sold and repaired televisions and small appliances.

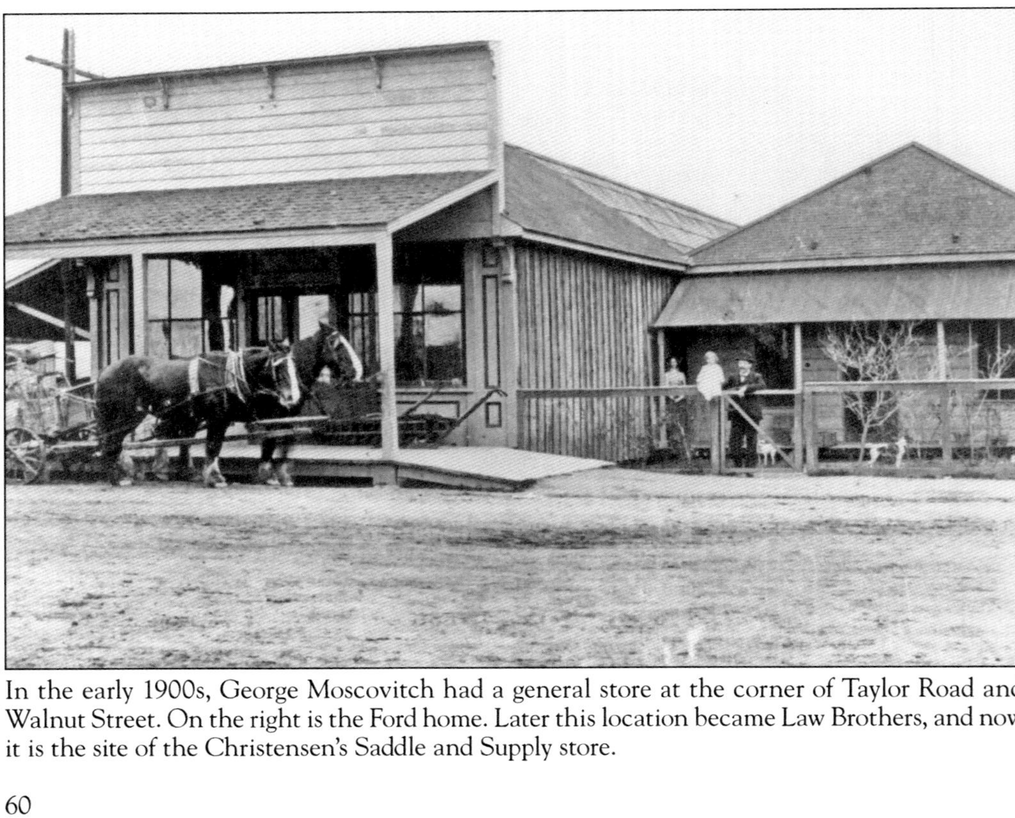

In the early 1900s, George Moscovitch had a general store at the corner of Taylor Road and Walnut Street. On the right is the Ford home. Later this location became Law Brothers, and now it is the site of the Christensen's Saddle and Supply store.

The first bank in Loomis was named the Bank of Loomis. It was located in the Andrew Ryder Building. The men in this 1913 photograph are believed to be (from left to right) James Callison, cashier; Dick Cook; Andrew Ryder; Samuel Day; James Brennan Sr., president; Edmund Lee Rippey; and George McCauley, an Auburn banker and friend of James Callison.

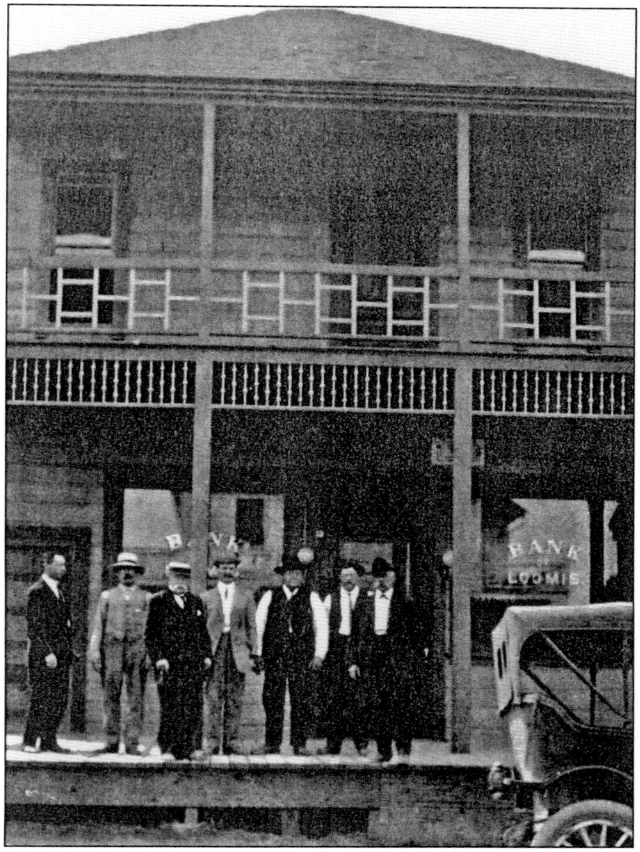

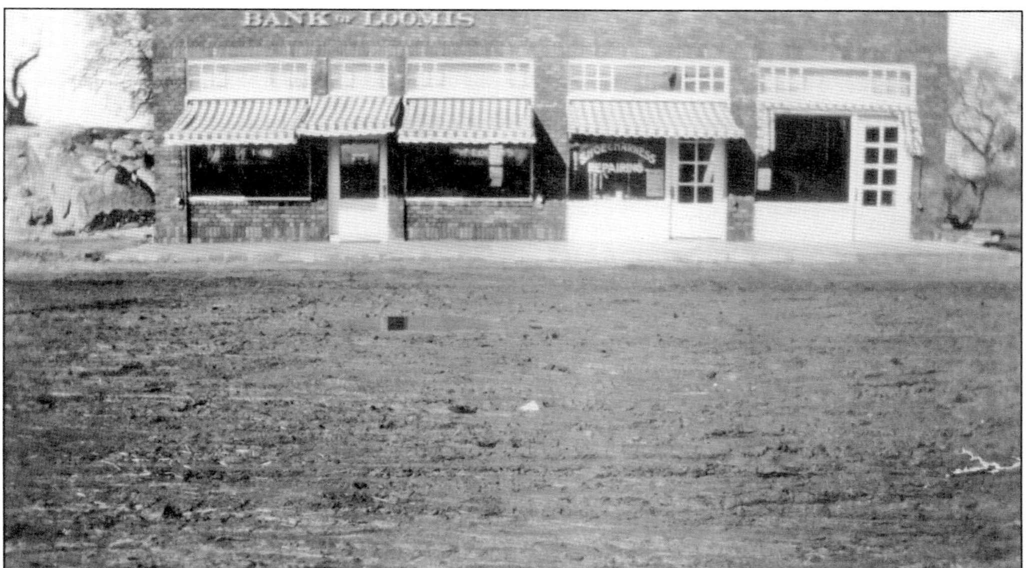

After the 1915 fire, the bank was rebuilt. This later became the site of the Nelthorpe and Son store. The rock on the far left is still a landmark in downtown Loomis.

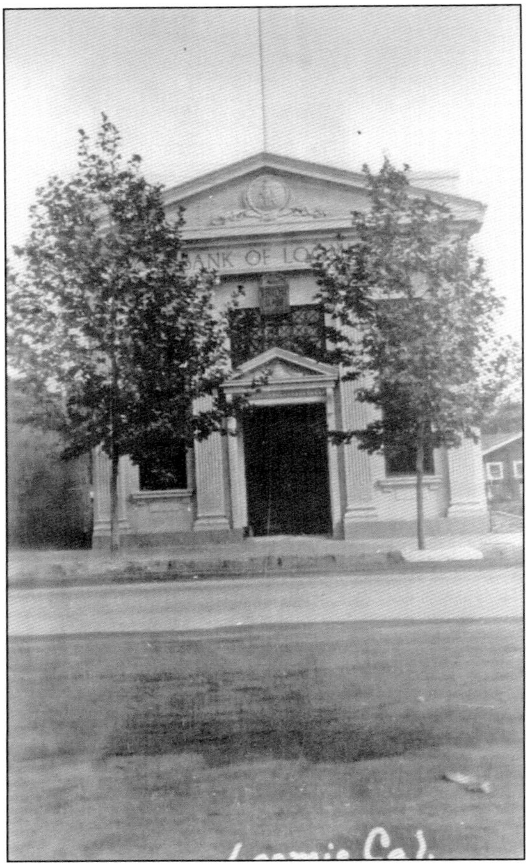

The Bank of Loomis is pictured in the early 1920s. This much grander and more visible bank was built across the street from the brick bank in the previous photograph. It is still standing. It eventually became the Rocklin Loomis Municipal Utility District and in 2008 became the future home of the Town of Loomis offices.

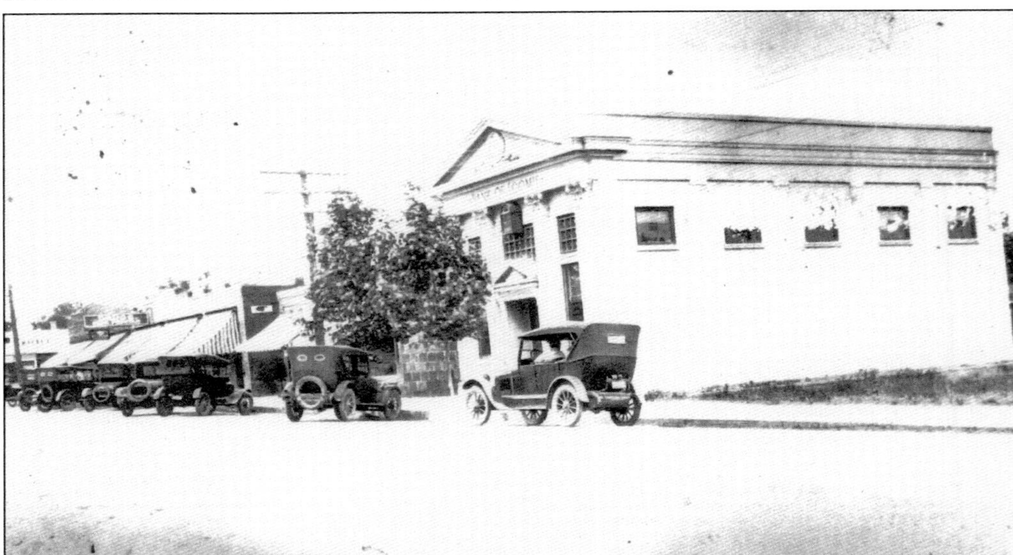

This is a street scene of Taylor Road in front of the Bank of Loomis. The open field to the right of the bank later became the site of the U.S. Post Office.

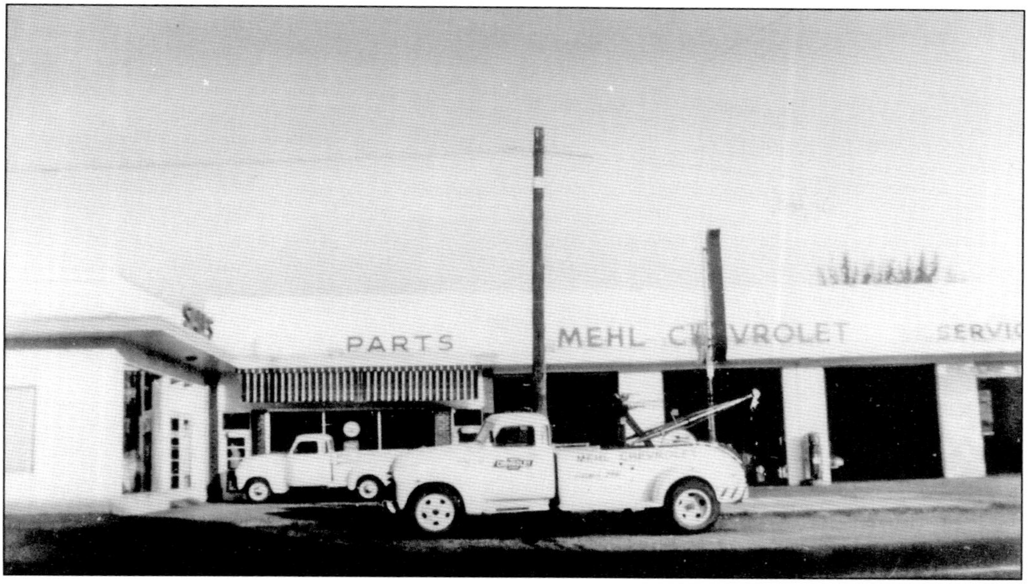

The Mehl Chevrolet agency building was located at 3701 Taylor Road. This building was across from the Main Drug Store. The Mehl family had this agency since 1929. The dealership sold the fire department one of the department's pumper trucks. Mehl Chevrolet was sold in 1956 and became Allton Chevrolet in October of that year. The far left portion of the building was constructed in 1919. The Mehl family still owns an extensive amount of real estate in the Loomis area.

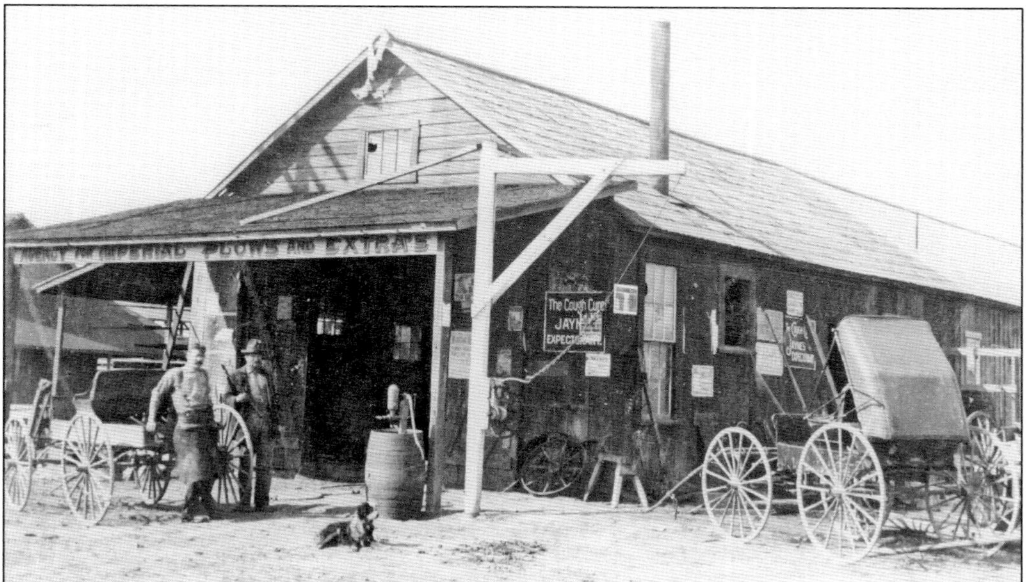

George Boller is the blacksmith leaning against the wagon. The other man's identity is not known. The blacksmith shop sold Imperial Plows and Jayne's Expectorant, which the sign says is the cure for the cough. The old blacksmith shop had a town well and a stone watering trough for all to use. In the early days of Pino, this was very important to the town, as it supplied drinking water. Ditch water was supplied by the South Yuba ditch line for other uses. The town well had a water dipper that hung on the side of the well house for everyone to use.

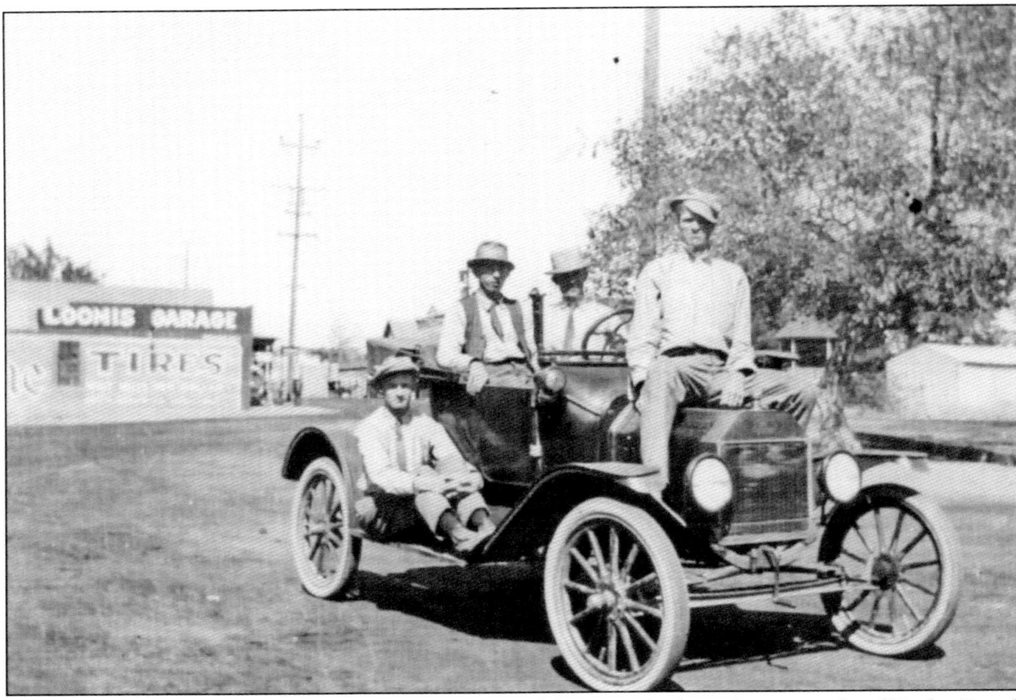

This is a quaint photograph of the times. The Model T is parked on the west side of Taylor Road. The Loomis Garage in the background was the site of the Boller blacksmith shop.

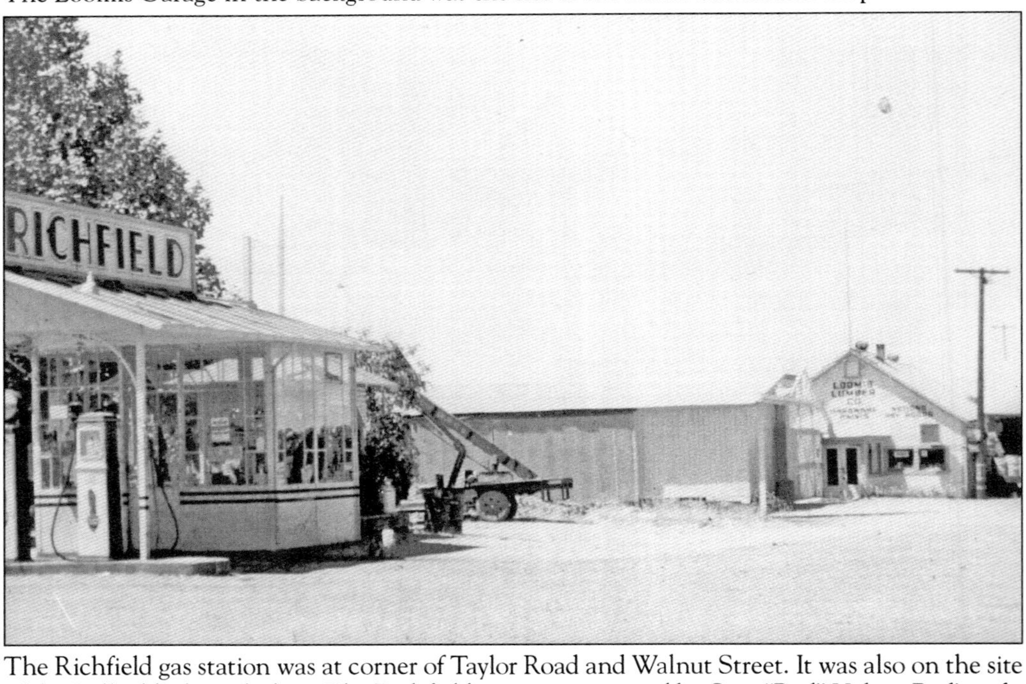

The Richfield gas station was at corner of Taylor Road and Walnut Street. It was also on the site of the Boller blacksmith shop. The Richfield station was owned by Otto "Red" Helms. Red's wife, Jessie, was the town librarian for decades. The Loomis Lumber Company is in the background. The spur track for the fruit sheds was between these two buildings.

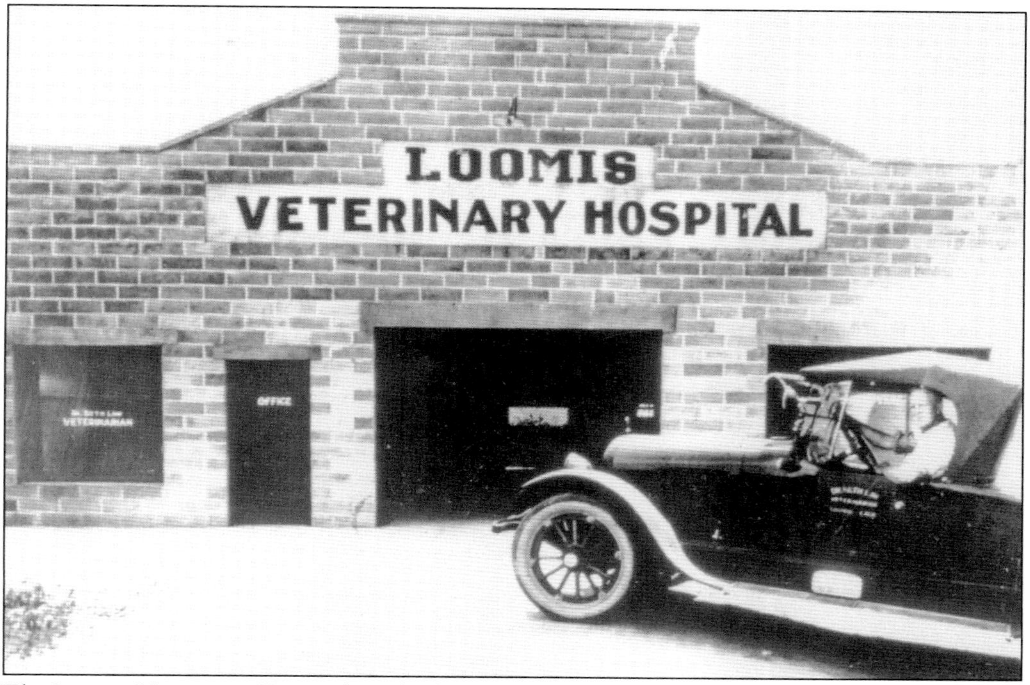

The Loomis Veterinary Hospital was built around 1918. People of the community had a dance in the new structure at its completion, as was often the custom. Dr. Seth Law was the veterinarian in the area. He is seen in his car, which he used to drive from ranch to ranch to take care of the animals. This building also housed the Reeves and Doty garage, the *Loomis News*, and Rippey's Marine.

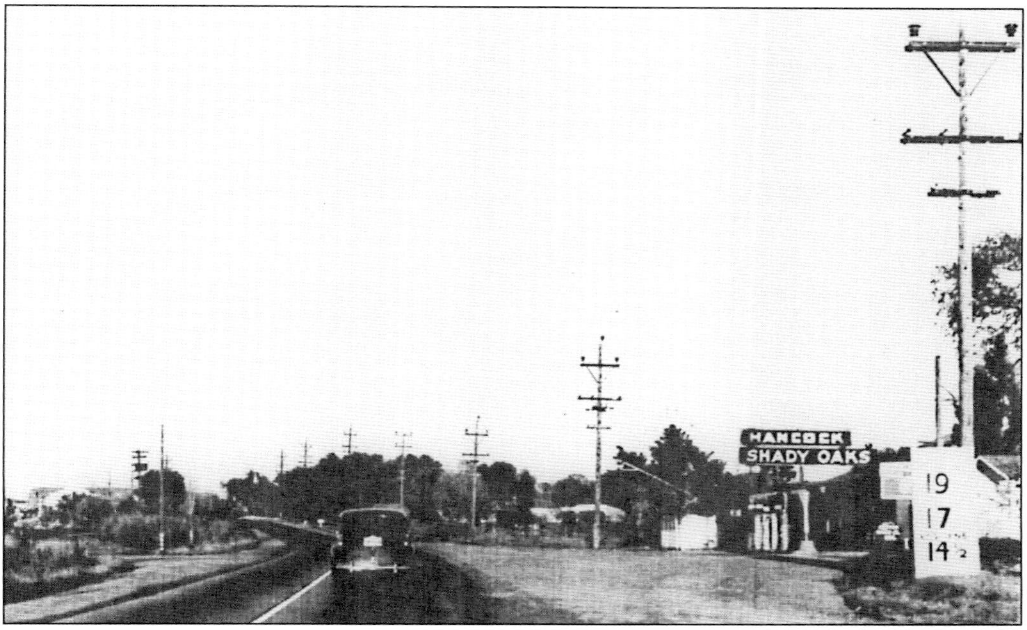

This photograph was taken on Taylor Road at the south end of town. The Hancock gas station is on the right. The prices for gas shown on the sign have not been seen for decades.

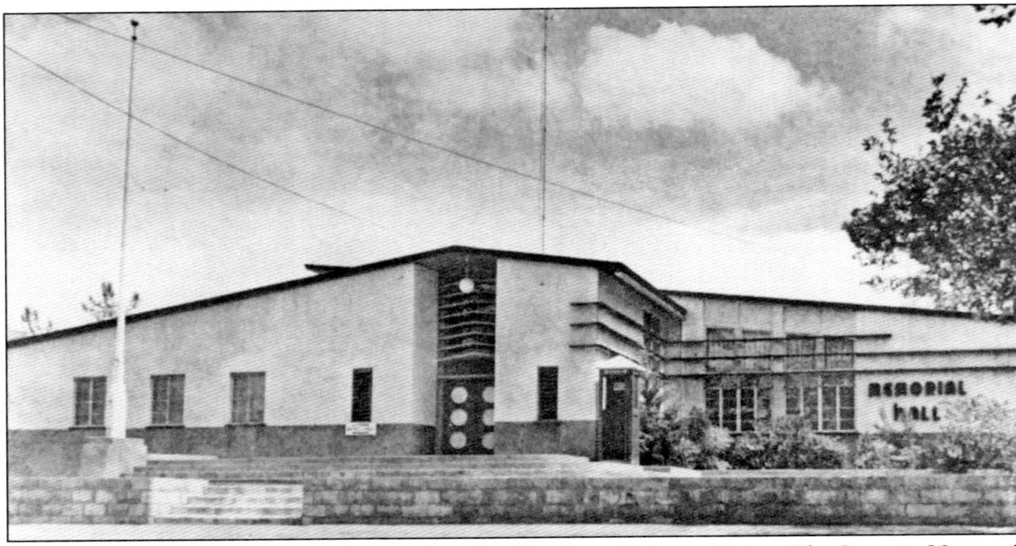

This building is at the curve of Horseshoe Bar Road and Library Drive. The Loomis Veteran's Memorial Hall was built in the 1950s. Note the round windows in the front doors. Other than the doors being changed to all glass and what looks like a phone booth being removed, the building looked much the same as it does today.

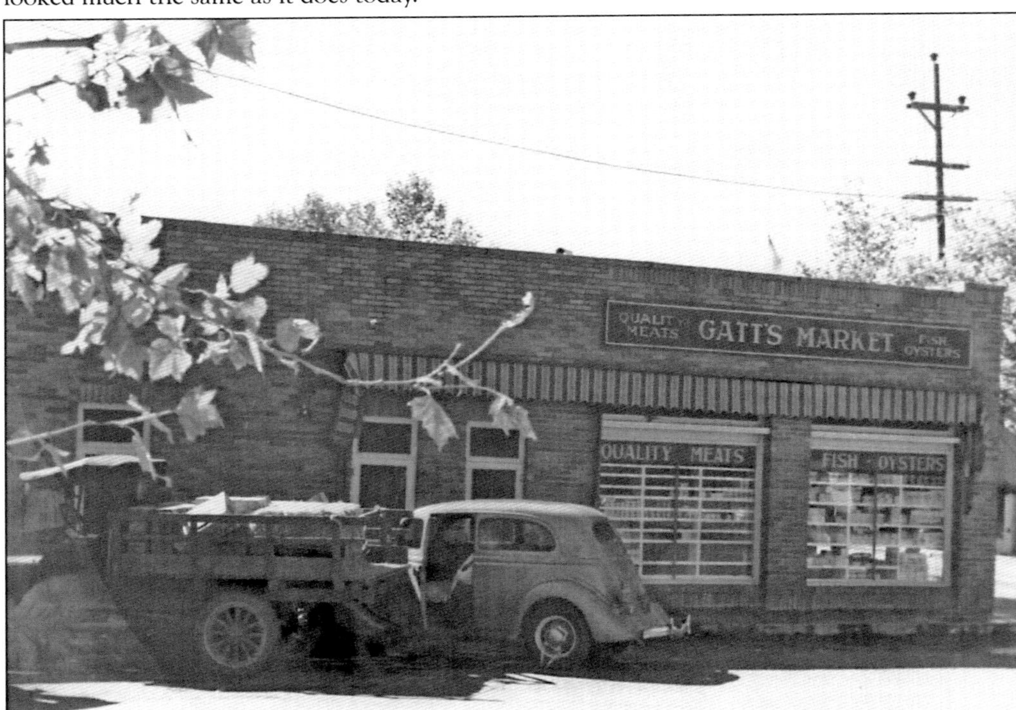

Jess Noia and George Gatt were the original owners of what became Gatt's Market. This brick building on the corner of Taylor Road and Horseshoe Bar Road was built by Charley Dolce. As the business grew, George Gatt bought out Jess Noia and became the sole proprietor in 1926. The business was commonly referred to as Gatt's Meat Market.

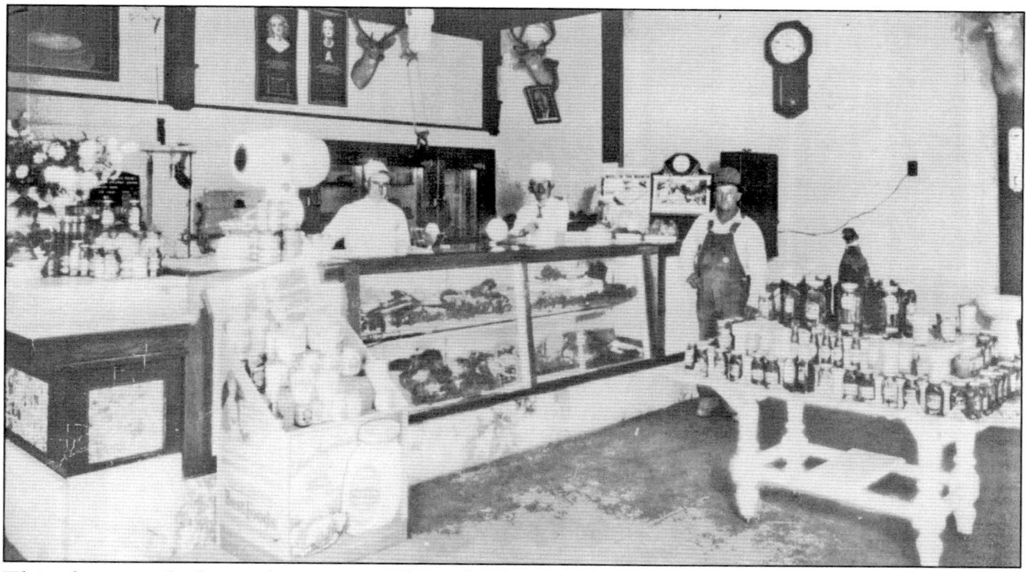

This photograph shows the interior of Gatt's Meat Market. It was taken about 1933. Behind the counter are George Gatt, left, and Louie Brenzo. The customer is Iolin Porter, a hay farmer. The store was always a clean, cool place to visit after a long day's work. The store featured a cold water fountain and always had bouquets of beautiful flowers from Ina Gatt's garden.

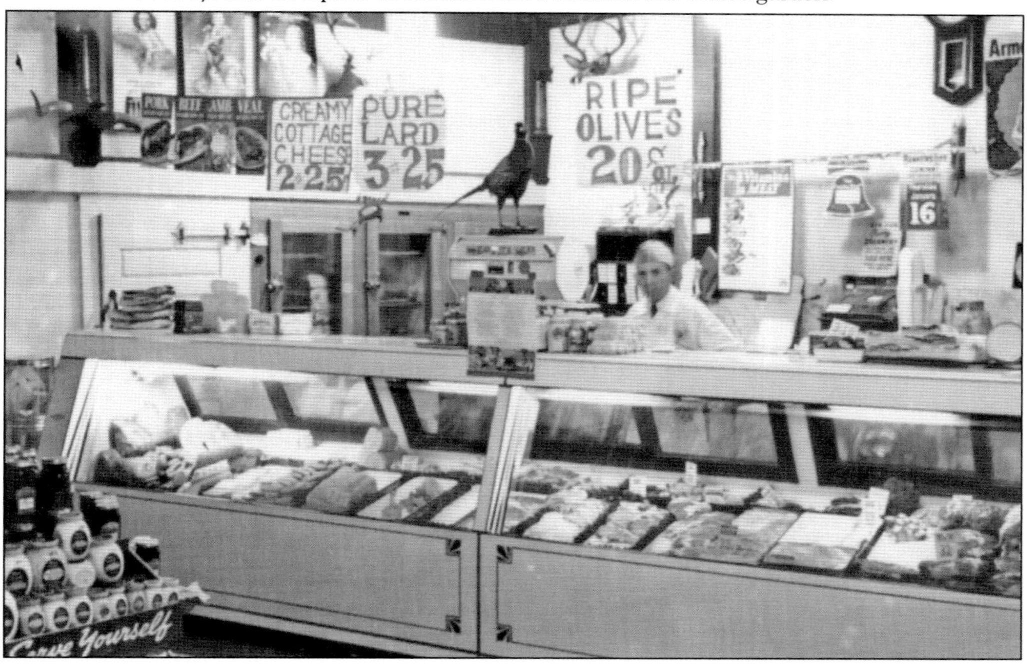

This is an interior photograph of Gatt's Market in 1937. George Gatt is the butcher and the owner of the store. George was born in Newcastle, California, on December 24, 1884, the son of Joseph Gatt and Mary Noia Gatt. Joseph, of German descent, was a stonecutter and worked for the Griffith Quarry in Penryn. He at one time owned the site of the Newcastle School and built the stone wall that surrounded the place. Much of this stone wall is still in place. Joseph and Mary had four children: George, John, Louise, and Marie.

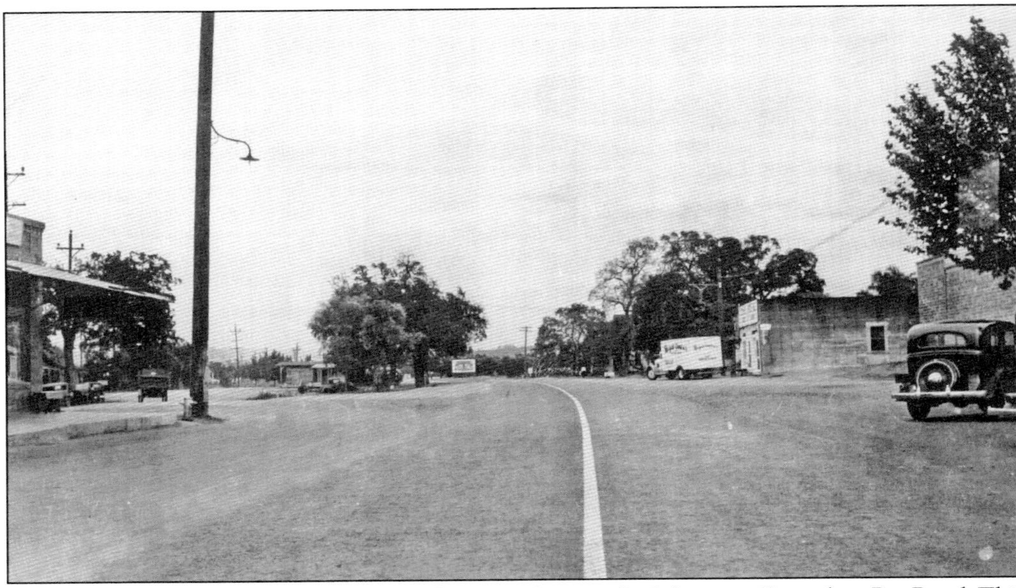

This is a view of U.S. 40 (now Taylor Road) at Pine Street, which became Horseshoe Bar Road. This was taken in the mid-1930s, after U.S. 40 was straightened out. The power pole that is prominent on the left shows in all the photographs, whether taken in the early 1900s or in 2009.

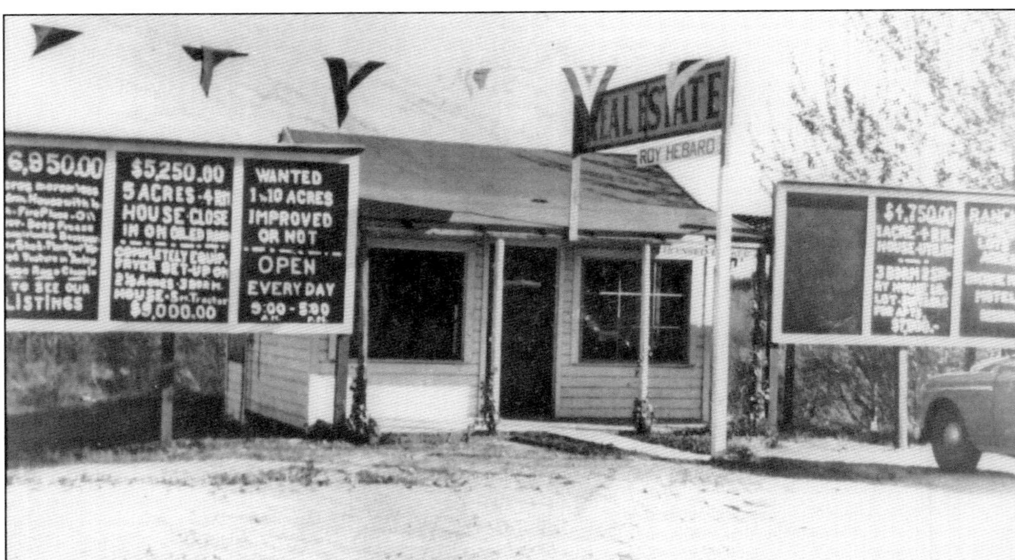

This photograph was taken of the Roy Hebard Real Estate office on Taylor Road below Circle Drive. The prices are reminiscent of times gone by.

Four

The Fire Department

Like most small settlements, Loomis's buildings were mostly wooden. As the history of the town progressed, fire was no stranger. After a fire, reconstruction followed. With no organized fire suppression system in place, the town was tempting fate. In 1915, a major fire hit the downtown core. The fire wiped out many businesses and buildings. This time, the reconstruction was accomplished with granite, cinder block, or brick; wood was not used. The Loomis Fire Protection District was formed prior to 1930, and commissioners were elected by popular vote. William Dearborn was named president, and Garrett Doty was the secretary of the board of commissioners. They rented a fire truck from the Nugent-Covey Wagon Company of San Francisco for $1,700. By August 21, 1930, a fire department was formed, and Victor DeCampos became the chief. Hugo Mehl was first assistant chief, and Earl Vance was second assistant. By October 8, 1930, rules and regulations for efficient operation were formed. Among the first pieces of equipment was a 1930 Ford Model A Pumper. The old Reeves and Doty Ford Garage was the first fire station. In 1959, a cinder block station house was built. In 2009, that cinder block structure holds the fire equipment, and a new station has been built next door. In 1945, a new Ford pumper was added, and in 1951, a Chevrolet fire truck was purchased from Mehl Chevrolet in Loomis. It was equipped with a two-speed axle for low speed when used off-road and when climbing steep hills. In the 1950s, a Jeep equipped with a small water tank was added. A large siren mounted on the roof of the Reeves and Doty garage and later on the roof of the fire station was activated when the volunteers needed to fight fire. There was also a telephone calling system that summoned the volunteer firemen. Nick Mangiaracina, Frank Nute, and Wes Barnes have all contributed more than 40 years of volunteer work with the department.

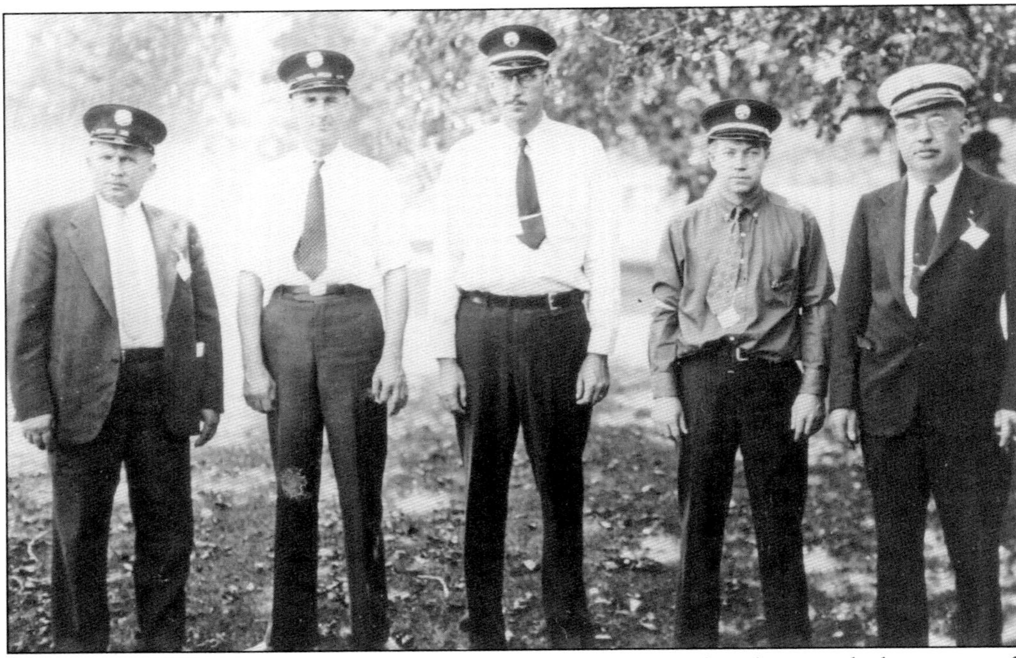

This photograph shows men of the Loomis Fire Department. From left to right, they are Howard Ogden, Art Stokes, Albert Fieser, Earl Vance, and fire chief Garrett Doty. Doty was chief from 1935 to 1953.

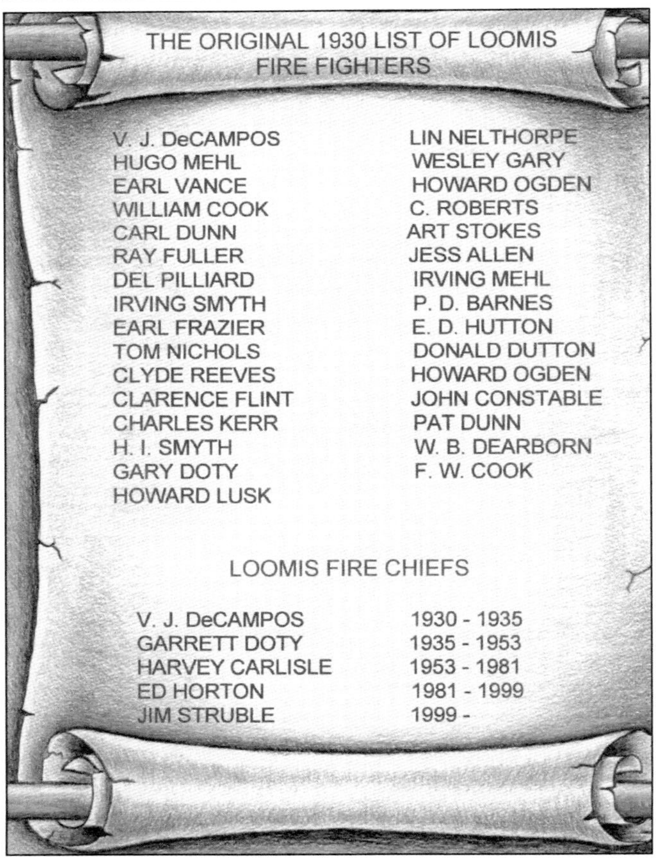

THE ORIGINAL 1930 LIST OF LOOMIS FIRE FIGHTERS

V. J. DeCAMPOS	LIN NELTHORPE
HUGO MEHL	WESLEY GARY
EARL VANCE	HOWARD OGDEN
WILLIAM COOK	C. ROBERTS
CARL DUNN	ART STOKES
RAY FULLER	JESS ALLEN
DEL PILLIARD	IRVING MEHL
IRVING SMYTH	P. D. BARNES
EARL FRAZIER	E. D. HUTTON
TOM NICHOLS	DONALD DUTTON
CLYDE REEVES	HOWARD OGDEN
CLARENCE FLINT	JOHN CONSTABLE
CHARLES KERR	PAT DUNN
H. I. SMYTH	W. B. DEARBORN
GARY DOTY	F. W. COOK
HOWARD LUSK	

LOOMIS FIRE CHIEFS

V. J. DeCAMPOS	1930 - 1935
GARRETT DOTY	1935 - 1953
HARVEY CARLISLE	1953 - 1981
ED HORTON	1981 - 1999
JIM STRUBLE	1999 -

This scroll lists the names of the original 1930 Loomis firefighters. The fire chiefs are listed below the names.

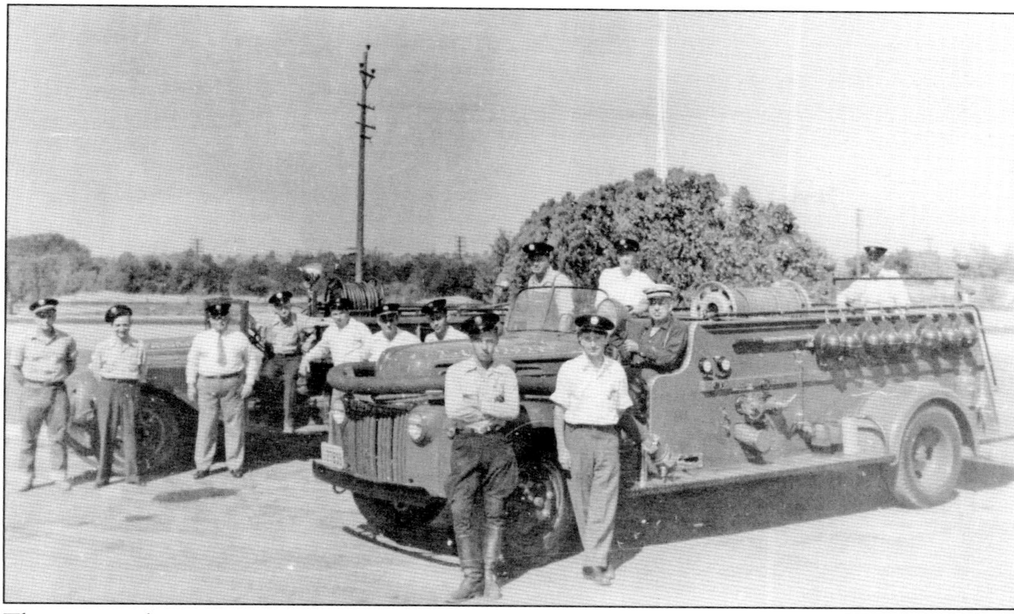

This picture shows two Loomis fire trucks, including the 1945 pumper truck, and some of the men of the fire department. Starting on the left are Frank Nute, Paul Sagaser, and Howard Ogden. In the truck are Robert Todd and Merle Coburn. By the truck in the foreground are Harvey Carlisle Jr. and Ed Rippey. On the fender in bib overalls is Robert Tudsbury, and behind him is Art Stokes. Chief Garrett Doty is at the wheel. At the back of the truck is Ed Court. Standing in front are Wes Barnes and an unidentified man.

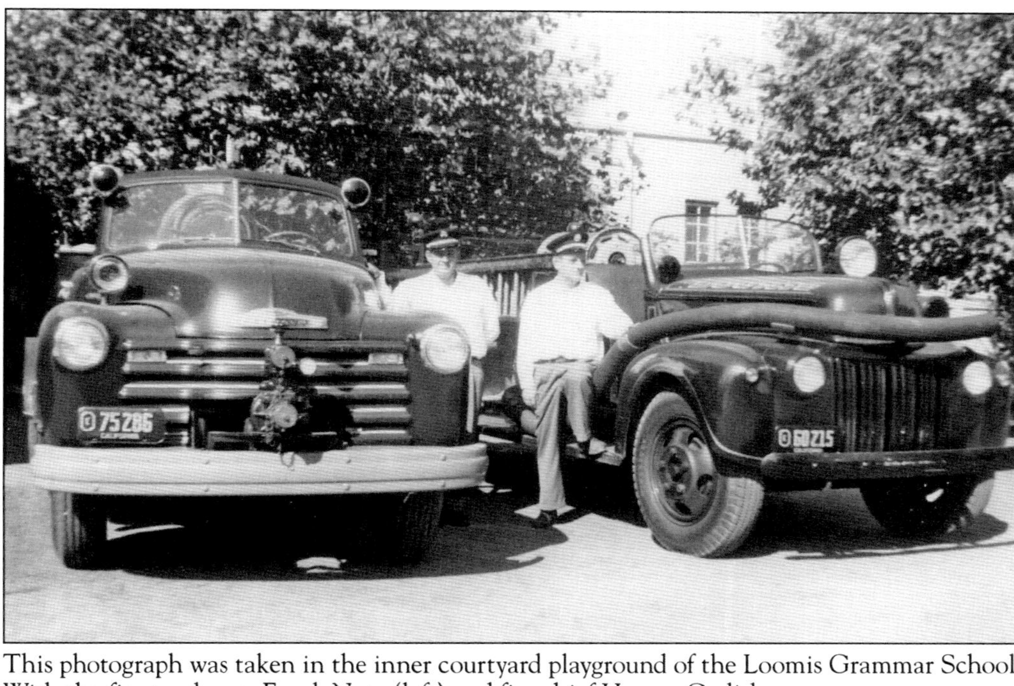

This photograph was taken in the inner courtyard playground of the Loomis Grammar School. With the fire trucks are Frank Nute (left) and fire chief Harvey Carlisle.

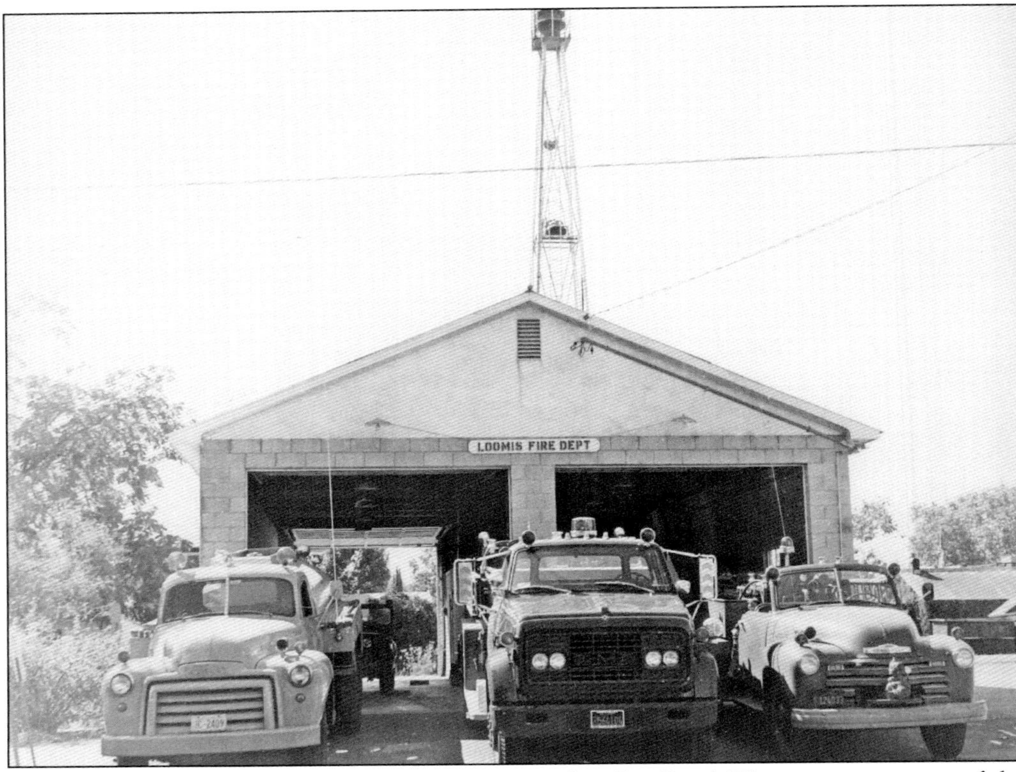

This shows the current fire station garage on Horseshoe Bar Road. The structure on top of the building houses the siren. This siren blew when a fire was reported. The volunteers were notified by a phone tree. Dorothee Law Johnson was one of the callers on the phone tree.

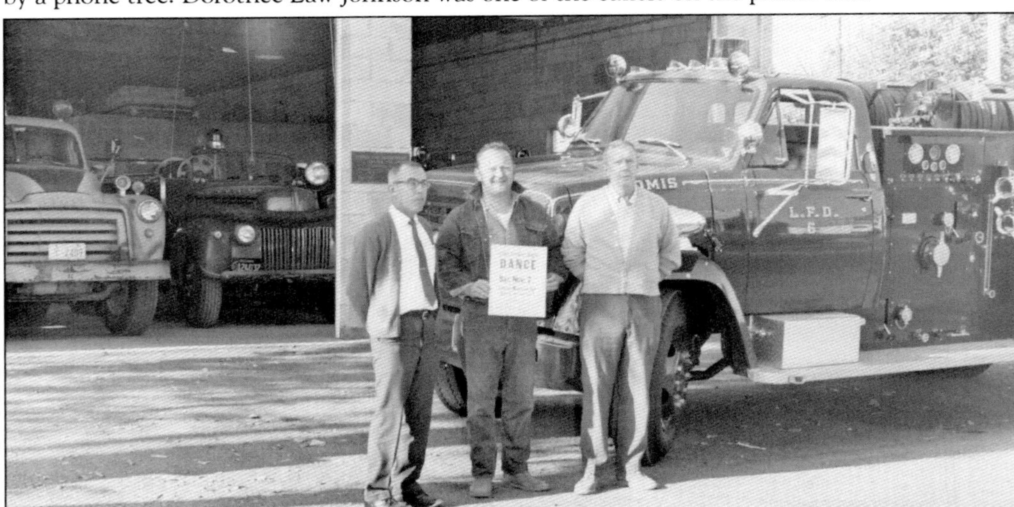

The three firemen in front of the station are Wes Barnes, postmaster; John Lee, postal carrier; and Jim Johnson, co-owner of Law Brothers. These men are shown in a publicity photograph for the fireman's dance. This dance was held for many years as a main fund-raiser for the volunteer department. The dances were held about half a block down the street from the fire department at the Memorial Hall. The firefighters were close to the station house if a fire occurred.

Five

SCHOOLS

From the very beginning, the families that settled the area were concerned with education for their families. The Franklin School District was organized in 1862, according to the *Superintendent of Schools Ledger Book*, but the *Board of Supervisors Book B* states that it was created on May 9, 1863. Other sources suggest that a group of mining families joined together in 1852 at Doton's Bar to form the Franklin School District and built one of the earliest public schools in the county. The school was relocated farther west when mining failed at Doton's Bar. The second location was on the old Sacramento Wagon Road (now Auburn Folsom Road). In 1884, fourteen pupils were taught by Mary McKay. In 1967, the third school of the Loomis Union School District was built off Laird Road and named Franklin School after the original school. Another of the earliest schools to be built was called Pine Grove School, near Secret Ravine. The first building was constructed in 1856 on the Grant property near what is now the intersection of Brace and Barton Roads. P. Lynch, L. Stout, and J. Turner were the first trustees. There were 85 children between the ages of 4 and 18 living in the district in 1856. In 1862, the town changed its name from Pine Grove to Placer for three months and then to Smithville. The school was renamed to Smithville, as was the district. A second school was built on property between Brace and Horseshoe Bar Roads just north of the Loomis Methodist Church. In 1869, the new Central Pacific Railroad convinced the businessmen of Smithville to relocate the town westward toward the present site of the railroad tracks, after which the town was renamed Pino. Smithville School was closed for a short time, and the students in the area had to go elsewhere. George Turner, who lived less than a half-mile from the school, had to ride a mule cross-country to Monte Rio School, near Rattlesnake Bar on the American River, to attend classes. The Smithville School was reopened by December 21, 1872. When Mary Neubaumer, who became Mrs. George Turner, taught there in 1886, it was known as Pino School. When the town changed its name from Pino to Loomis in 1890, it became Loomis School. Thankfully there were no more name changes, and the Loomis School is still in existence.

PINE GROVE SCHOOL.

Christmas Exercises,

FRIDAY EVENING, DECEMBER 24, 1886.

PROGRAMME.

1. Song—Happy Greeting to All . . . . *School.*
2. Opening Address . . . . *Frank Webb.*
3. Poor Little Jim . . . . *Nellie Cook.*
4. What I Found in a Kitchen Drawer . . . . . *Melbourne Callahan.*
5. Room at the Top . . . . *Edward Leahy.*
5. Dialogue—Four Seasons
   Spring . . . . *Maggie Hoffman.*
   Summer . . . . *Birdie Callahan.*
   Autumn . . . . *Maria Hickey.*
   Winter . . . . *Joseph Cordel.*
7. Dialogue—Preparing for School . . . . *Willie Webb, Jesse Bankhead.*
8. Song—In The Star Light . . *Maggie Bankhead, Nellie Cook, Birdie Callahan, Maria Hickey.*
9. My Watch . . . . *Willie Turner.*
10. Dialogue—A Place for Everything . . . *Katie Hickey, Lily Turner.*
11. A Fragment . . . . *John Files.*
12. Willie and Annie's Prayer . . . . *Blanche Hawk.*
13. A Fast Friend . . . . *Elmer Himes.*
14. A Little Girl . . . . *Katie Burns.*
15. The Old Home . . . . *Walter Callahan.*
16. Twenty Years Ago . . . . *Lily Turner.*
17. Dialogue—Spelling Class . . *Maggie Bankhead, John Files, Thomas Leahy, Willie Turner, Charlie Himes, Walter Callahan, Frank Webb, Elmer Himes, John Leahy, Melbourne Callahan, Joseph Cordel, Frank Himes, Maxwell Hiser.*
18. Song—Hail to the New Year . . . . *School.*
19. My Machine . . . . *Charlie Himes.*
20. Remember, Boys Make Men . . . . *Maxwell Hiser.*
21. Dialogue—Amateur Farming. . . . *Mary Bankhead, Blanche Hawk.*
22. Dialogue—Patrick's Love . . . . *Agnes Bankhead, John Leahy.*
23. Dialogue—The House Jack Built . . . *Frank Himes, John Leahy, Paul Orslin, Celestine Cordel, Arthur Hawk, Minnie Orslin, Maggie Hoffman, Walter Himes, Claudie Hoffman, Johnnie Leahy.*
    MAIDEN, *Emma Orslin;* MAN, *Michael Leahy;* PRIEST, *Edward Leahy*
    FARMER, *Maxwell Hiser.*
24. Christmas . . . . *Nellie Leahy.*
25. Little Boy's Speech . . . . *Claudie Hoffman.*
26. Song—Merry Merry Christmas . . . . *School.*

MARY T. NEUEBAUMER, TEACHER.

Doors open at 6 P. M. Exercises begin at 7 P. M.

Admission, Free.

The Pine Grove School presented a Christmas program on December 24, 1886. Students participated, and families came to share in the holidays. Mary Neubaumer was the teacher. The Pine Grove School is the second oldest school in the area. The school belonged to the Secret Ravine School District in 1856. The first school building was on the Grant property not far from the present intersection of Barton and Brace Roads.

Pine Grove School

CHRISTMAS EXERCISES,

Saturday Evening December 24, 1887

PROGRAMME.

1	Song—Happy Are We	School
2	Welcome	Agnes Bankhead
3	First Speech in Public	Thomas Bolton
4	Charity Begins at Home	Nellie Cook
5	How Many Miles to Baby-Land	Willie Webb
6	Country Farming	Celestine Cordel
7	The French Man	Paul Robinson
8	The Christening	Lily Turner
9	To-day and To-morrow	Frank Davis
10	Song—Ring the Bells	School
11	A Nameless Hero	Winnif ed Robinson
12	Sowing Wild Oots	Walter Callahan
[illegible]	[illegible]	Maggie Bankhead
14	Boy's Ambition	Maxwell Hiser
15	Dialogue—"The Sevens."	
	Seven Times One	Jessie Bankhead
	" " Two	Maggie Hoffman
	" " Three	Blanche Hawk
	" " Four	Nellie Cook
	" " Five	Mary Bankhead
	" " Six	Katie Hickey
16	Song—Follow Me	Primary Pupils
17	Christmas Morn	Paul Orsolini
18	That Other Fellow	Elmer Hines
20	The End of the Season	Maggie Hoffman
21	Pride	Frank Hines
22	Two of Them	Emma Orsolini
23	Dollars Does the Business	John Files
24	Guilty or not Guilty	Katie Hickey
25	Song—Keep to the Right	School
26	Beautiful Things	George Bolton
27	Grown up Land	Walter Hines
28	Making Up	Katie Burns
29	Horse Shoe of Good Luck	Melbourne Callahan
30	School Master's Guests	Lily Turner
31	Christmas	Claude Hoffman
32	Christmas Stockings	Arthur Hawk
33	Santa Claus Knew	Celetine Cordel
34	Song—Christmas Song	School

Mary T. Neuebaumer, Teacher.

Doors open at 6 P. M. Exercises at 7 P. M.

The Pine Grove School presented an annual Christmas Eve program for the students and their families. Mary T. Neubaumer was still the teacher. She later married George W. Turner.

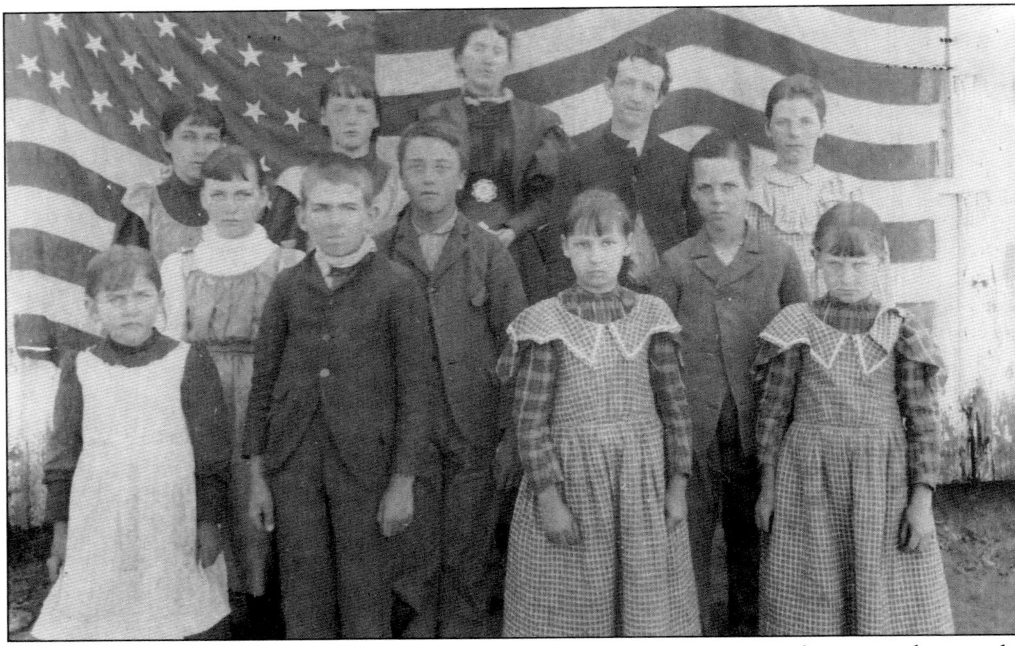

This is a photograph of Franklin School taken about 1896. William Crossley is standing in the middle in front of the teacher. The following names do not match this picture but are the names from the September 1897 class. The names are Maud Gossett, Zella Gossett, Chester Gossett, Elmira Gossett, Catherine Ferguson, Pearl Miller, Ernie Darling, Elfrida Darling, Charley Lucas, Arthur Stark, Roy Fletcher, George Schwerdtle, Dora Schwerdtle, Mamie Schwerdtle, Maud Bridges, Willie Crossley, and teacher Cora Light.

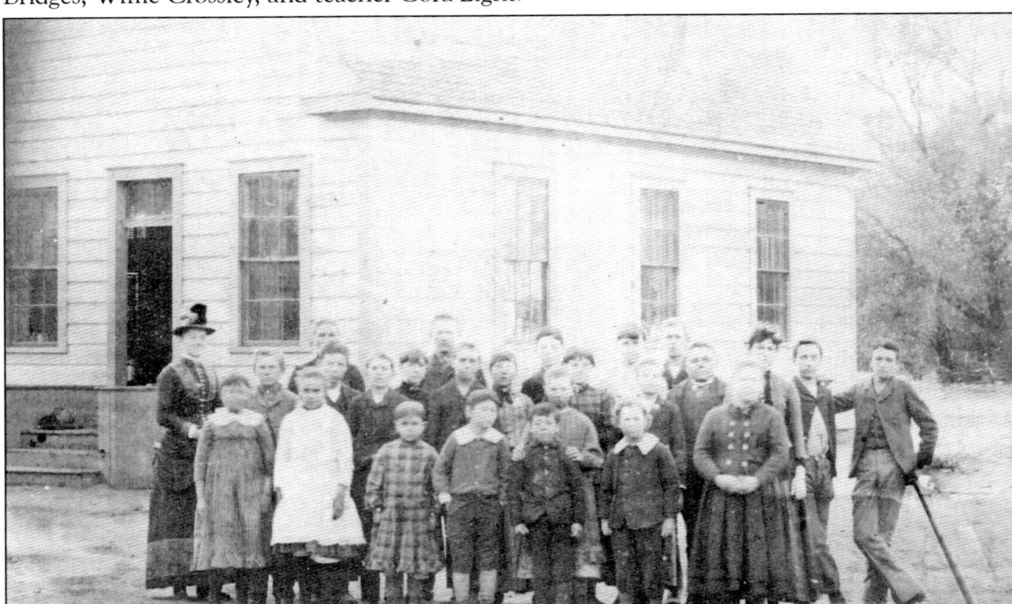

The Smithville Schoolhouse is seen as it stood in 1887. The Smithville School District was formerly part of the larger Secret Ravine School District. The Smithville School District closed on November 19, 1886.

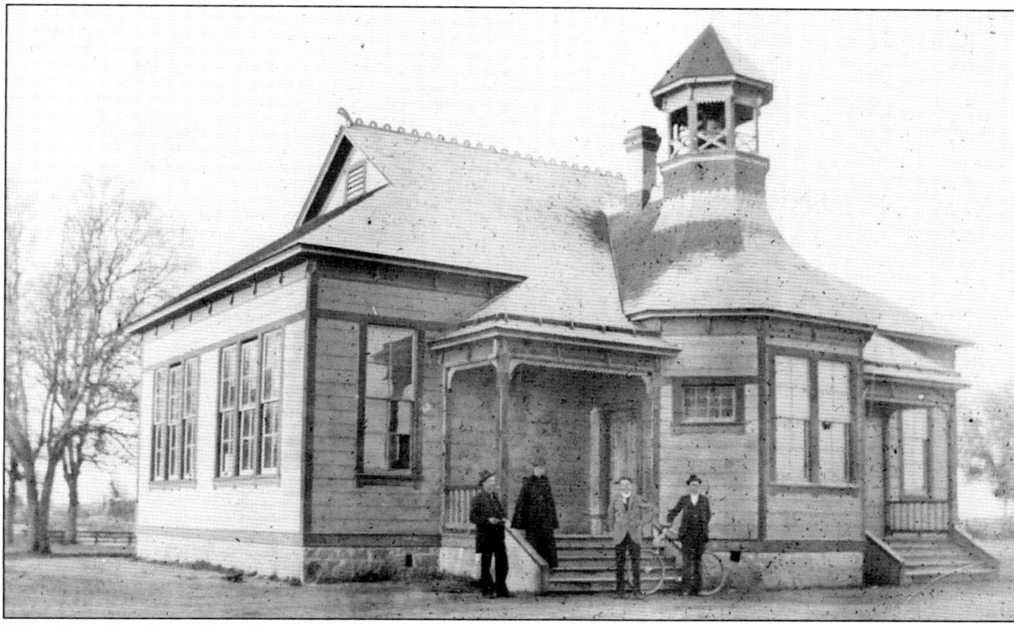

The Smithville Schoolhouse became the Loomis Grammar School as of August 28, 1898. It is located on a 3-acre parcel between Horseshoe Bar and Brace Roads across from the Loomis Methodist Church. The 1924–1925 school term was the last at this site.

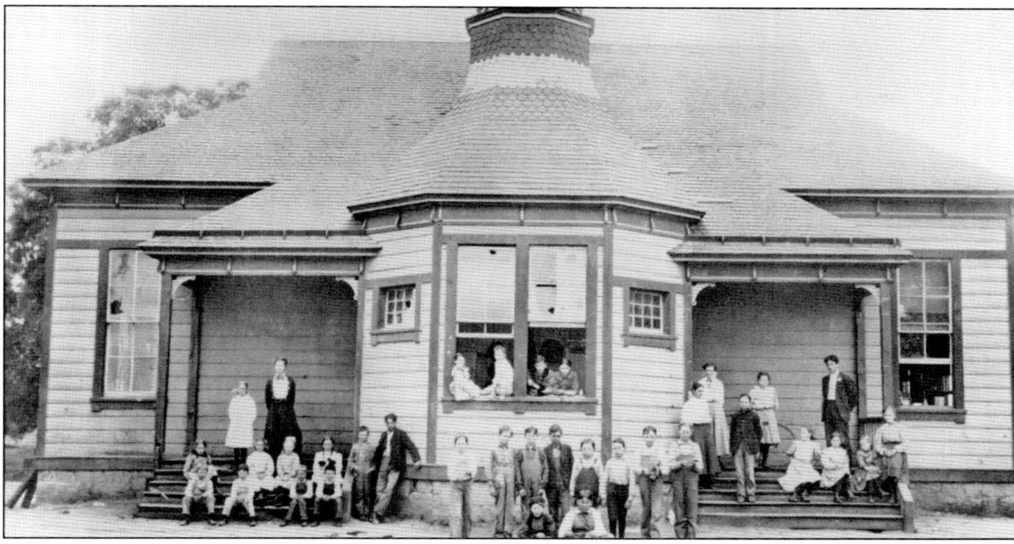

The Loomis School class of 1903–1904 was taught by Edna Fisher and James Bunker. The students are (sitting on steps) Jean Laird, Ethel Fisher, Norma Himes, and Helen Renicke; (boys) George Bock, Joe Turner, Kenneth Laird, and unidentified; (against the wall) Charles Cushman and Angelo Dolce; (in window left to right) Edith Sheppard, Helen Gilmore, Bessie Federoff, and Jessie Gilmore; (left to right) Blanche Quinn, Ora Turner, teacher James Bunker, Verna Laird, and Charles H. Turner; (sitting) Jessie Rowell, Thelma Johnson, Dorothy Fassett, and Olga Kutchiker; (boys standing in front, left to right) Harold Misley, Bert Cook, unidentified, James Laird, Charles R. Turner, Audrey Cook, Glen Gilmore, and Ferdinand Bock; (sitting in foreground) Carroll Roddan and Eugene Lawrence.

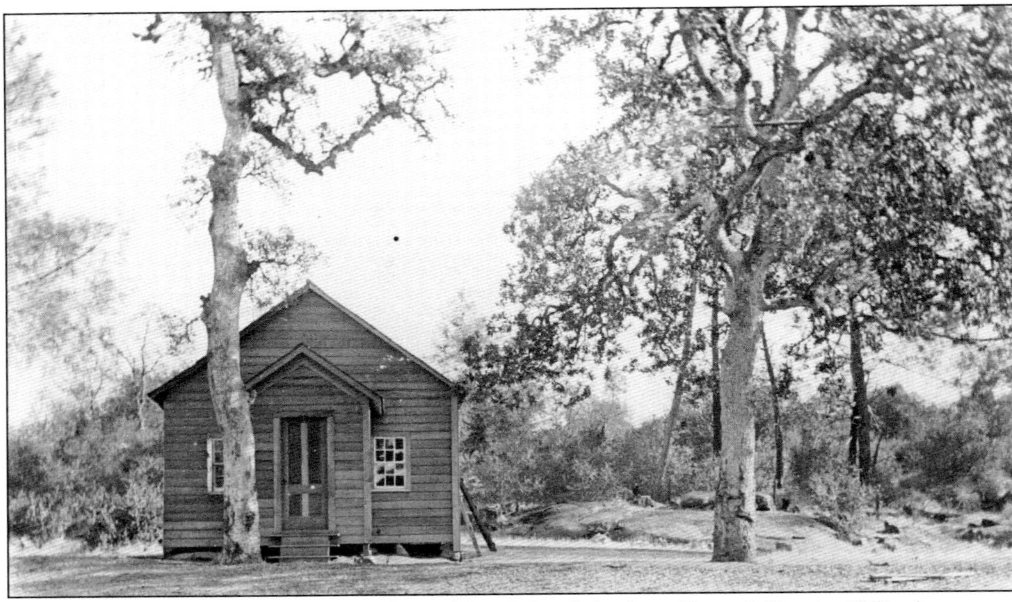

This photograph shows the original Franklin School, built at Dotan's Bar in 1852. A group of mining families joined together to form the Franklin School District and built one of the earliest public schools in Placer County. Later a woodshed was added to store the wood needed to heat the school. Franklin received its first public money in 1862. Fourteen students attended the school. It closed in 1920.

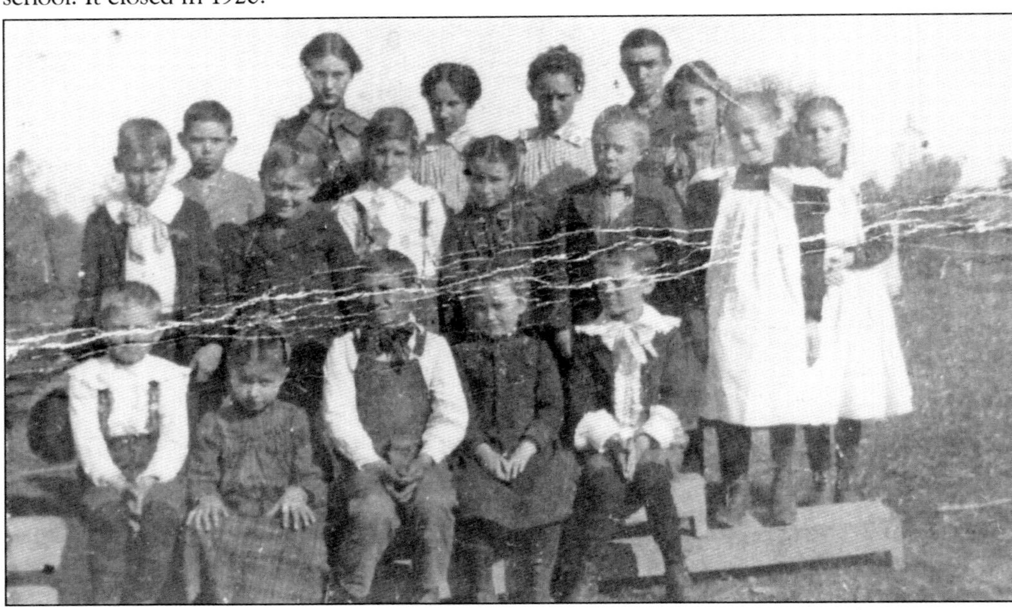

This is a photograph of the pupils of Franklin School taken on Lincoln's Day, February 12, 1901. Cora E. Light was the teacher. From left to right are (first row) Henry Lucas, Lilly Prisser, Tony Prisser, Zella Quinn, and Clarence Quinn; (second row) Fred Colgrove, Harry Hill, Charlie Lucas, Blanche Quinn, Arthur Stark, Gertie Hill, and Francis Lucas; (third row) Tom Payne, Pearl Miller, Erma Darling, Elfie Darling, Ben Payne, and Myra Gossett. (Photograph courtesy of Tony Prisser.)

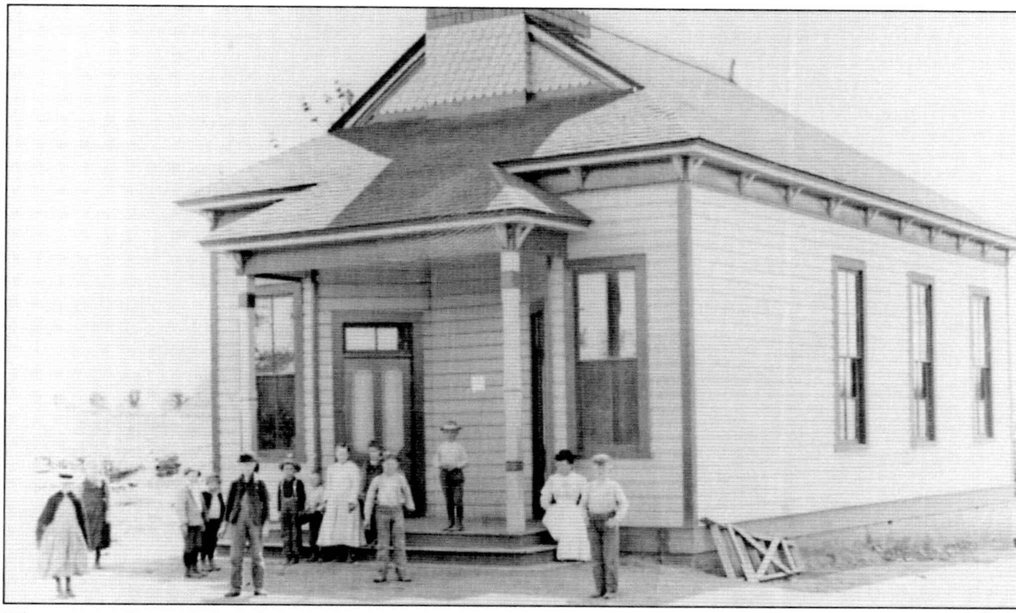

This was taken of the Placer School. The school is still located at the Tudsbury and Horseshoe Bar Roads intersection. The first class picture was in 1894. That year, a group of farmers joined together to build a one-room schoolhouse. The cost of the building was about $1,000. Mamie Starbuck, seated on the porch, was the teacher. She is remembered by Kate Fieser Leak, one of her students, as a "very stern looking woman, over 6 feet tall." A minimum of 12 students was required to collect county money to pay the teacher. Four-year-old Fred Fieser was sent to school that first year so there would be 12 students. Students would fill a bucket with water from the well at the Tudsbury home so they would have drinking water for the day.

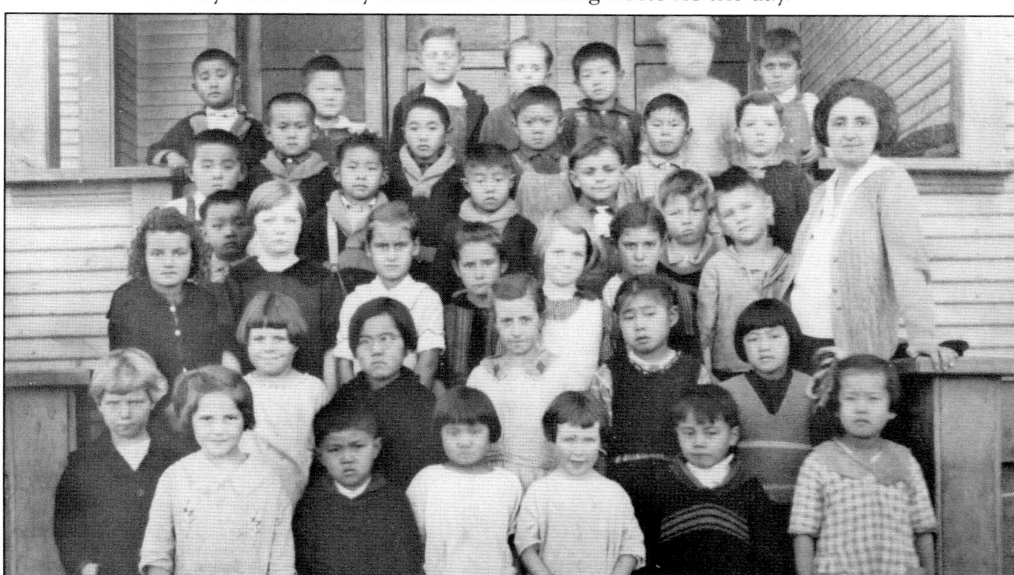

This photograph was taken at the Japanese Methodist Church at Barton and Brace Roads. It dates to February 10, 1924. Mrs. Parsons is the teacher. Frank Crossley is in the second row from the top, standing next to the teacher.

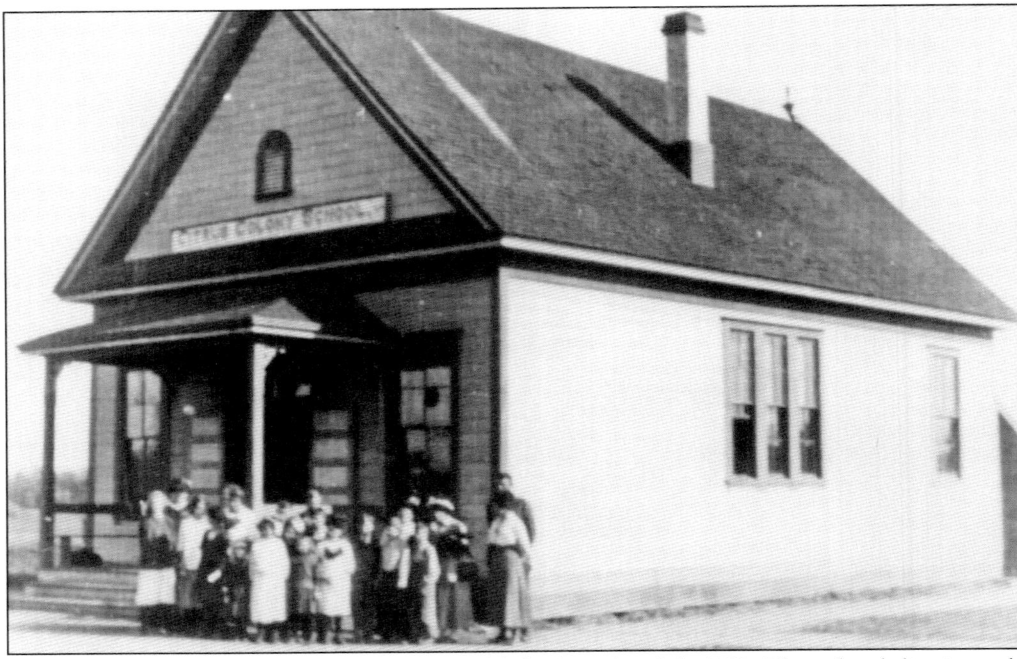

The Citrus Colony School District was established on April 5, 1893. The school district only lasted about one year. In 1904, it was reformed and continued until 1925. Early trustees were E. C. Coburn, J. D. Lewis, Frank Galloway, J. H. Swetzer, William S. Williams, R. J. Layton, and W. J. Bock. In 1909, the estimated value of the school was $1,975. By 1915, the value had risen to $3,175.

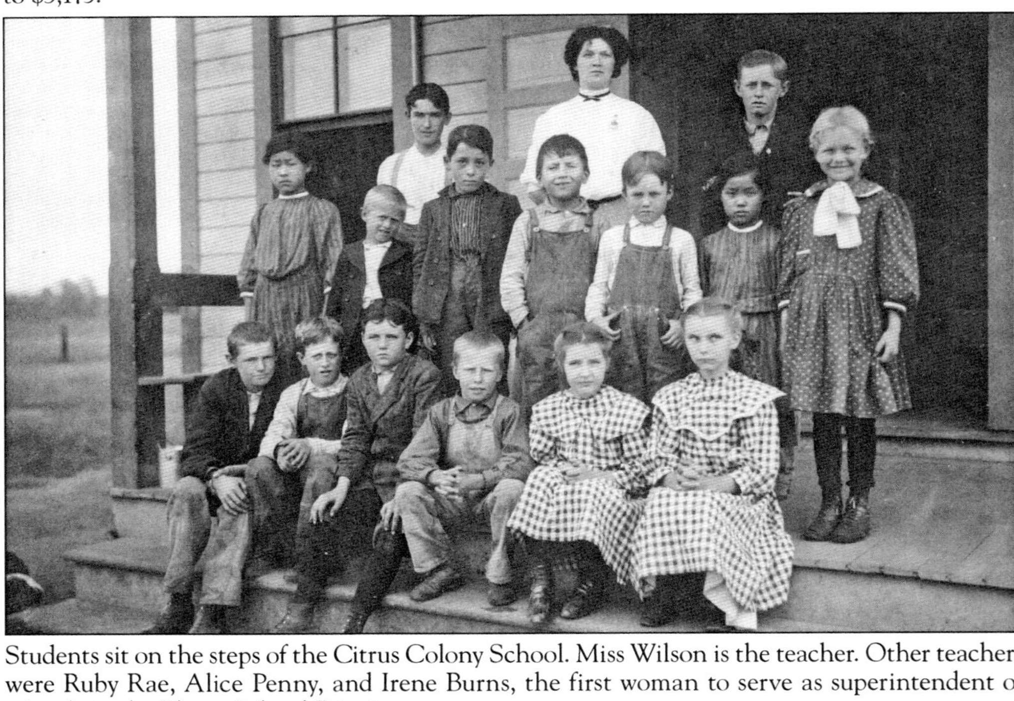

Students sit on the steps of the Citrus Colony School. Miss Wilson is the teacher. Other teachers were Ruby Rae, Alice Penny, and Irene Burns, the first woman to serve as superintendent of schools in the Placer School District.

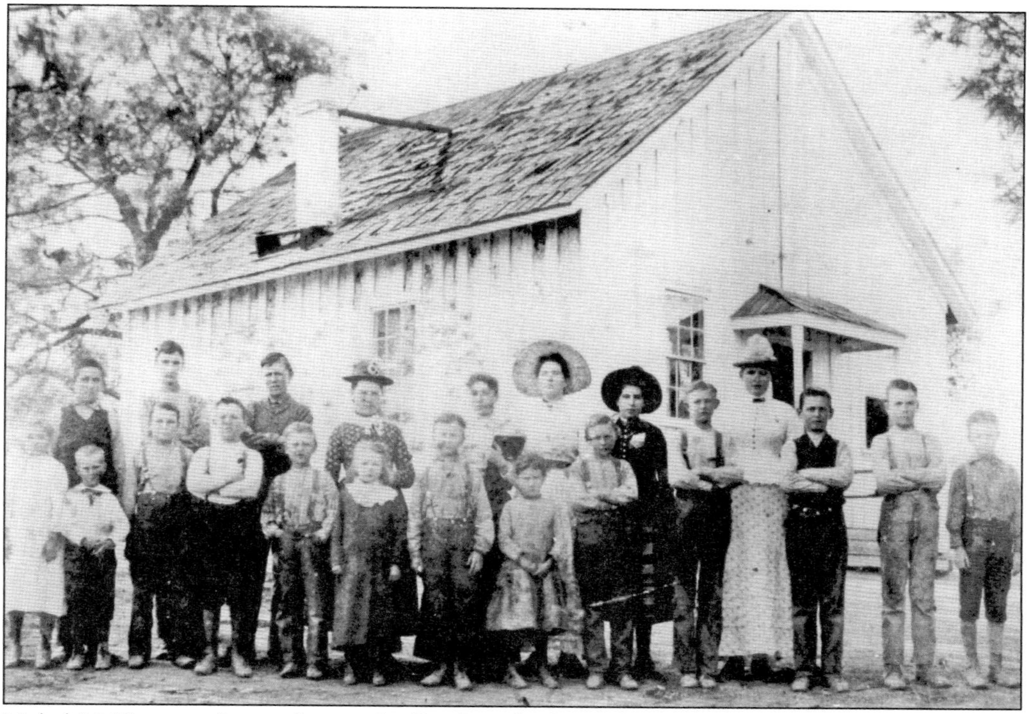

Mabel McKay was the teacher at the Rattlesnake Bar School when this picture was taken on October 28, 1888. The schoolhouse was then located on Rattlesnake Road about a half-mile up from the American River. The school was built in 1857 on what was actually Lacy's Bar. Mary Turner taught 40 pupils on a pay-as-you-go basis for 50¢ per week. The next year, 1858, the school was moved to Sexton's ranch on Rattlesnake Road. The school was burned by arsonists on October 8, 1870. Insurance of $300 covered rebuilding costs. However, insurance had not yet been purchased when arsonists torched it in November 1870. This time it was a complete loss.

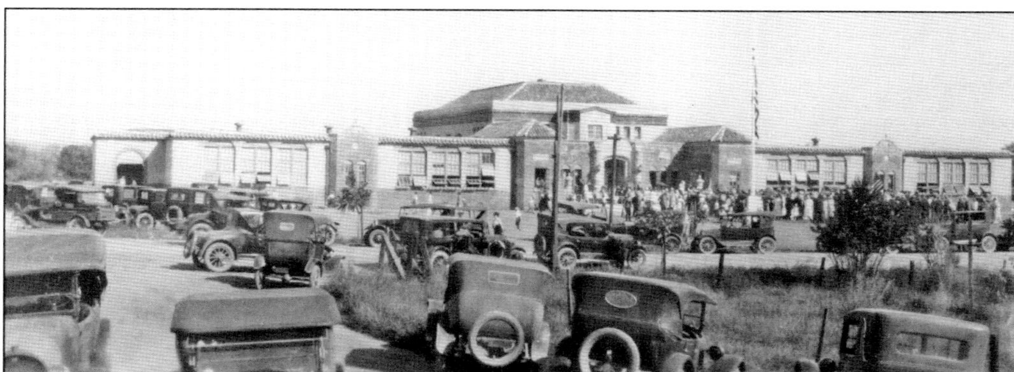

In 1920, Loomis and Franklin Schools consolidated, and the old Franklin School was closed. In 1923, Earl Gates was hired as principal. The teachers that year were Gertrude Williams, Jessie Hannis, Mrs. Parsons, and Harry L. Reese. The trustees at that time included R. L. Tudsbury, J. A. Ferguson, H. J. Smyth, Mary Williams, and Olive Fisher. The dedication of the new school on May 1, 1925, was an all-day celebration. Music was provided by the Loomis Community Band, the laying of the cornerstone was completed by the grand master of the Masonic lodge, and there were numerous speeches.

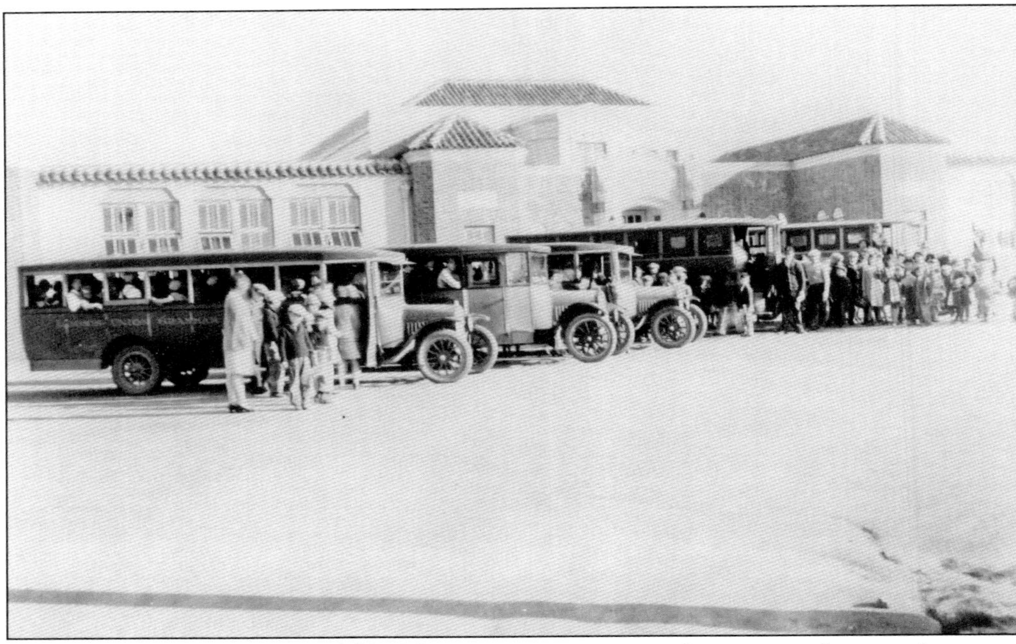

In 1927, school busses were available. This same year, two more classrooms and a second entrance were added to the south end of the building. Soon a cafeteria program was organized, offering hot lunches to students and staff. The kitchen and the dining room were located in the basement of the auditorium under the stage. Blanche Stark was the first cook.

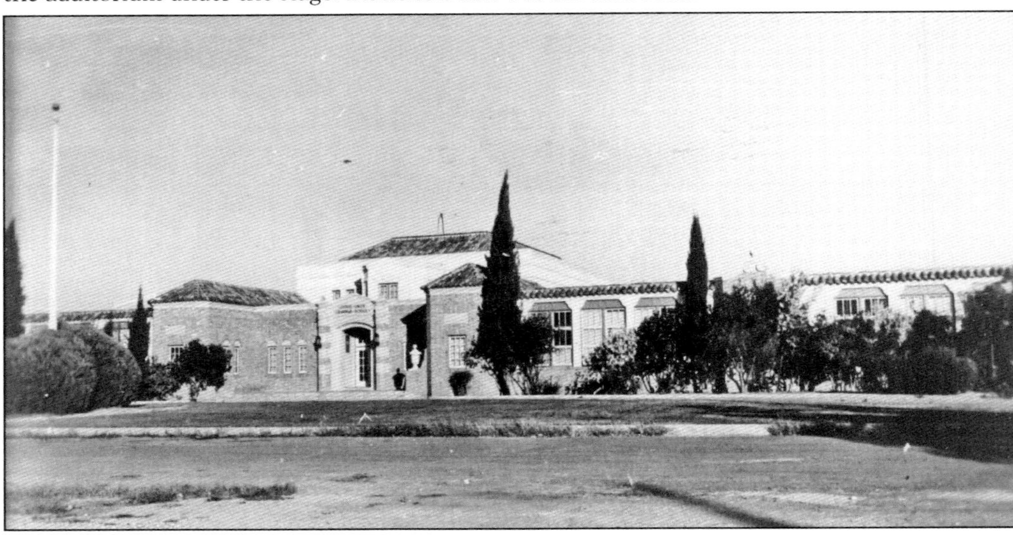

The Loomis School is pictured as it looked in 1941. It looked very similar to this until it was torn down and replaced by the current building in 1975. Richard T. "Dick" Brown was the principal and superintendent in 1948. During his administration, a new building was added at the north end of the campus that contained a large cafeteria and one classroom. In 1953, Thomas Ross replaced Dick Brown. There were 14 teachers that year. Lack of space forced the school board to rent classroom space at the Loomis Methodist Church for two kindergarten classes. Thomas N. Howell became principal and superintendent in 1955. Another wing east of the cafeteria was added with five classrooms, restroom facilities, storage space, and a small conference room.

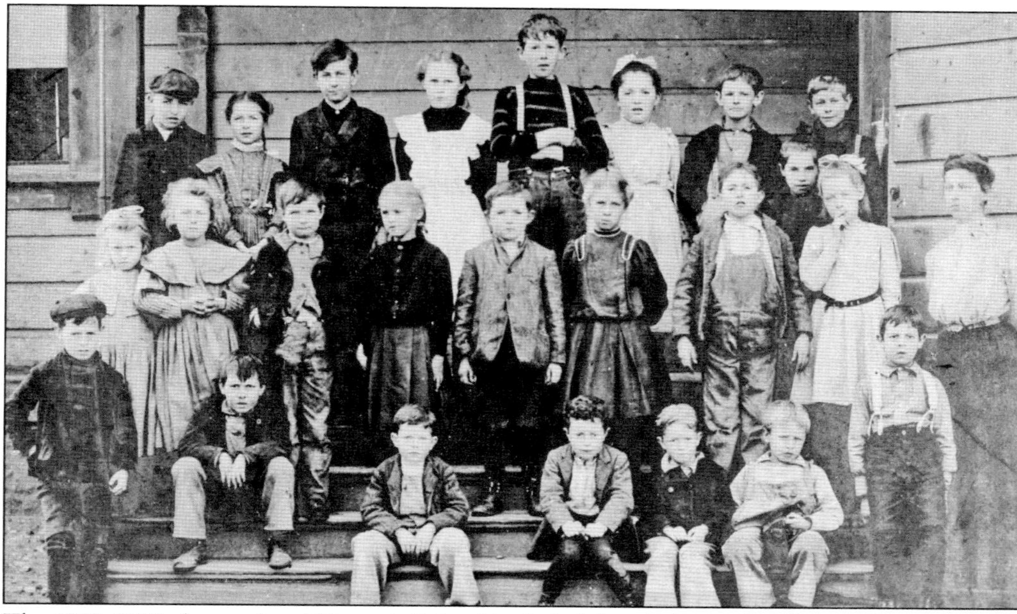

The 1902–1903 class at the old Loomis School included, from left to right, (first row) unidentified, Charles Cushman, Joseph Turner, Fred Turner, Kenneth Laird, George Bock, and Audrey Cook; (second row) two unidentified DeSheil girls, unidentified, Jenny Scroggs, Charles R. Turner, Ethel Fisher, Harold Misley, unidentified, and Dorothy Fassett; (third row) Glen Gilmore, Hazel Cushman, unidentified, Jessie Rowell, ? Dyke, Ora Turner, and Robert Brock.

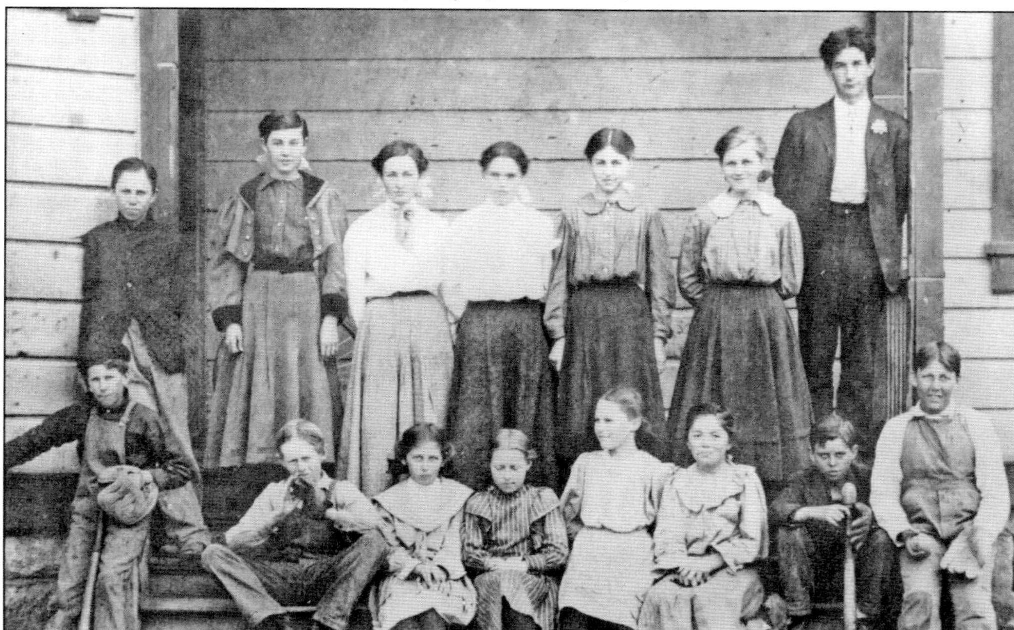

Students from the 1903–1904 class at the old Loomis School include (first row) Carol Roddan, Ferdinand Bock, Thelma Johnson, Dorothy Fassett, Jessie Rowell, Ora Turner, James Laird, and Eugene Lawrence; (second row) Charles H. Turner, Bessie Federoff, Blanch Quinn, Verna Laird, Jessie Gilmore, Olga Kutchiker, and teacher James H. Bunker.

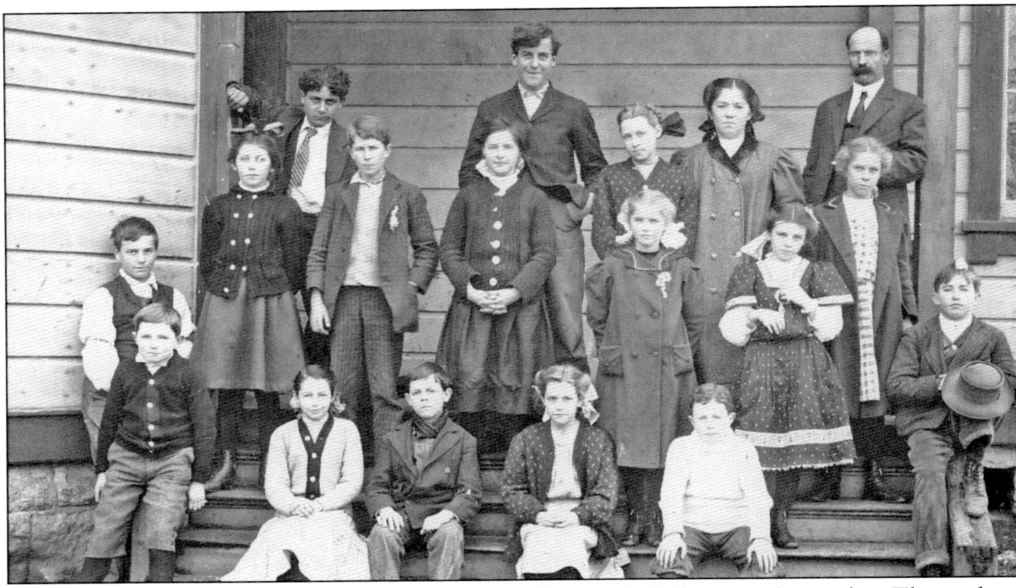

In this January 4, 1907, picture at the Loomis Schoolhouse, W. E. Bacon is the teacher. The students include Roscoe Rasmussen, Angelo Dolce, Andrew Rasmussen, Carroll Roddan, Thelma Johnson, Dorothy Fassett, Ora Turner, Hazel Cushman, Audrey Cook, Edith Shapard, Harold Misley, Fred Turner, Charles R. Turner, Winefred Fassett, Jean Bacon, Ethel Fisher, and Jenny Scroggs.

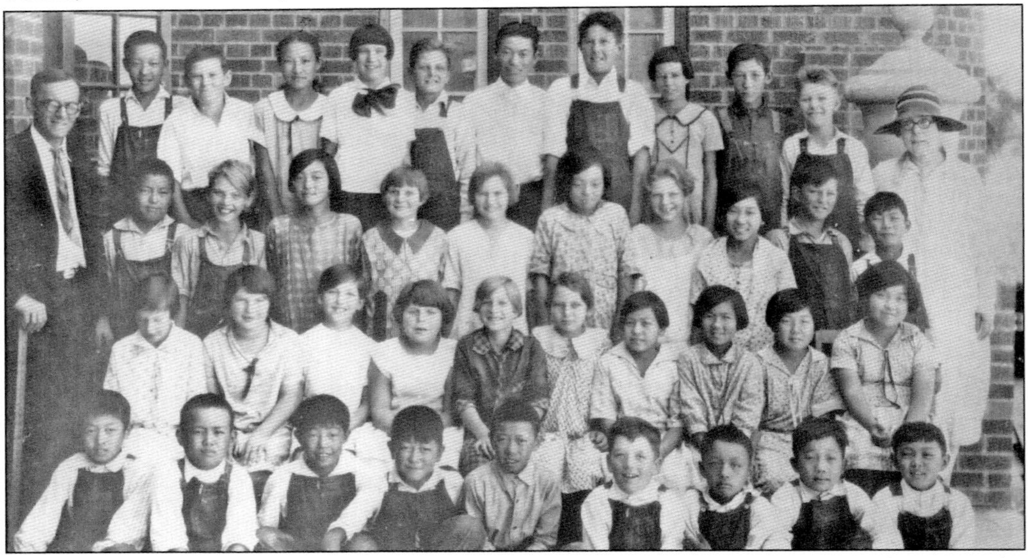

The fifth-grade class of 1928 was taught by Anna King. The principal was Earl Gates. The students are (first row) Shigeo Takahashi, Sakaye Hamamoto, Samuel Takagishi, Sandy Yokote, Valie Marr, Frank Crossley, Lung Quong, Shigeo Yokote, and Aster Kondo; (second row) Jessie Moulton, unidentified, Betty Tuft, Helen White, Marie Doring, Mickie Oseto, Gloria Hamai, Shigeyo Minahato, and Masayo Takuma; (third row) principal Earl Gates, Fred Shimizu, George Kaiser, May Kurahara, Ella Gilbert, Dorothy Lindsay, Marie Kurahara, Elise Pilliard, Teruko Takahashi, George Kessler, and George Suzuki; (fourth row) Takeshi Hamamoto, Glen Leavitt, Grace Ishihara, Dolores Carmassi, Clyde Stone, Frank Mayeda, Perry Leavitt, Mary Tonella, Pedro Nevarro, Robert Laird, and teacher Anna King.

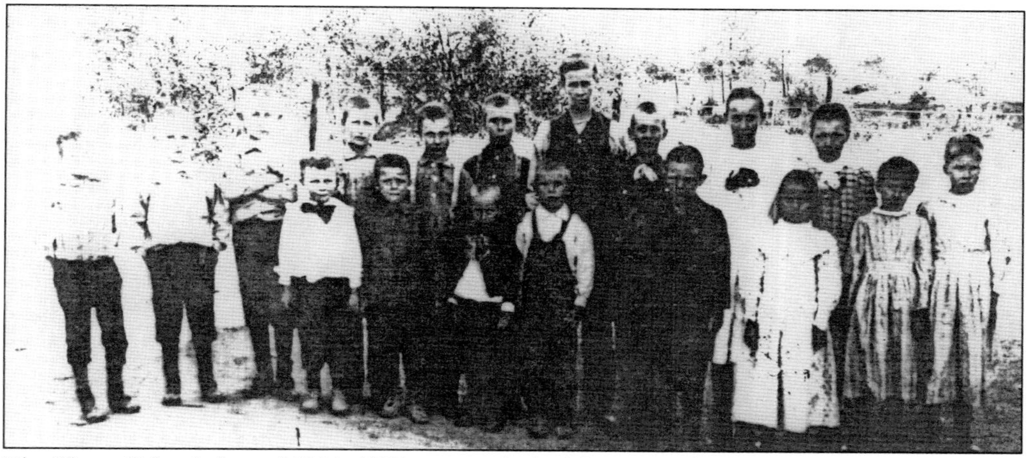

The Placer School class of 1894–1895 was taught by Mamie Starbuck. She is not in the picture, but her students were (first row) Howard Tudsbury (to the right a bit), George Errens, Kate Fieser, Ella Hansen, and Lena Hansen; (second row) Lee Tudsbury, Vigg Jensen, George Jensen, Don Wilson, Nick Hansen, George Higson, Jonnie Elery, Hazel Elery, and Jessie Wilson.

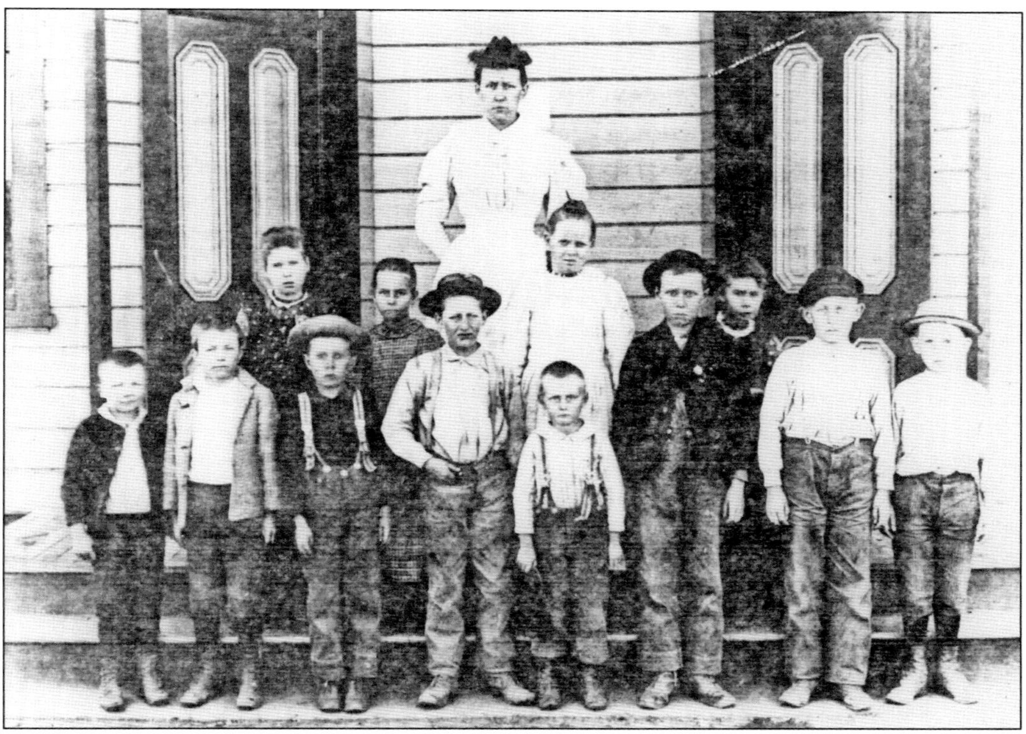

These are the students of the Placer School of 1895–1896. The teacher, Mamie Starbuck, is in the back with the hat with a net on it. The boys almost always wore hats.

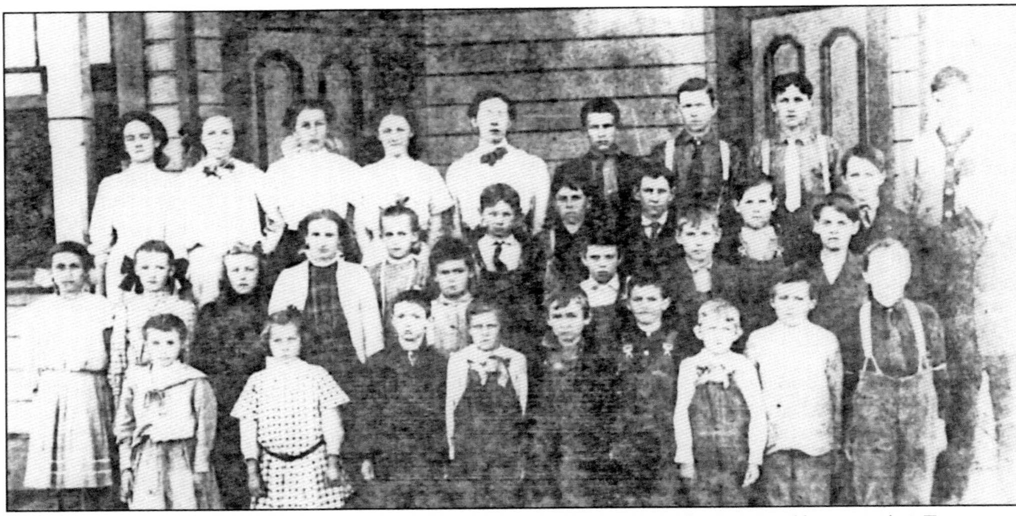

The Placer School class of 1910 was taught by Ada Lan. Students are (first row) ? Emerson, Nellie Wales, Charlie Shapard, Willie Woods, Lawson Brainerd, Fred Wales, Earl Wods, Markey Rasmussen, and Elmer Woods; (second row) Florence Wales, Ida Shapard, Beryl Tudsbury, Marion Nixon, Theresa Braham, Linn Nelthorpe, Willie Wilson, Robert Wales, Harold Brainerd, Albert Fieser, Harry Emerson, Wendell Day, Fred Keeley, Edward Larsen, and Frea Denton; (third row) Mildred Brainerd, Mae Fieser, Olga Jensen, Anitta Goddard, teacher Ada Lan, Rudoff Braham, Clelle Woods, Willard Wales, and Andrew Rasmussen.

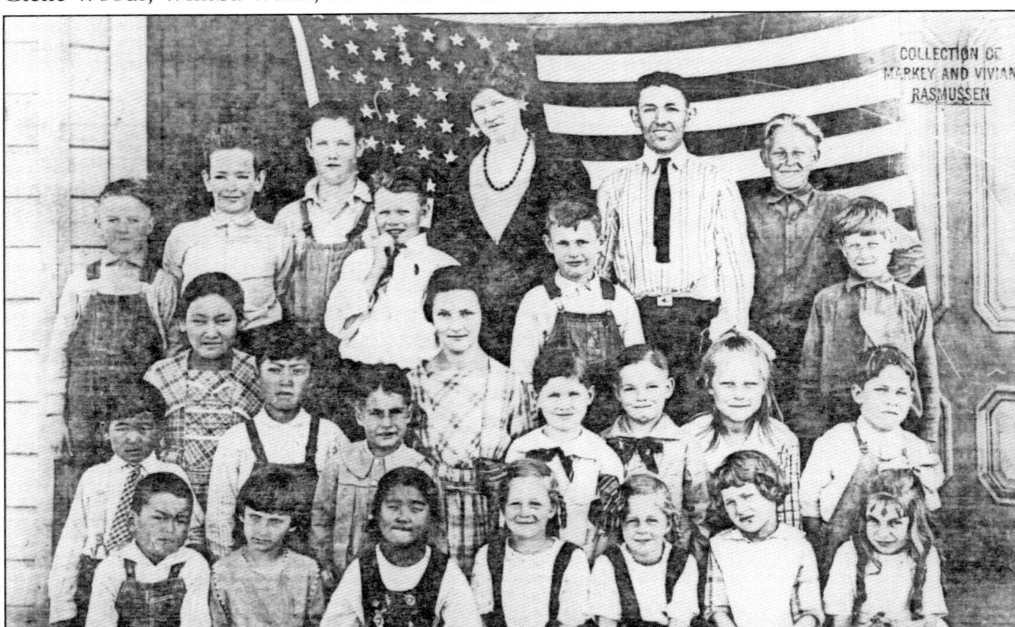

This is the Placer School class of 1921–1922. The teacher is Jessie Hannis. Students are (first row) unidentified, Helen Kiss, Tomiko Sakamoto, Geneva Tudsbury, Gene Tudsbury, unidentified, and Virginia Fassett; (second row) Park Wilson, Jack Brainerd, unidentified, Robert Tudsbury, Jessie Hannis, Charles Branstetter, Joe "Big Joe" Manzano, Kirk Fredricksson, Grace ?, Victor Marr, Joe Montero, Norma Crocker, Wilson Hannis, George Crocker, Anna Sipploa, and unidentified.

Six

HOMES

There are many stately homes in the Loomis area. In 1908, L. F. Atwater published *Pen Sketches and Camera Shots of Loomis, California, and Vicinity—A Magazine Illustrating Beautiful Homes and Prosperous Communities.* Stately, palatial, and beautiful are words used to describe many of the homes. Some of them have stood the test of time and are still lived in today. The businessmen and ranchers built lovely homes that were frequently reminiscent of the country of their heritage. Naming homes and ranches also was common. Some of the names included Rich Hill, High Home, Oakdene, Orange, Golden Rule Farm and Nursery, Oak Knoll, Brookside, Moonshine, Home, Alba Sepes, Sunnyslope, Indian Hillock, Kingmont, Lone Pine, and Falls Orchard.

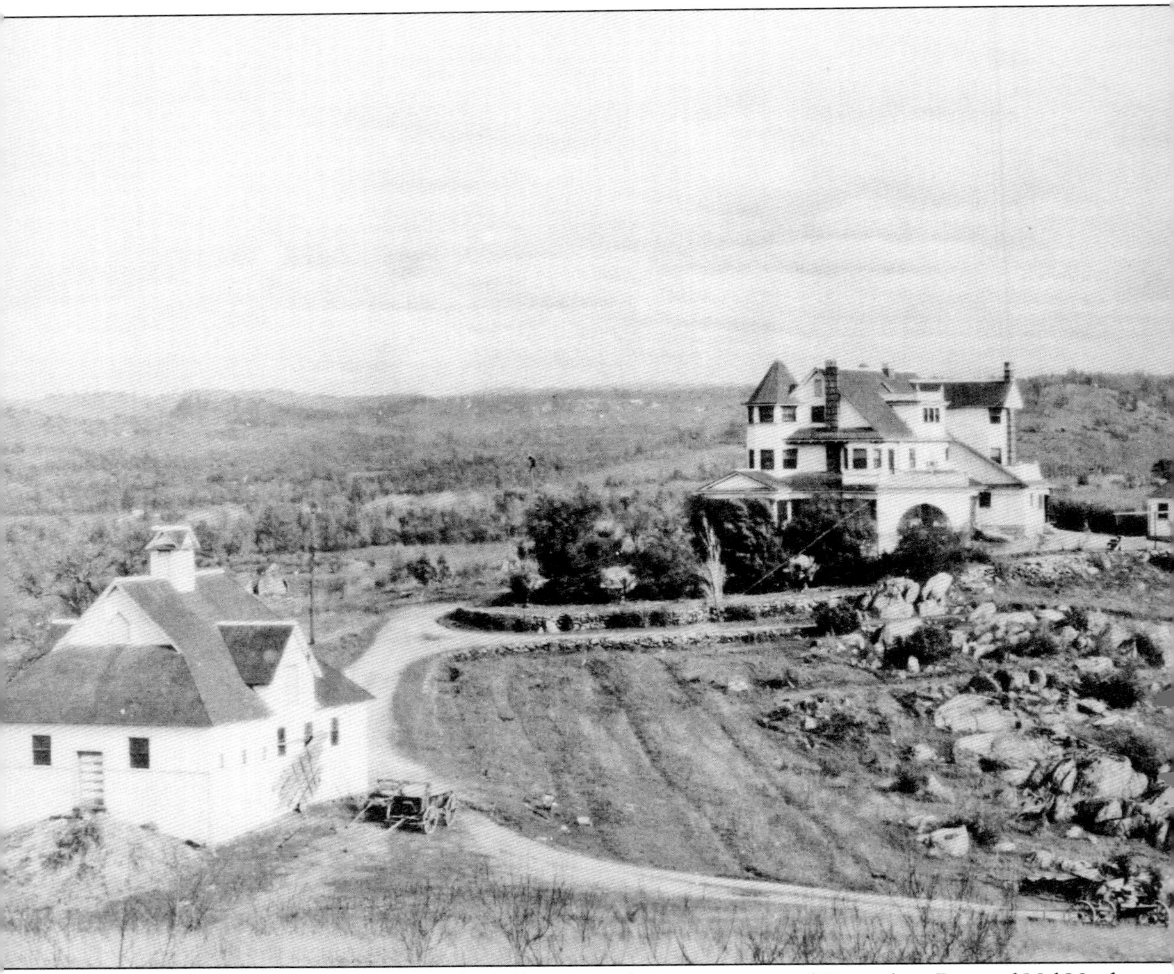

This lovely home still stands on the hilltop near the intersection of Horseshoe Bar and Val Verde Roads. The Pendleton home was built about 1904. George Pendleton was the manager of the only drugstore in town. The Pendletons built the bandstand for the cornet band and furnished the band with winter and summer uniforms. William Courtland Pendleton was 57 years old in 1904, when the house was being built. He planted 75 acres in cling peaches. When the fruit was of good bearing age, the orchard was rented out for sharecropping. In the 1920s, the home was owned by the Samuel Day family. They called it Hyholme Ranch. They had acreage in plums and peaches. In the fall of 1976, Daniel and Glenna Haley bought the home, and they have restored it to its original splendor. The house comes complete with a dumbwaiter.

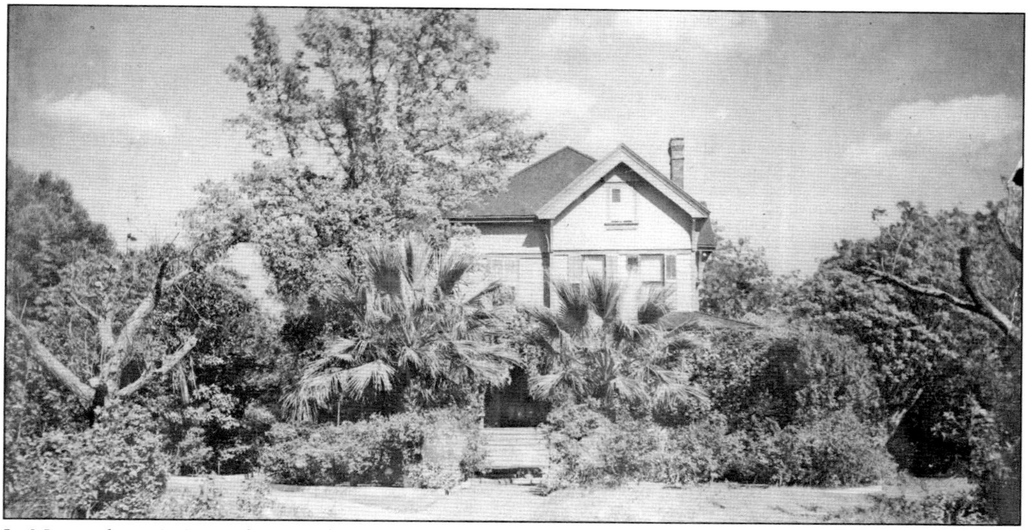

In November 1883, Andrew Ryder, a former resident of Jamaica, Long Island, New York, was looking for land in the Pino area. Born in 1842, he was a veteran of the Civil War and had helped his uncle as a ticket agent for the Long Island Railroad. He worked for the Central Pacific in Sacramento and was the baggage master on the line that ran to Colfax and eventually was built over the Sierra. He became a rail conductor in 1866. He was on the train that carried Leland Stanford, Collis P. Huntington, Mark Hopkins, and Charles Crocker—the "Big Four"—to Promontory Point in Utah when the golden spike was driven in at this historic ceremony in 1869. In 1889, Ryder and his wife, Frances, moved onto 160 acres he had purchased from P. Pringle northwest of Pino.

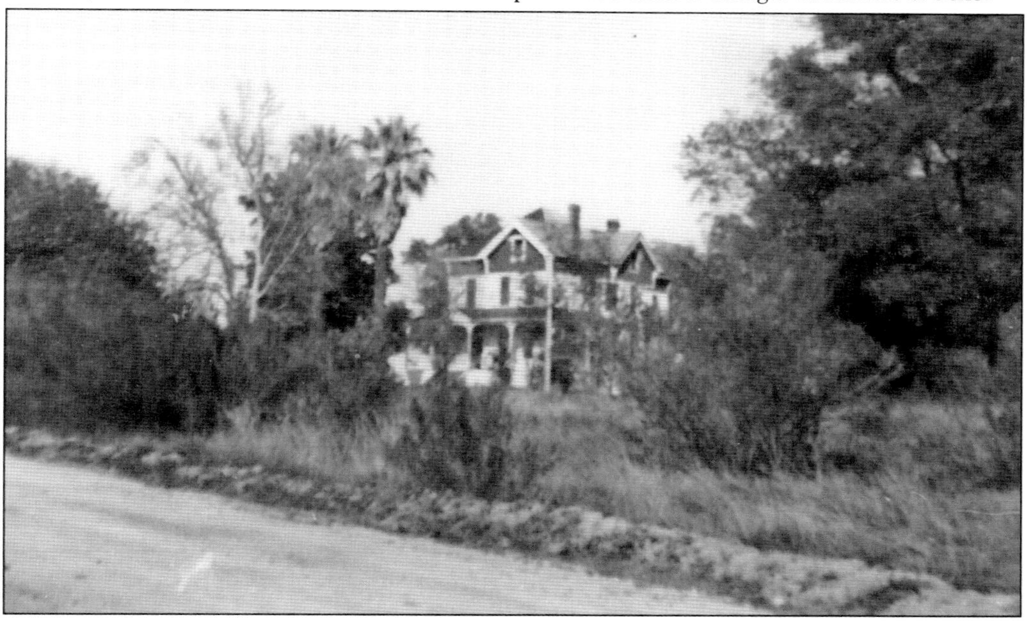

Graystone Orchard belonged to Andrew and Frances Ryder. In 1908, there were 57 acres in peaches, 13 acres in plums and 20 acres of table grapes. Ryder was very civic minded. He owned the large building in town that was partially used for the first Bank of Loomis in 1913. He was vice president of the bank and a large stockholder. The building burned in 1915, and Ryder rebuilt with hollow tile bricks.

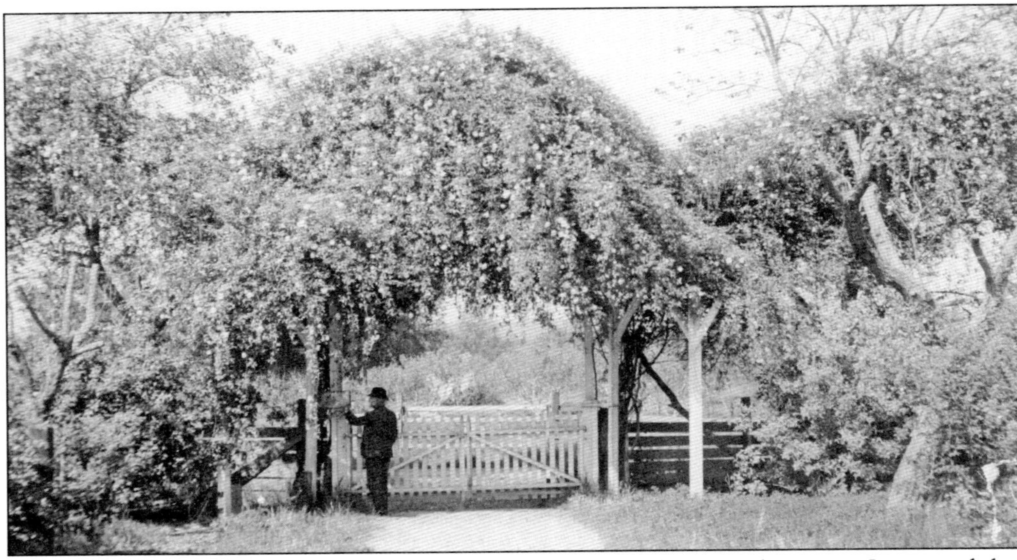

The home of Frances and Andrew Ryder was well known for the rose arbor entry. It was said that a wagonload of different kinds of roses could be picked at one time. The spacious yard was planted with all kinds of flowers and shrubs. The Ryders celebrated their golden wedding anniversary in May 1919. Andrew passed away on October 7, 1920, at the age of 78 1/2. Frances was one of the founders of the Women's Christian Temperance Union in Loomis. During World War I, she spent many hours knitting garments for the soldiers. Alice Law lived with Frances Ryder after Andrew's death until Frances died on July 13, 1932.

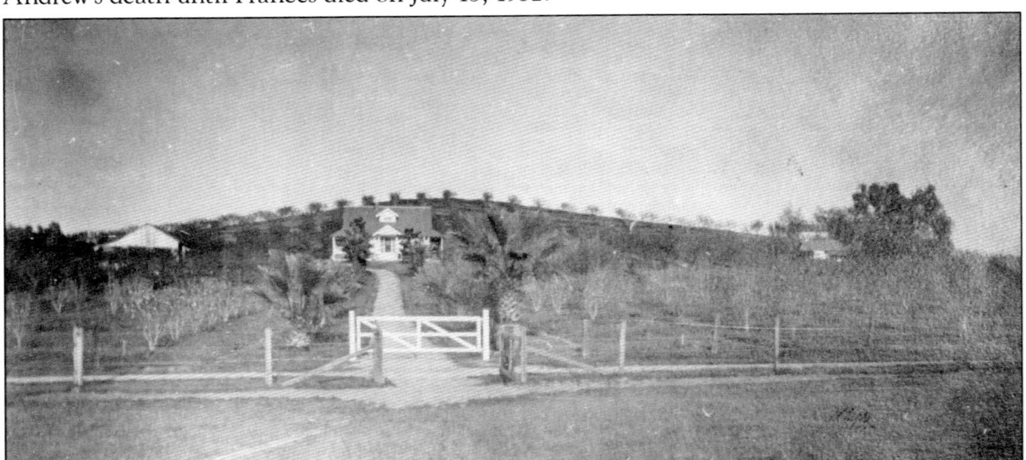

Albert Law was born in Liverpool, England, in 1872 and attended Liverpool College. He also worked for his father in the grocery business. He came to America in 1892 and worked for J. M. Free in Penryn and in 1894 bought 20 acres on brushland in the Hickey tract at Loomis. He cleared the land and planted deciduous trees. In 1908, Albert and his brother, Seth, who came to the United States in 1895, started to ship fruit under the Law Brothers name and label in a building owned by Andrew Ryder. In 1922, Albert bought seven lots on Olive Street (Taylor Road) and Walnut Street. He built a large concrete building, which was completed in 1923. He and Seth sold hardware and farm equipment. Albert married Ethel Greenwood Smith in 1916. They had two children, Frank and Dorothee. Frank married Maxine Turner of Sacramento, and Dorothee married James Johnson.

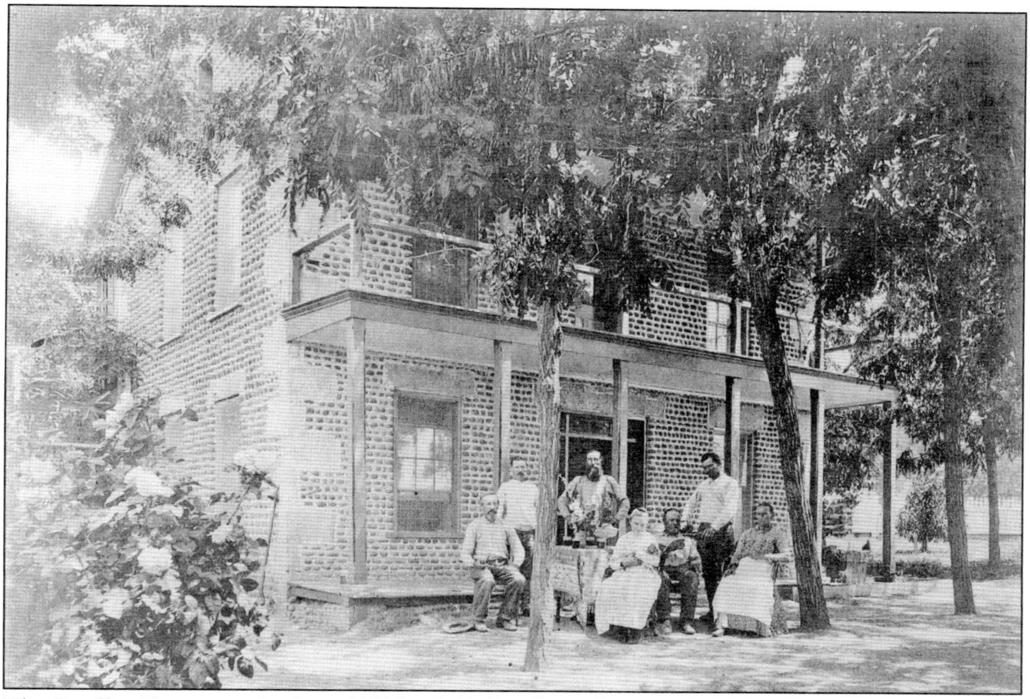

The Bradley House was built in 1852 by S. R. Bradley, who came to the area from New England. This home served as a Wells Fargo and stage stop. The house was an eight-room building made mostly of small stones brought to the location by horseback in saddlebags from the surrounding territory. The barn was built of cobblestone in the 1850s. There was an arch over the large barn doorway. A small portion of the wall still exists on Barton Road, which was originally known as Lee Mine Road. In later years, the ranch was owned by Nevada Omahundro and her family.

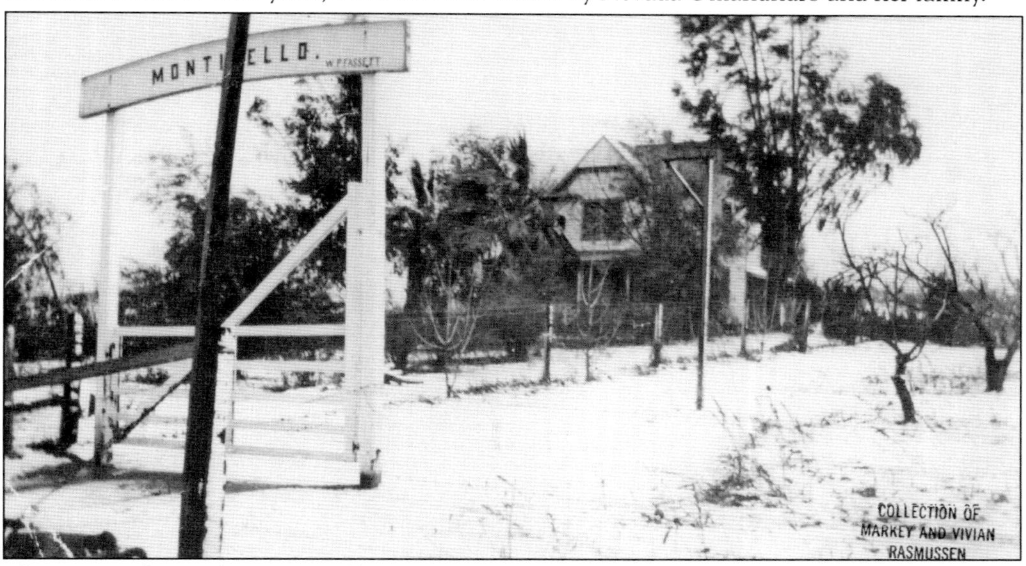

The Monticello ranch was owned by W. P. Fassett in the Val Verde Road area near Auburn Folsom Road. The Fassett family owned a store on Taylor Road in the building that is now the Horseshoe Bar and Grill. This photograph was probably taken during the 1912 snowstorm.

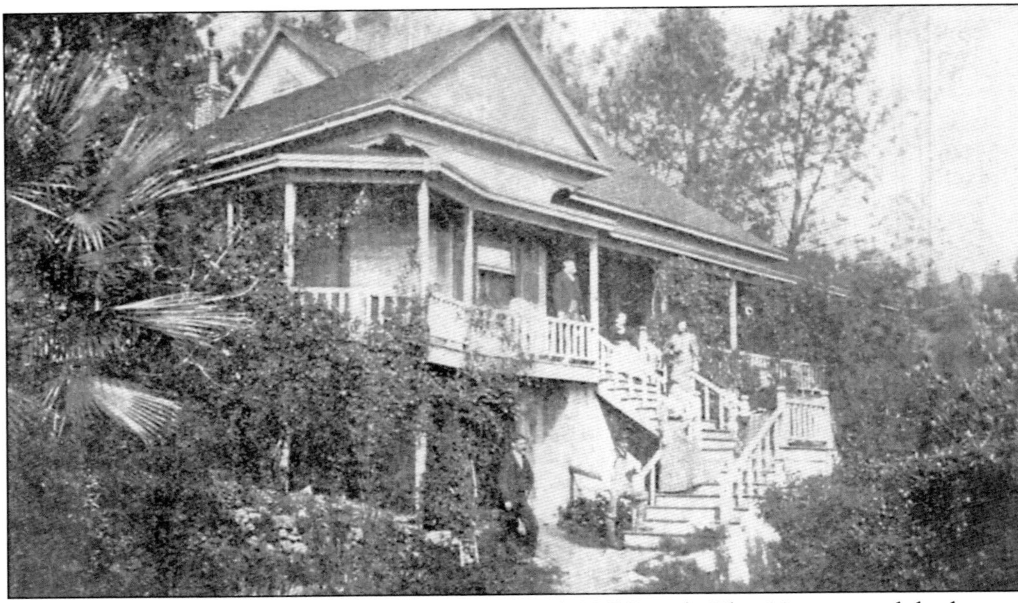

The property of L. B. Daingerfield was known as Rich Hill Ranch. This 20-acre ranch had one of the finest lemon groves in the area, of which 90 percent were absolutely seedless. There was also a grove of early-ripening oranges. Grapes and deciduous fruit were also grown on the ranch.

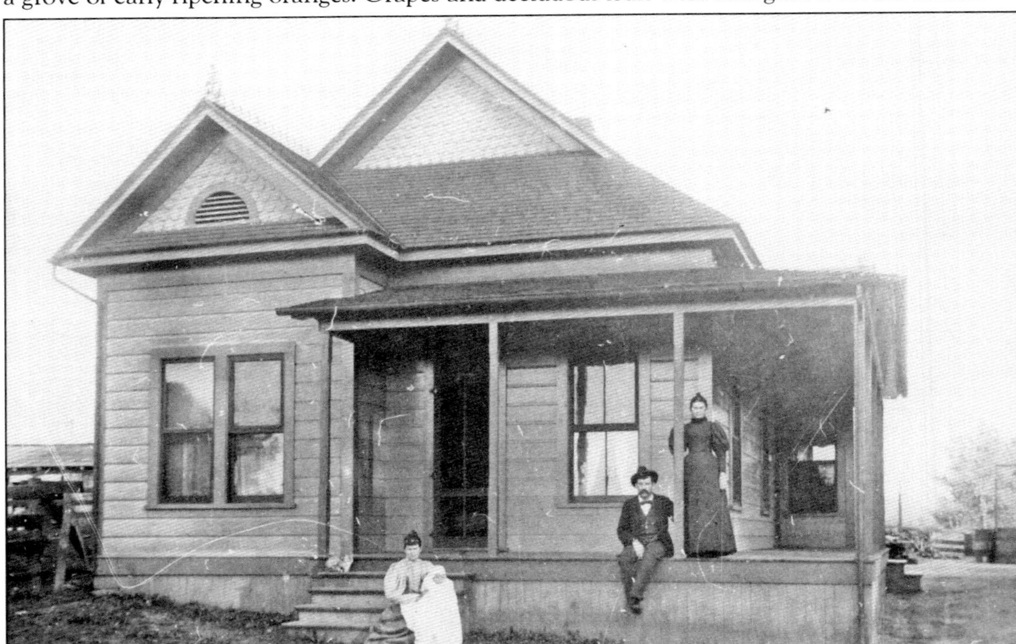

This home on Magnolia Street was owned by Frank and Clara Grigsby Cook. The photograph was taken about 1896. On the steps is Ella Grigsby, Clara's mother, who is holding her grandson Audrey. Frank is sitting on the porch, and Clara is standing behind him. Other children were William, Clarence, Claire, Claude, twins Ella and Ellen, and Mary. Frank owned the Peach Tree Inn and the grocery store at Taylor and Walnut Streets. In 1907 or 1908, he built a new home at Magnolia and Walnut Streets. This home now belongs to Jim and Dorothee Law Johnson.

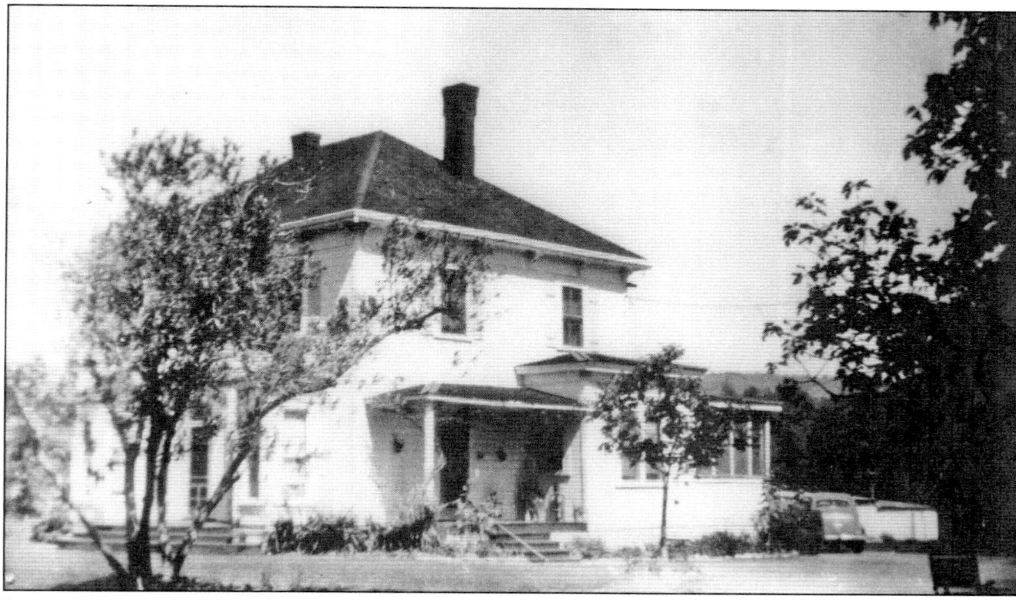

James W. Smyth opened a store in 1855 near the Franklin House and Stable. When he first married, he had many men, including Chinese, working for him mining using the long tom method. Smyth and his workers turned the channel of the river over 28 times. In 1860, he bought this house, which is in the vicinity of King and Auburn-Folsom Roads, from Mr. Woodworth. Smyth introduced the Alexander peach and planted the first oranges in Placer County. He also grew pears and apples.

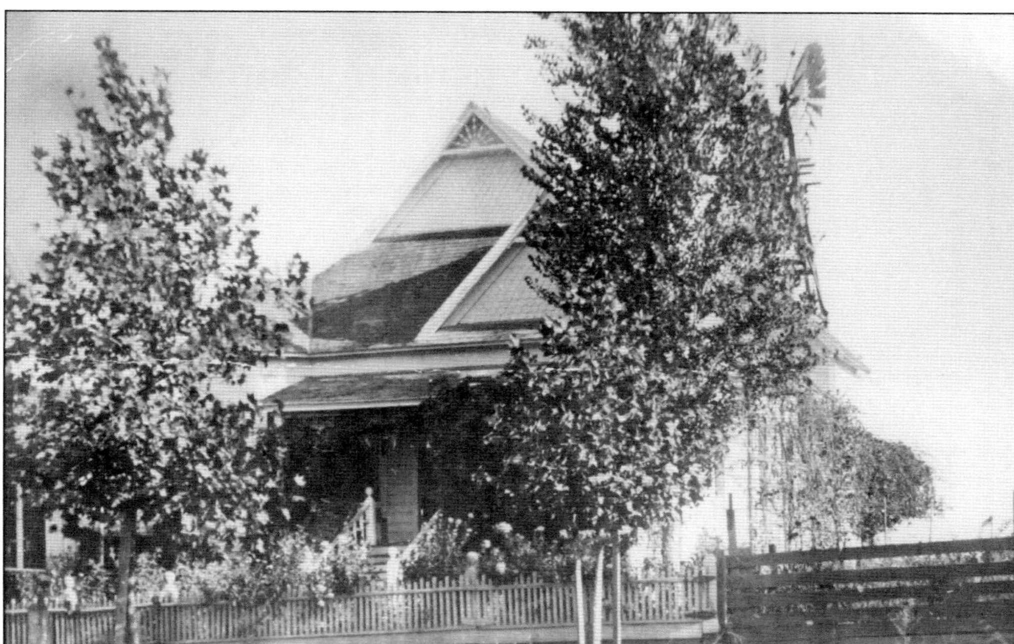

The Dunton family home was in town on Magnolia Street near Horseshoe Bar Road.

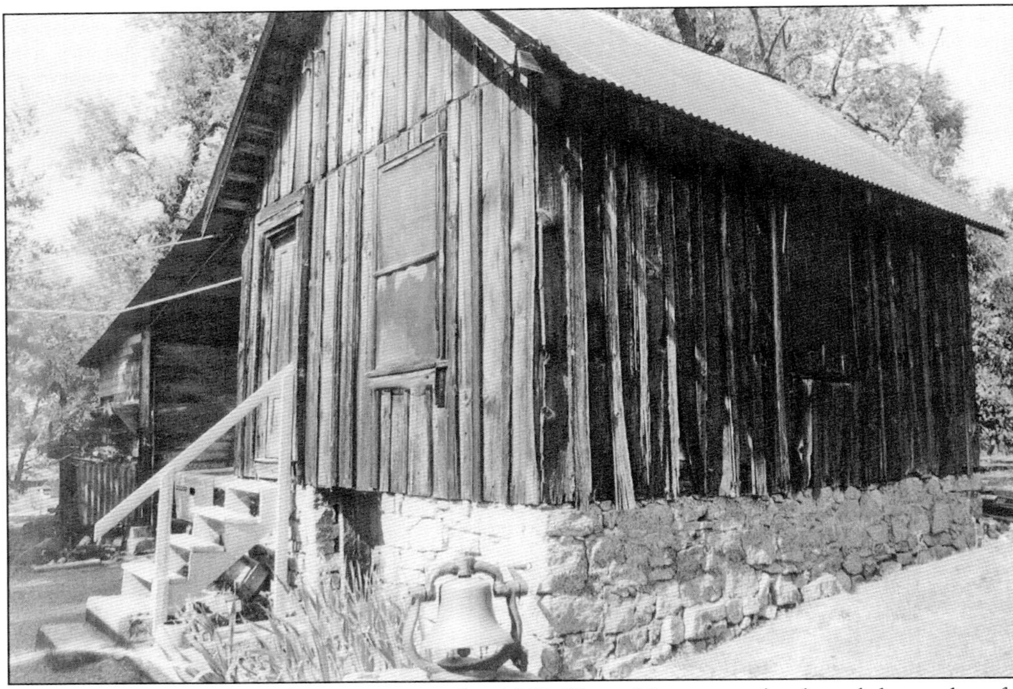

Joseph Turner built this cabin some time after 1860. The cabin was used to board the workers for the Carlaw quarry and for farm workers. It is still standing.

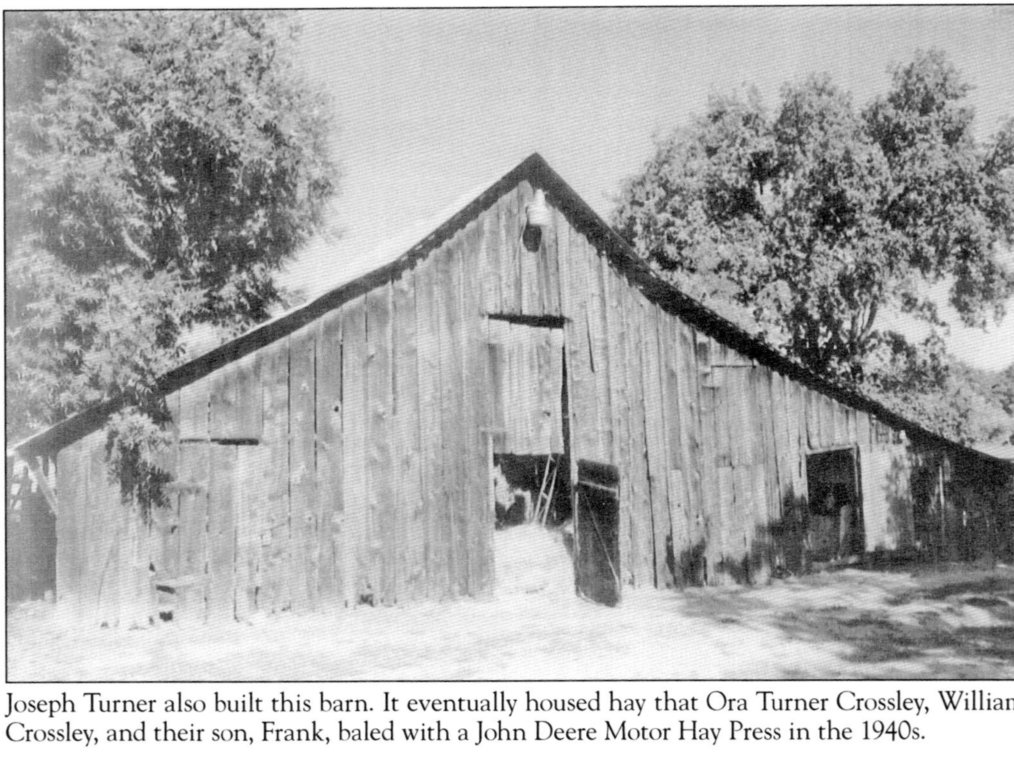

Joseph Turner also built this barn. It eventually housed hay that Ora Turner Crossley, William Crossley, and their son, Frank, baled with a John Deere Motor Hay Press in the 1940s.

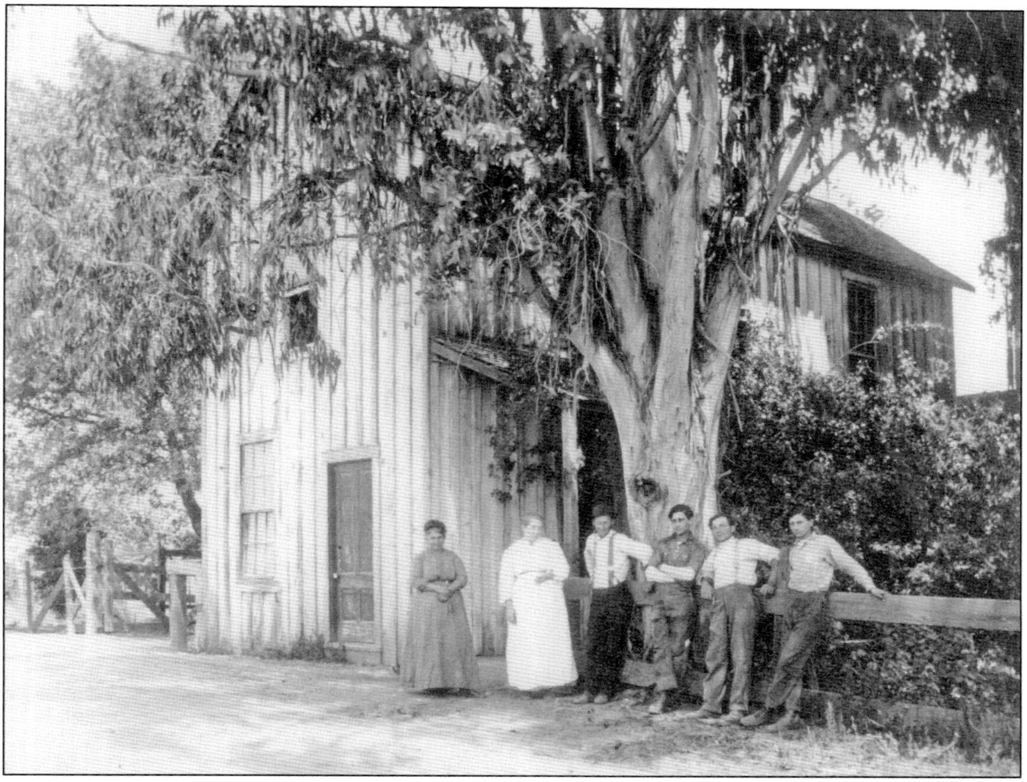

The Dolce Home was built at Taylor and King Roads across from the Loomis Grammar School. In the photograph are, from left to right, Mary Dolce, Rachel Bywater, Amos Hull, Angelo Dolce, Frank Dolce, and Ted Dolce. Since the 1990s, this site has been a dental office complex.

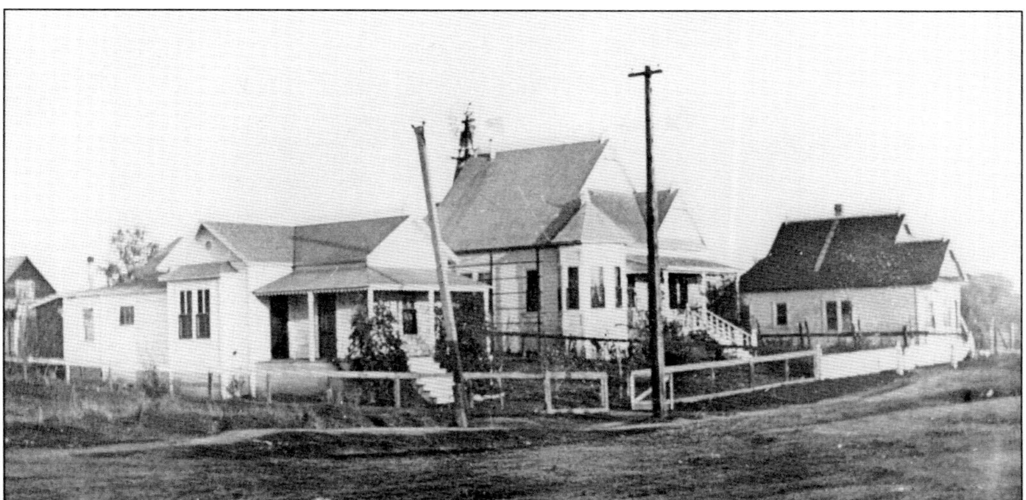

These three homes are located in town on Horseshoe Bar Road between Library Drive and Laird Street. They belonged to the Sexton, Howell, and Files families. The houses are still standing.

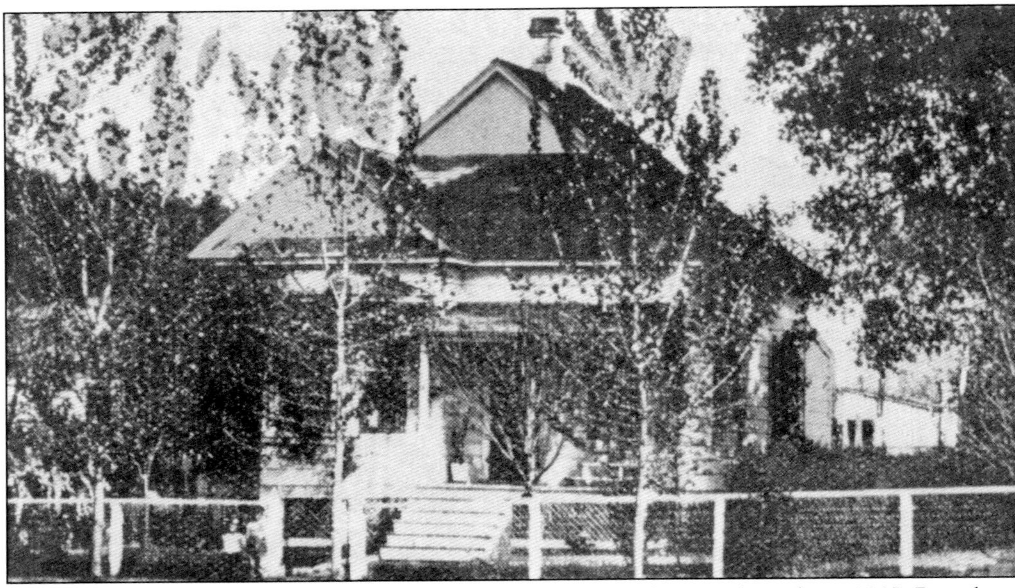

This is the home of Brazel and Clara Misley. The photograph was taken about 1907. Brazel was the local butcher. Clara kept a board and rooming house. It is said that many residents remember that the U.S. Department of Agriculture sent a Mr. Rutherford to get cuttings from fig trees belonging to Brazel Misley. The home was noted for the lovely garden of flowers. The home was located on Horseshoe Bar Road next to what became the Loomis Mutual Supply. It can be seen in the photograph of the Sexton Store.

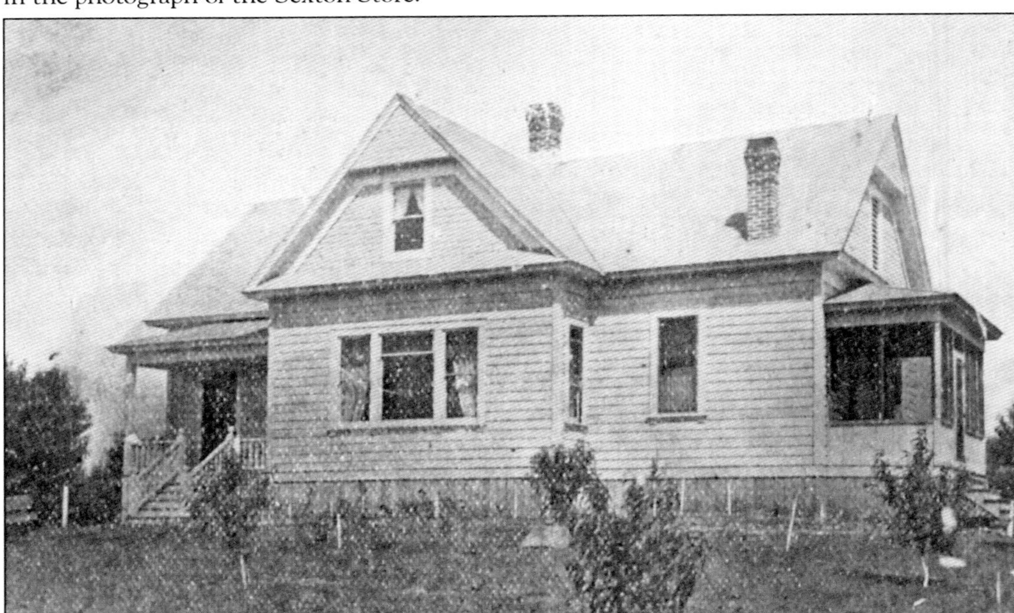

Indian Hillock was the name of the residence and orchards 3 miles east of Loomis belonging to J. T. Law. Many Native American grinding rocks are on the property. These would have been used by the Maidu Indians to grind food such as acorns and roots. At the Lewis and Clark Exposition held in Portland, Oregon, in 1905, Law took the gold medal for California cling peaches.

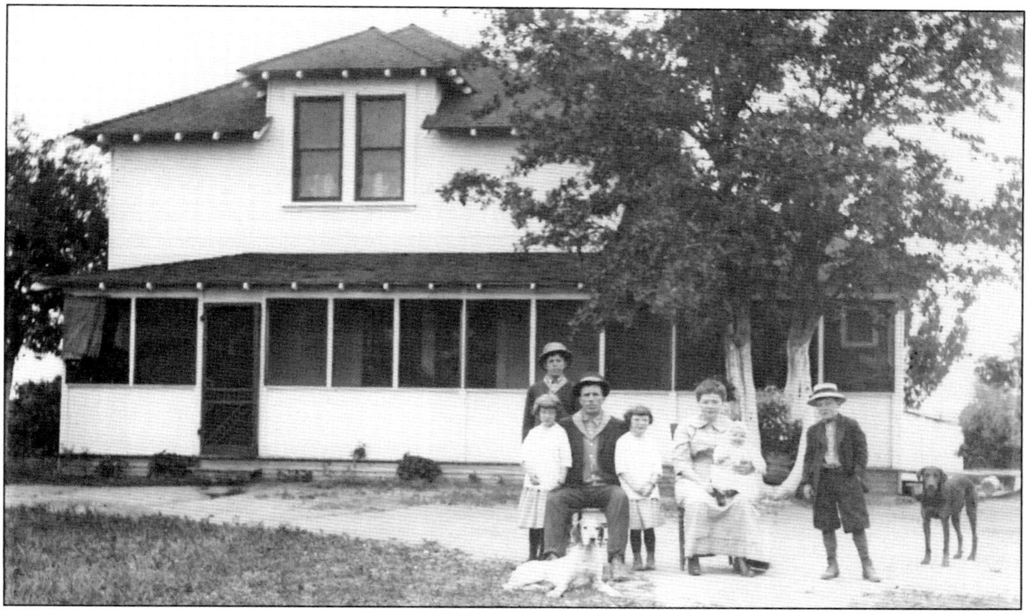

Moonshine was the home of Porter Lee and Allie Flesher Taylor. From left to right, Helen, father Porter, Inona, mother Allie holding Marguerite, and Milton Taylor. The boy in back is a friend of the family. The photograph was taken probably in late 1914, as Marguerite was born in August that year. This home still stands. It used to have a large "witch's pot" in the front yard, probably used for making tallow. Porter and his brothers came from Slickrock, Kentucky, and were ranchers and entrepreneurs.

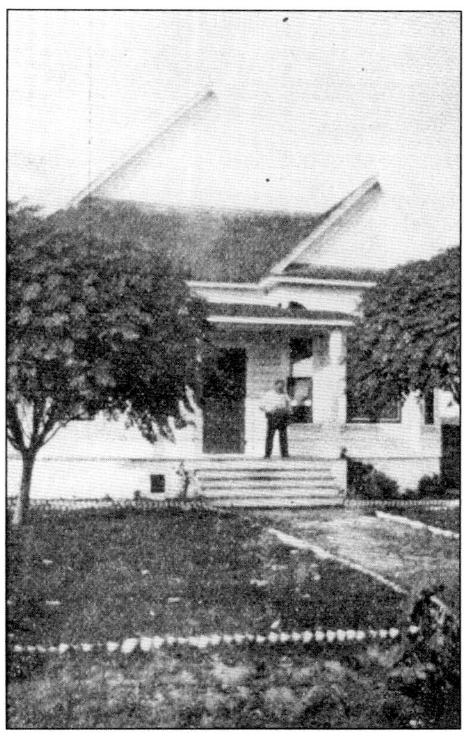

This is the home of Angelo Orsolini. The photograph is actually reversed, as the bay window is on the left side. Orsolini had 75 acres, all of which were planted in table and wine grapes. In 1908, most of the acres were young vines, most of which were too young to be bear fruit. However, Orsolini had returns of $2,300. This house was built in 1891 and has been owned since 1942 by Frank and Marge Nute and their family.

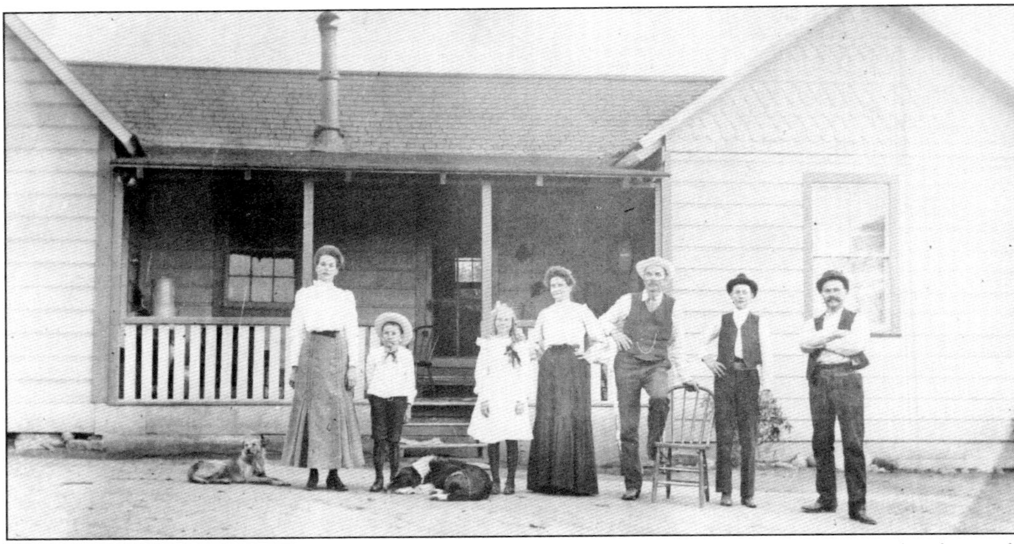

Frederick Fieser and his wife, Caroline, built their home in 1912. He was a wagon maker by trade and originally went to work for Baker and Hamilton, a plow and farm machinery company in Benecia, California. Fieser and some of his fellow workers bought property from Michael Hickey, east of Pino. The Hickey tract became a large Danish and German settlement. The Fiesers, with children Kate and Frederick Phillip, came to the area in November 1892. Other children included Mae, who married Irwin Mehl; Albert, who worked in the fruit industry and lived in Loomis with his wife, Grace; and Kate, who married Harold Leak in 1916. Kate and Harold lived all but the first year of their marriage in the home that her father had built. The 1905 photograph shows, at left, Kate, Albert, Mae, Caroline, father Frederick, and son Frederick. At the far right is the elder Frederick's brother.

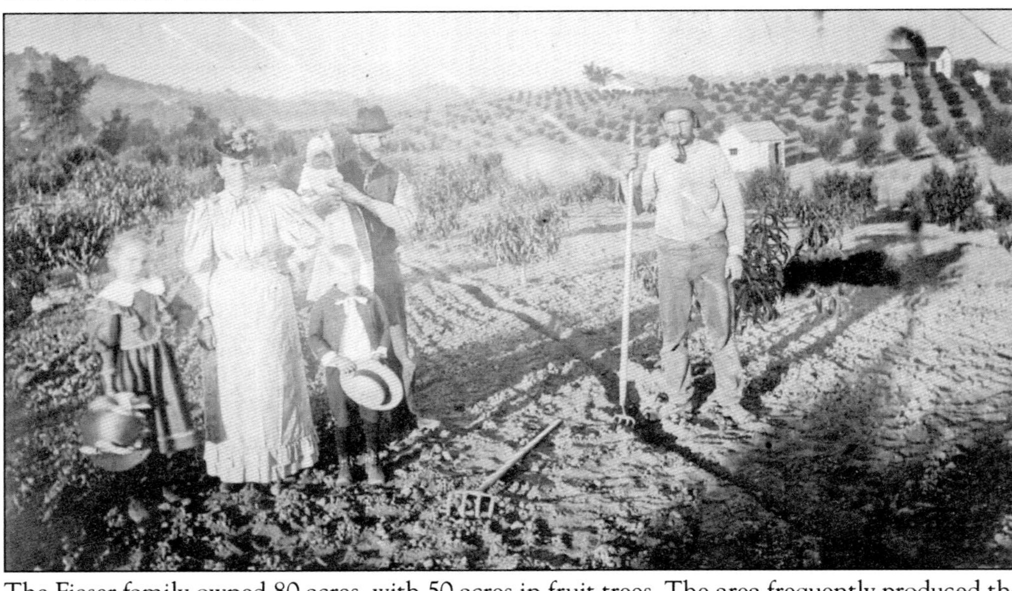

The Fieser family owned 80 acres, with 50 acres in fruit trees. The area frequently produced the first fruit of the season. Fieser also owned 200 acres near the American River at Dotan's Bar. This was all in hay and pasture in 1908. It was later put into fruit. Now the land is at the bottom of Folsom Lake.

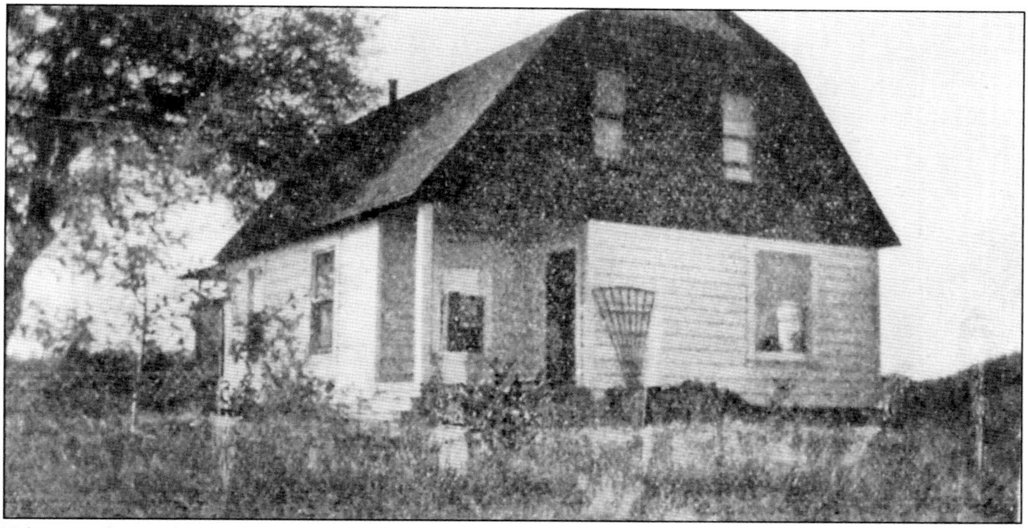

Edgar and Martha Nelthorpe built their home about 1909, on King Road, east of Loomis. Edgar worked for the Williamson Pen Company in Janesville, Wisconsin, prior to coming to California in 1902. He and Martha enjoyed the area enough to purchase 22 acres on Auburn-Folsom Road. They planted fruit trees, and Edgar learned carpentry and built their home in 1903. That home was sold to Martha's sister and brother. Edgar built this house along King Road on 15 acres and planted fruit trees. This 1913 photograph shows Martha and their daughter Mary. The couple also had a son, Lindsley, who worked in the appliance store they owned.

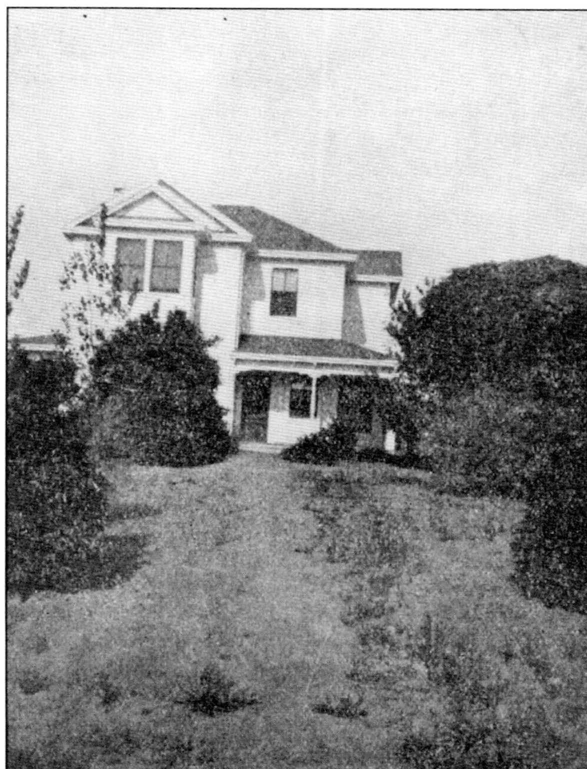

William Holder Tudsbury built this home in the 1890s off Horseshoe Bar Road. William's mother, Nancy Louise, applied for a homestead on 160 acres in 1857. Twenty years of hard work later, the deed was granted by Pres. Ulysses S. Grant. William was a horticultural commissioner for Placer County. William and his wife Isabelle's ranch was named Alba Sepes. William was also on the board of directors for the California Fruit Exchange and on the board of directors for the Loomis Fruit Growers Association.

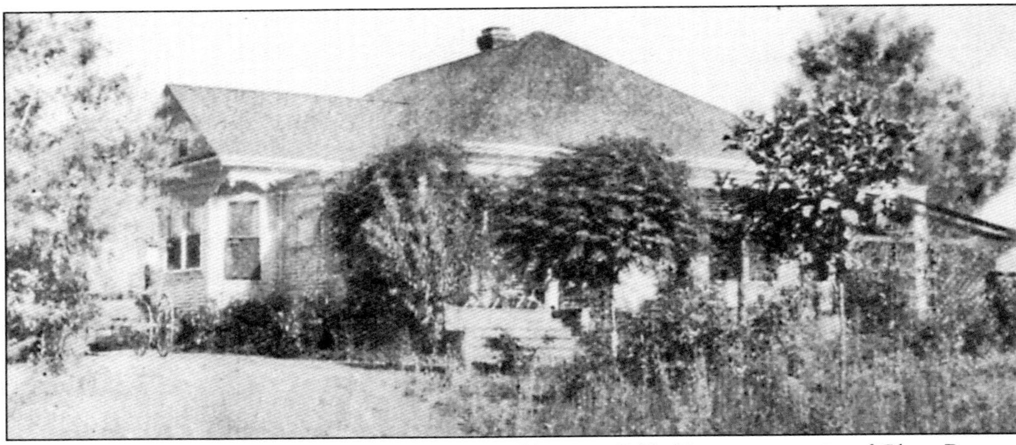

James N. Barton was born in Belmont County, Ohio, in 1930. He was a cousin of Clara Barton, the founder of the American Red Cross. James crossed the plains in an ox-team train in 1849 and settled in Sacramento County. He served in the California State Assembly for a time. He later did inside finished and cabinetwork on the state capitol building in Sacramento. The Bartons eventually came to Pino and were one of the first to start a fruit orchard here. They developed 40 acres into an orchard with house, barn, and other outbuildings, including a packinghouse and a cabin for workers. The Bartons had one daughter, Melissa, who married Henry Branstetter. The Branstetters also made their home in Loomis.

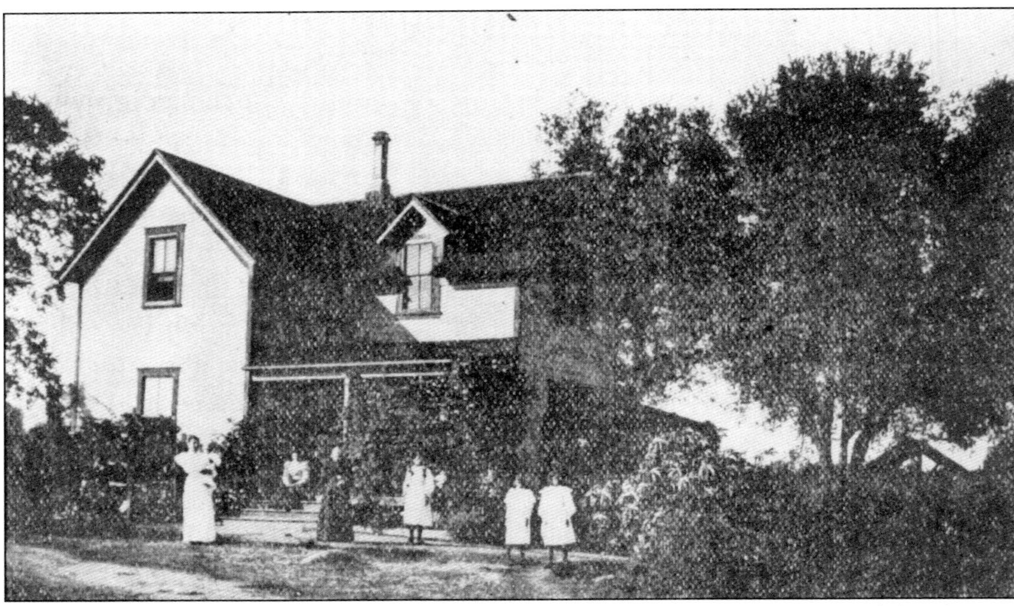

J. H. Nixon was one of the local pioneers. He was a native of Tennessee and crossed the plains in 1854. He settled at Dotan's Bar on the American River, about 2.5 miles below his present home. He had about 30 acres of fine orchard looked after by his son. He was the father of Senator G. S. Nixon of Nevada.

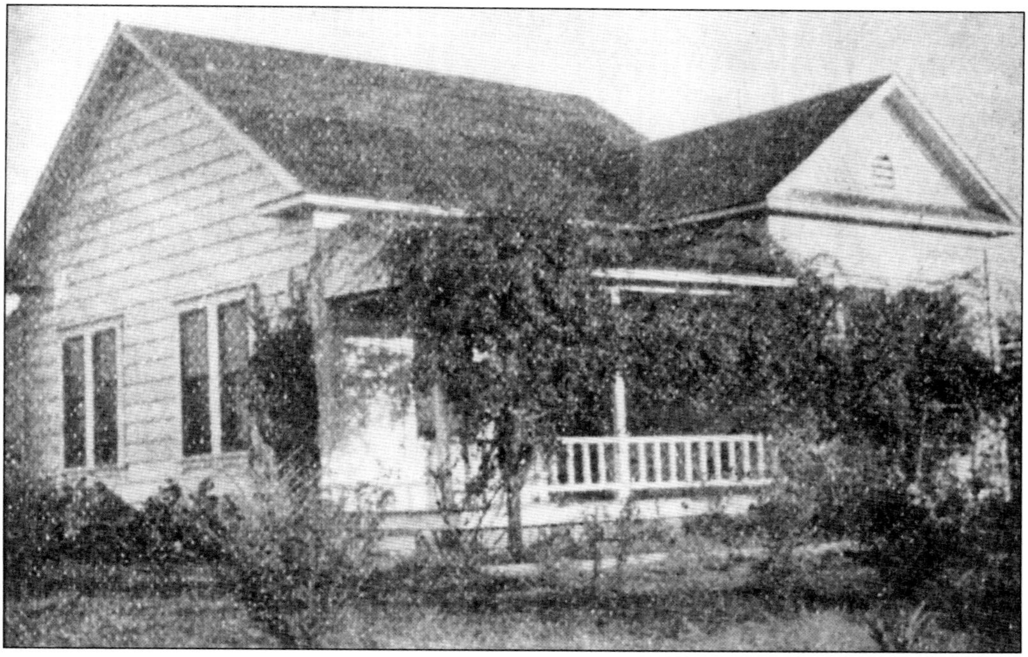

In 1854, Rudolph M. Nixon came from Arkansas with his parents to Placer County. He worked his father's fruit ranch for many years, and in 1906, he purchased 160 acres. He had 90 acres in peaches, 4 in pears, 10 in plums, 1 in oranges, 5 in quince, and 1 in apples. He marketed over 13,500 boxes of fruit around 1911. In 1910, he was deputy county horticultural commissioner. He served as secretary of the Loomis Fruit Growers Association.

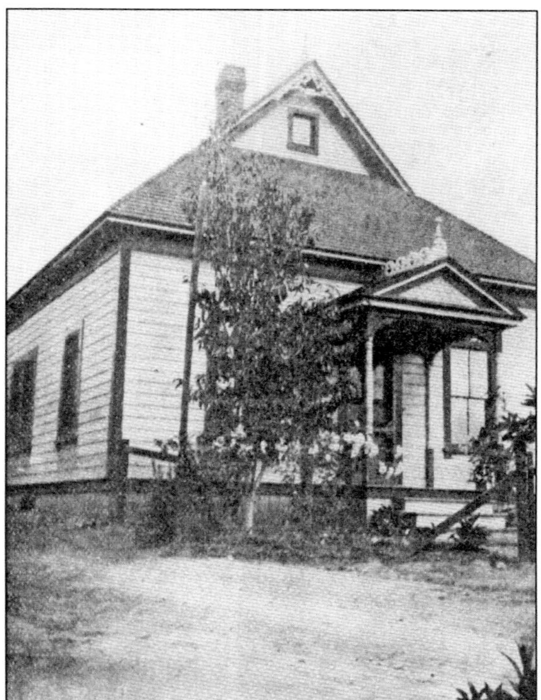

Neils Jensen had 15 acres of peaches and plums in 1908. He cleared the acreage by hand prior to planting the fruit trees. His home was on Leak Lane, formerly the residence of the Fieser family.

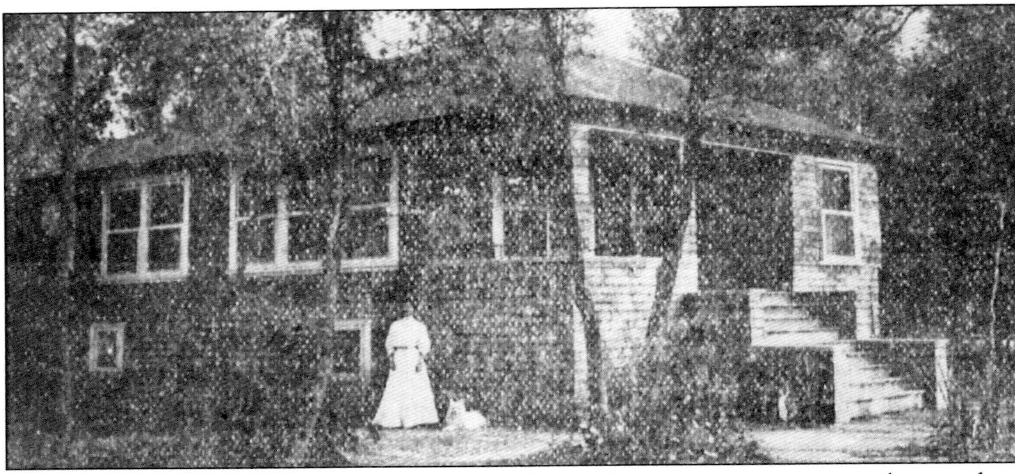

This home belonged to Mr. and Mrs. George B. Flint. The home sat on 11 acres about midway between Loomis and Rocklin near Del Mar Avenue. The house is nestled in a grove of live oak trees. There were splendid gardens and a vineyard.

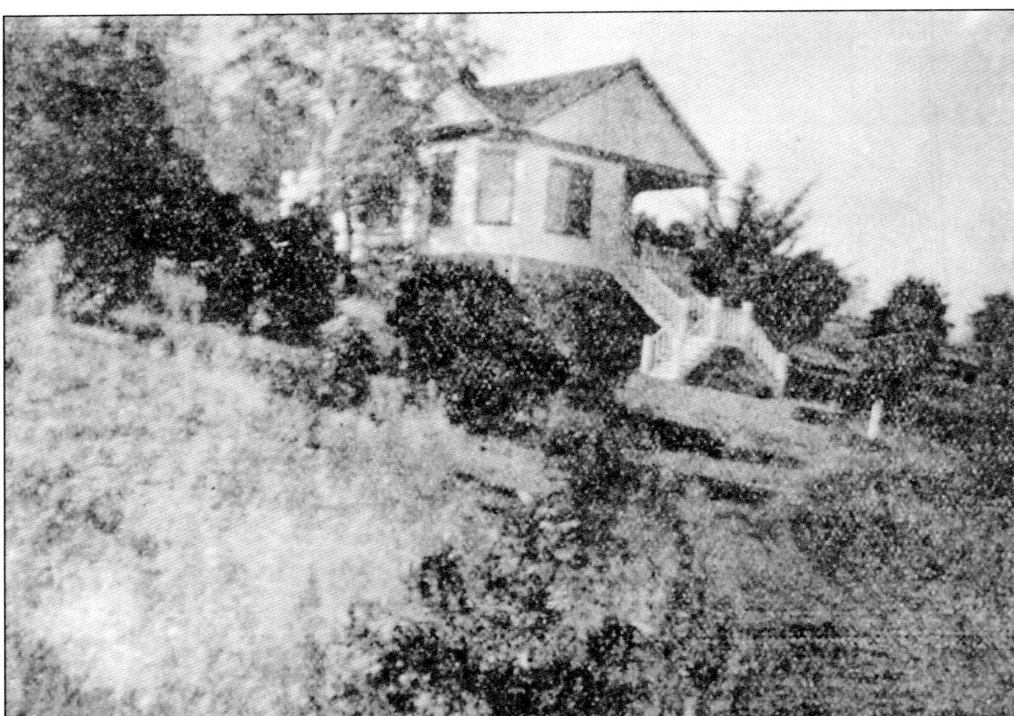

The home of F. J. Fitch lies among 19 acres of orchard. It is planted with peaches, plums, and tokay grapes. Fitch was the secretary of the California Fruit Exchange. Fitch's property was located on Hansen Road off Horseshoe Bar Road.

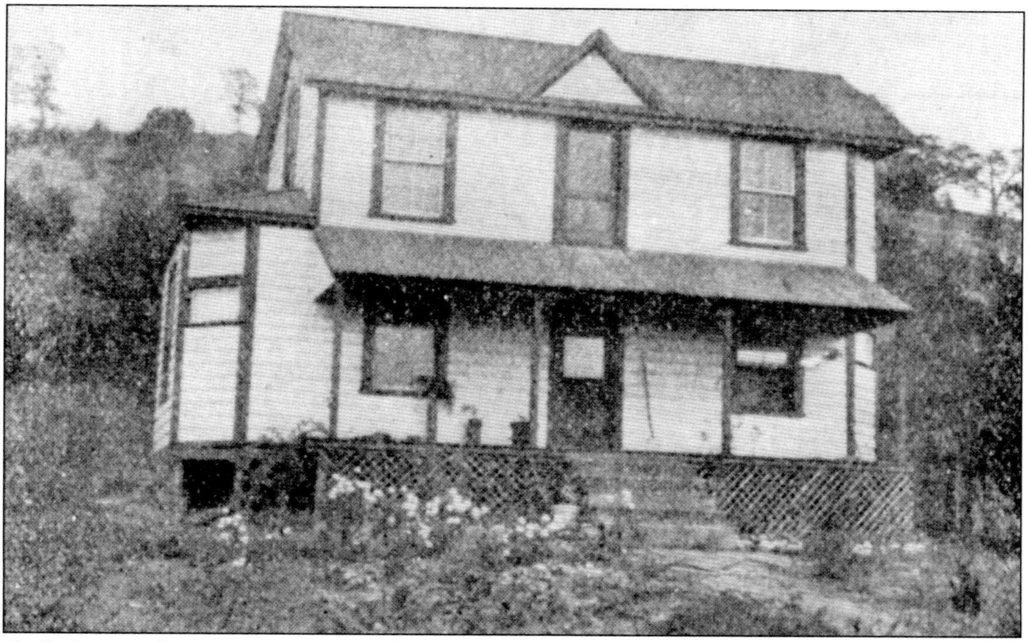

C. G. Brainerd was a newcomer to this area in 1908. His place was 49 acres, of which 20 were planted with fruit trees. He had 150 orange trees. This ranch was located on the south side of Horseshoe Bar Road west of Leak Lane.

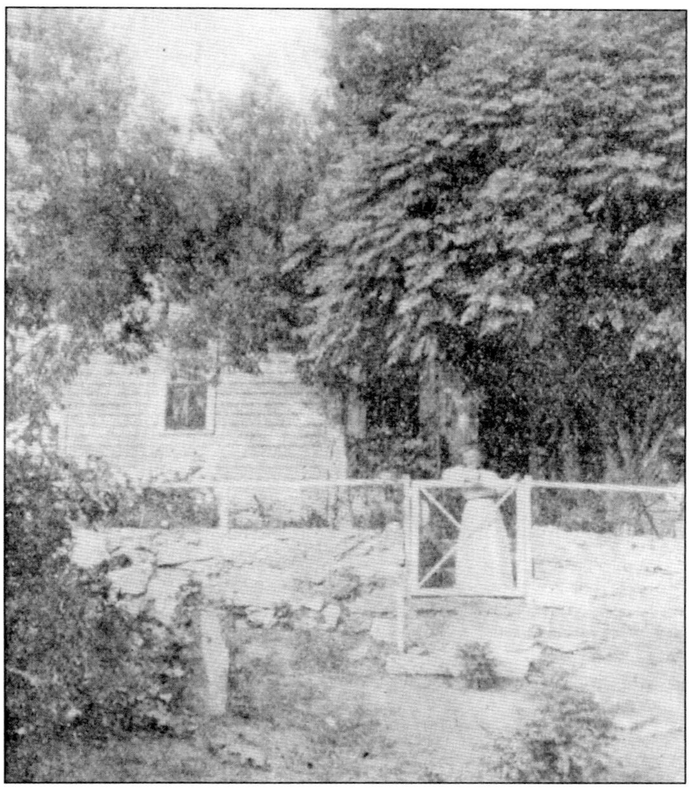

Sunnyslope was the home of John King and his wife. This ranch adapted well to peaches and plums. Because of the topography of the 20-acre orchard, the fruit trees were sheltered from frost. This property was later owned by Al Taylor and even later by Shig and Mitzi Takahashi. It is across from Placer School.

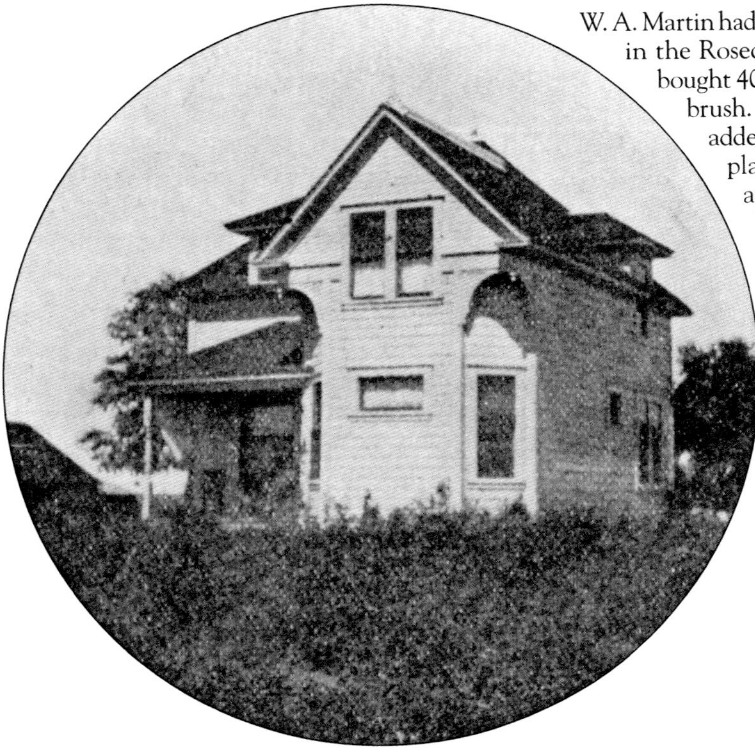

W. A. Martin had one of the finest vineyards in the Rosedale Colony. In 1900, he bought 40 acres covered with thick brush. He cleared the property, added another 120 acres, and planted 160 acres of tokay and mission grapes. The Rosedale Colony was near Auburn Folsom Road and Douglas Boulevard.

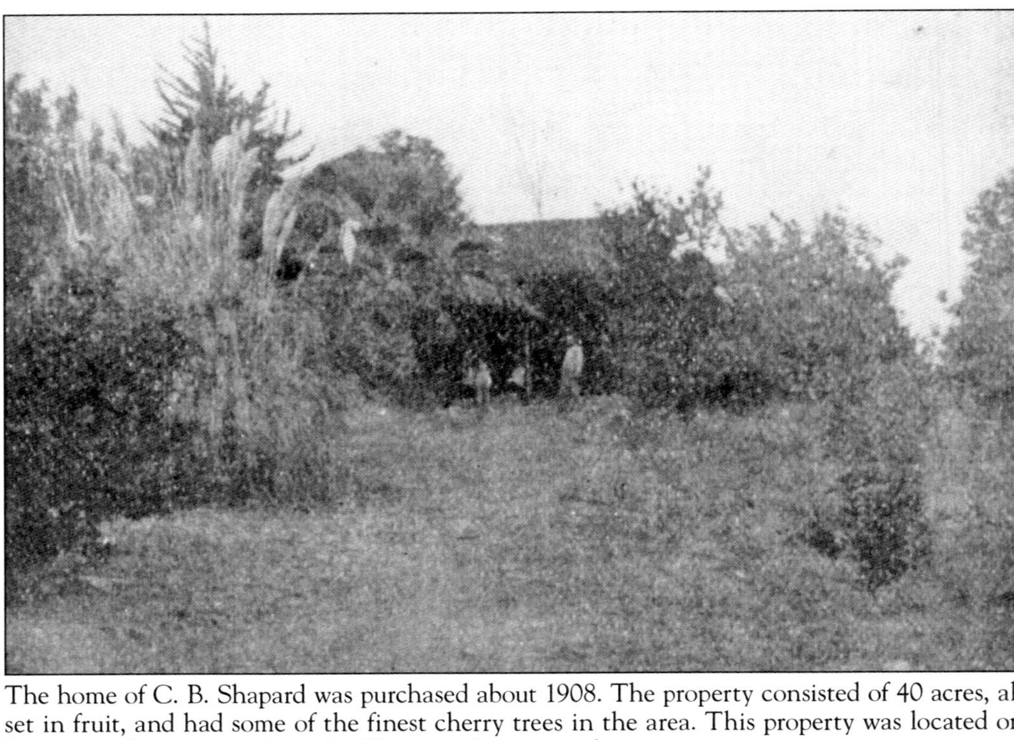

The home of C. B. Shapard was purchased about 1908. The property consisted of 40 acres, all set in fruit, and had some of the finest cherry trees in the area. This property was located on Rasmussen Lane across from the Christian Rasmussen home.

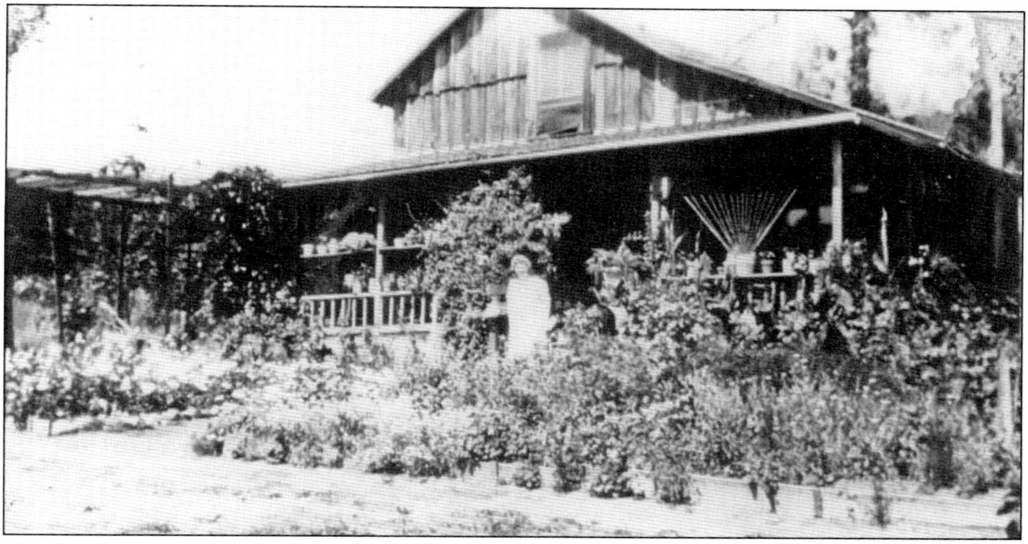

The W. P. Fassett home is pictured without the snow of a previous photograph. The Fassett family had a general merchandise store on Taylor Road next to the C. H. Plaus Drug Store. Fassett sold Syracuse brand plows. W. P. Fassett also played saxophone in the Ben Ali Shrine Band.

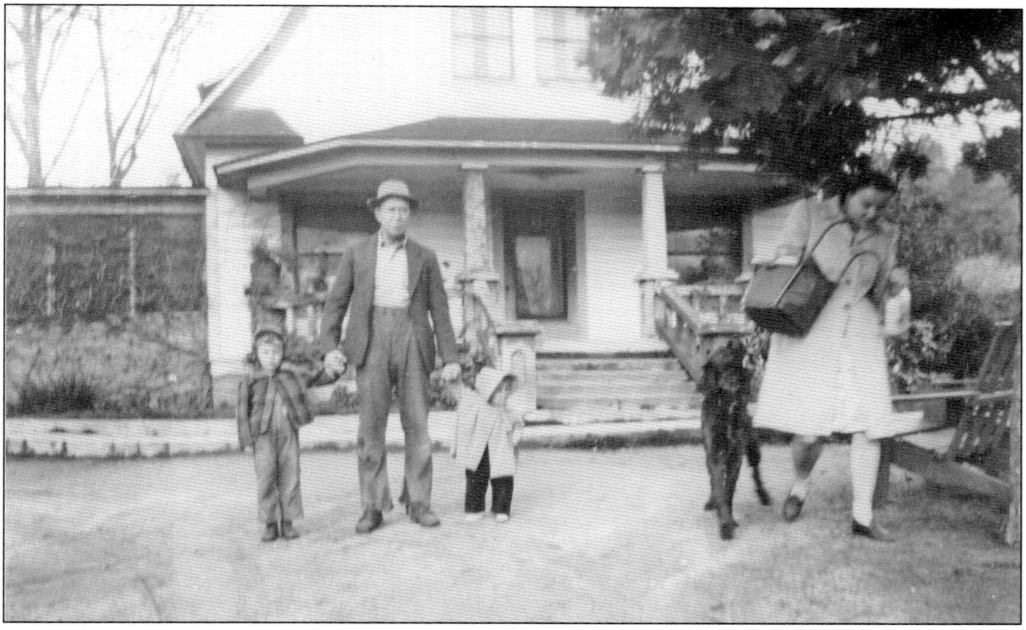

This is the childhood home of Robert, Jim, Lois, and Mildred Hansen. This picture shows Robert as a young child with his father, Hans Nicholas, his sister, and his mother, Adaline. Hans Nicholas was the child of Robert and Hannah Hansen. Robert and Hannah moved to the Loomis area from Benecia, California, in 1893 with Hans and the rest of their children, Harry Ulysses, Lena, Ella, and Kirsy Elizabeth. They started with 20 acres, with the first crop being strawberries. They gradually added peaches, pears, plums, grapes, and apples. Some of their holdings included Pine Hill and Magnolia Ranches. These are on Hansen Road, off Horseshoe Bar Road next to Placer School. Hans Nicholas's grandson, Randy, was the final manager of the Loomis Fruit Growers Association. Hans was president of Loomis Fruit Growers for 26 years prior to his death in 1952.

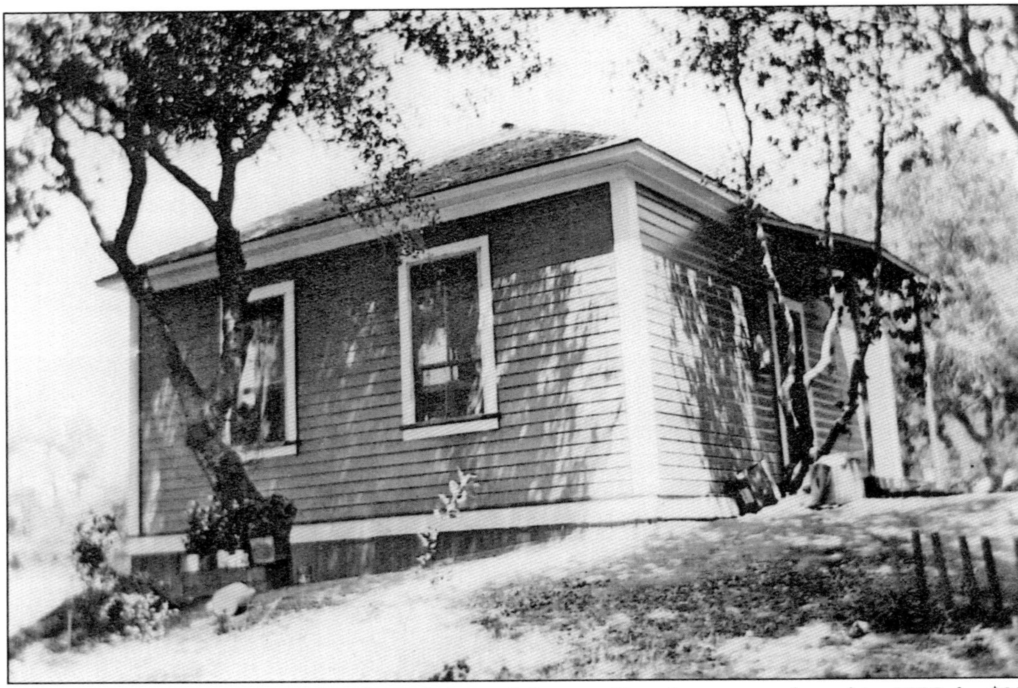

The 40-acre homestead of John A. and Anna Johanna Sippola was purchased in 1908 for $25 per acre. They originally grew plums, grapes, peaches, and pears.

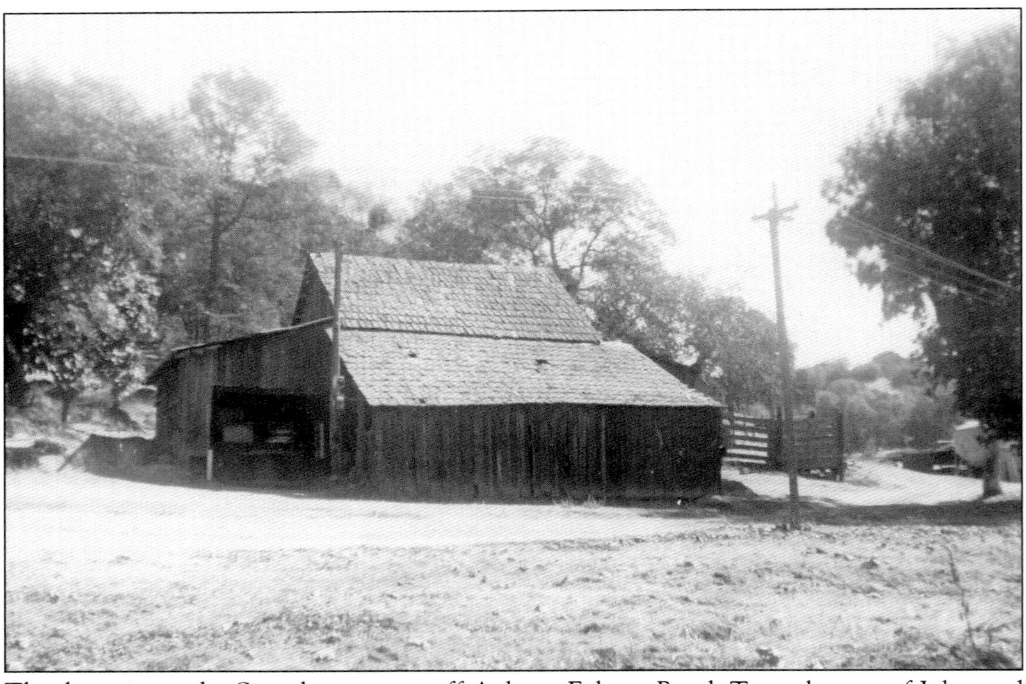

This barn is on the Sippola property off Auburn Folsom Road. Tom, the son of John and Anna, still lives on the ranch with his wife, Jean. There are many large granite outcroppings on the property.

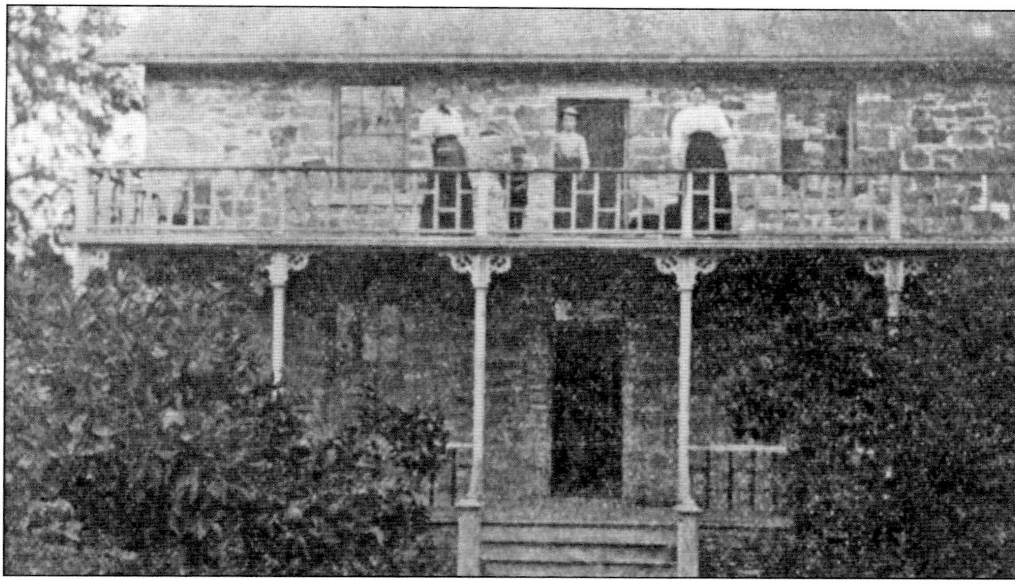

Owen King came to California a second time in 1854 after returning to his native New York to marry Bridget O'Shaughnessy. They came to California by way of the Isthmus of Panama. They built their home, Kingmont, from granite from the Griffith W. Griffith quarry in Penryn. They had four children, Katherine, Anna, James J., and Mary Elizabeth Brennan. James was well known in the fruit industry and was the county supervisor for years. He was also president of the California Fruit Exchange. He and his wife, Martha, lived in the two-story granite home.

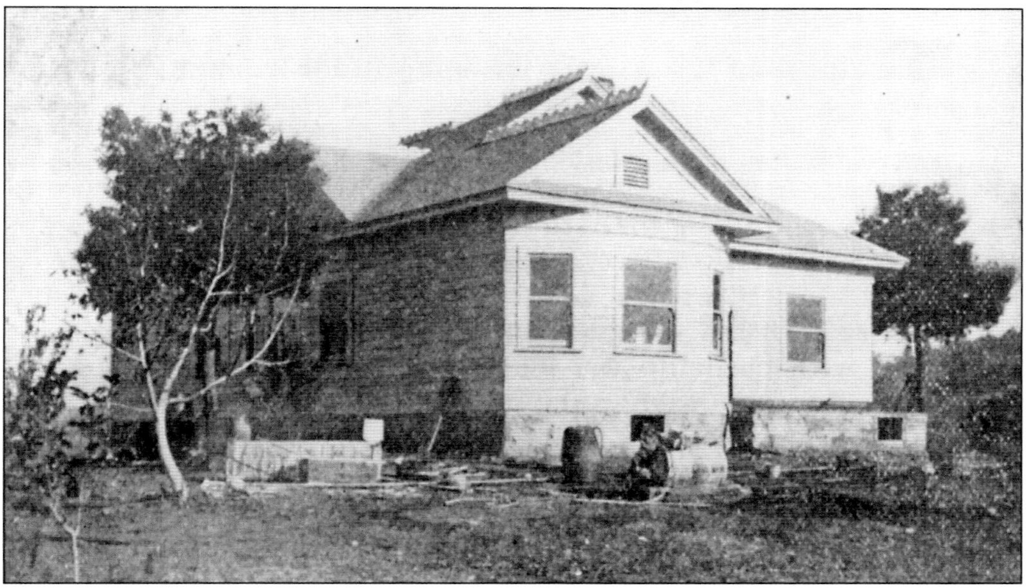

Christian Rasmussen and his wife came to this district after he left railroading. They bought 40 acres of brushland, cleared the property, and planted fruit, mostly peaches. Thirty-five acres of five-year-old trees in 1906 yielded $6,000. In 1908, with a light crop, the same trees netted $2,500 above expenses. Rasmussen had another 10 acres of orchard in another portion of the district planted in olives. This property is located on Rasmussen Road off Val Verde Road, between King and Horseshoe Bar Roads.

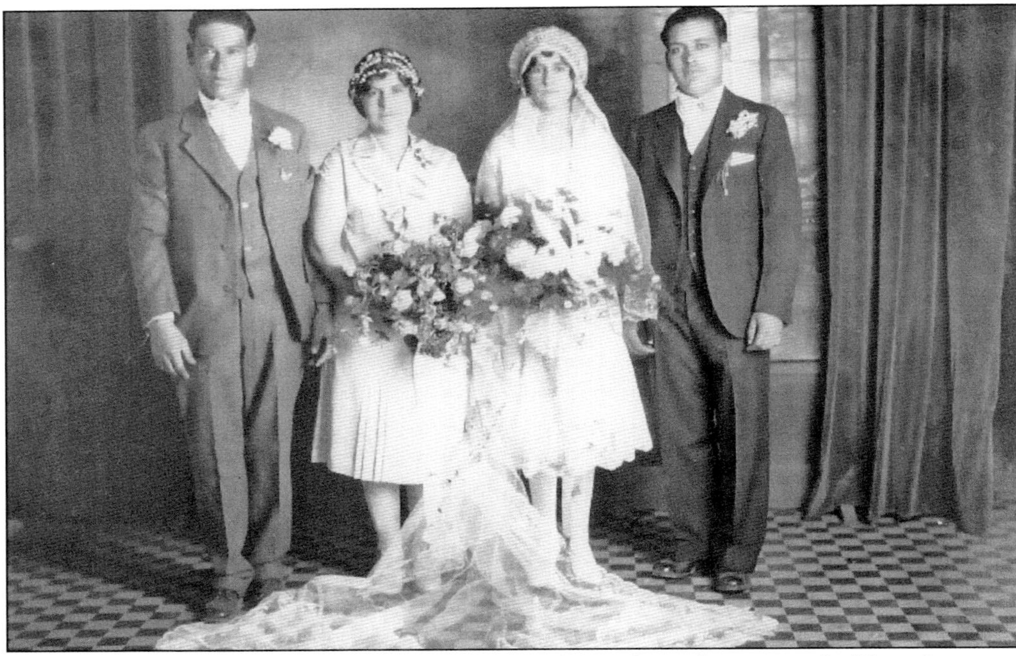

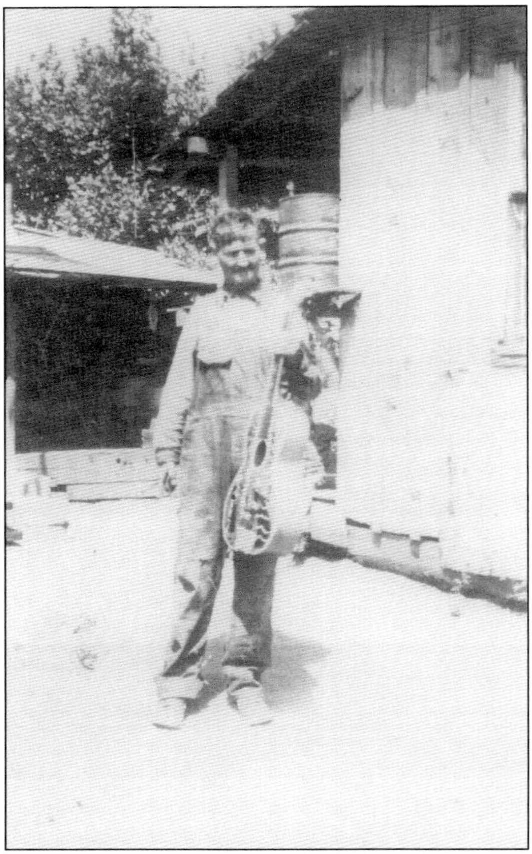

Many Spanish came to the United States by way of Hawaii. Raymond and Julia Lopez were married in Loomis shortly after they arrived from Spain.

Tony Montero lived off Del Mar Road, which at the time was County Road 53. He traveled to the United States by way of Hawaii in 1911 and in 1914 came to Loomis.

Seven

Churches

Churches were very important to the citizens of the community. The All Saints Episcopal Church was moved in three pieces from where it was built in Citrus Colony to Laird Street in town, a move of a few miles. The First Congregational Church was established from a gathering of early settlers. Eventually a small building was erected. The large stately building one block off Taylor Road was built in 1920. The Japanese Methodist Church was built in 1904 by the Issei of the area. Many of their descendants are still members of the church today. There are many other churches in the area, but these are the oldest. All Saints Episcopal no longer exists, but the other two are still in existence.

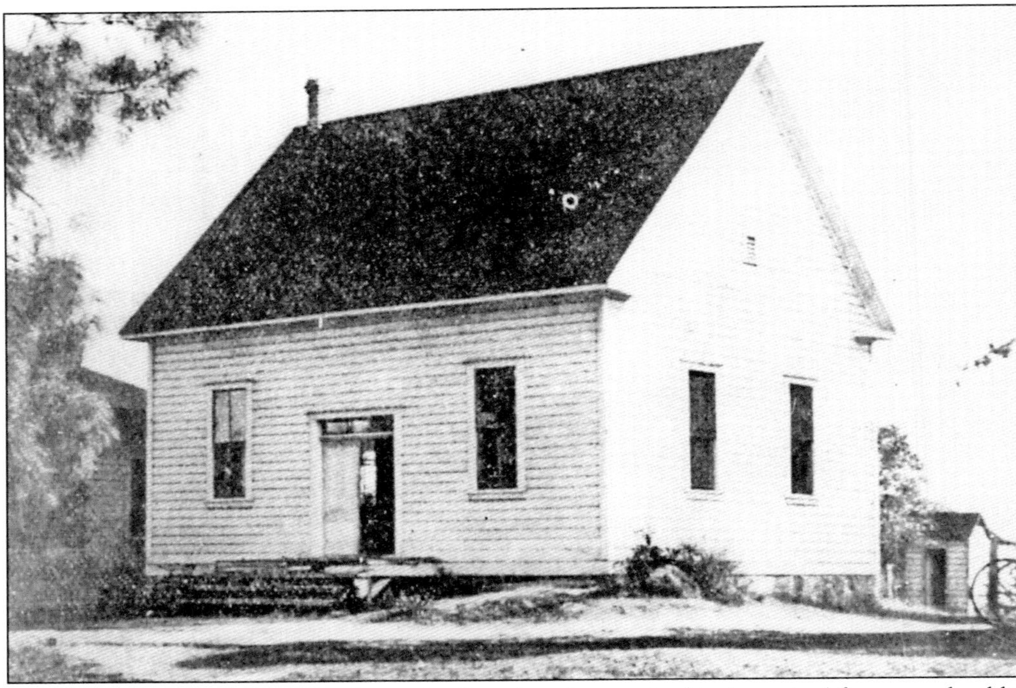

The First Congregational Church was the first church organized in Loomis. After several public meetings to discuss forming a united church, about 40 residents met at the Loomis Fruit House Hall on July 1, 1894, to vote on the church of choice. Congregational received the most votes. Charter members were Harry H. Caldwell, Maggie Bankhead, Belle Bankhead, Ida Emerson, Mr. and Mrs. John Tufts, Arthur W. Brown, C. L. Jensen, Mr. and Mrs. Peter Johnson, and Rasmuss Laurson. The first worship service was on March 24, 1895.

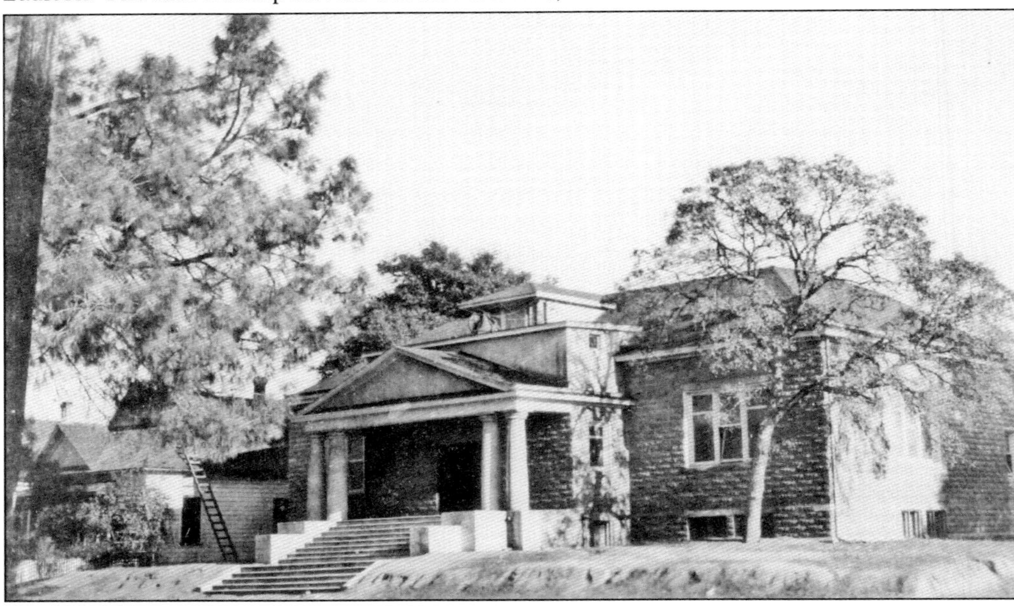

The First Congregational Church is pictured in 1948. The church on Magnolia Street was sold in 1980 and a brand-new church was built on King Road about a half-mile east of Taylor Road.

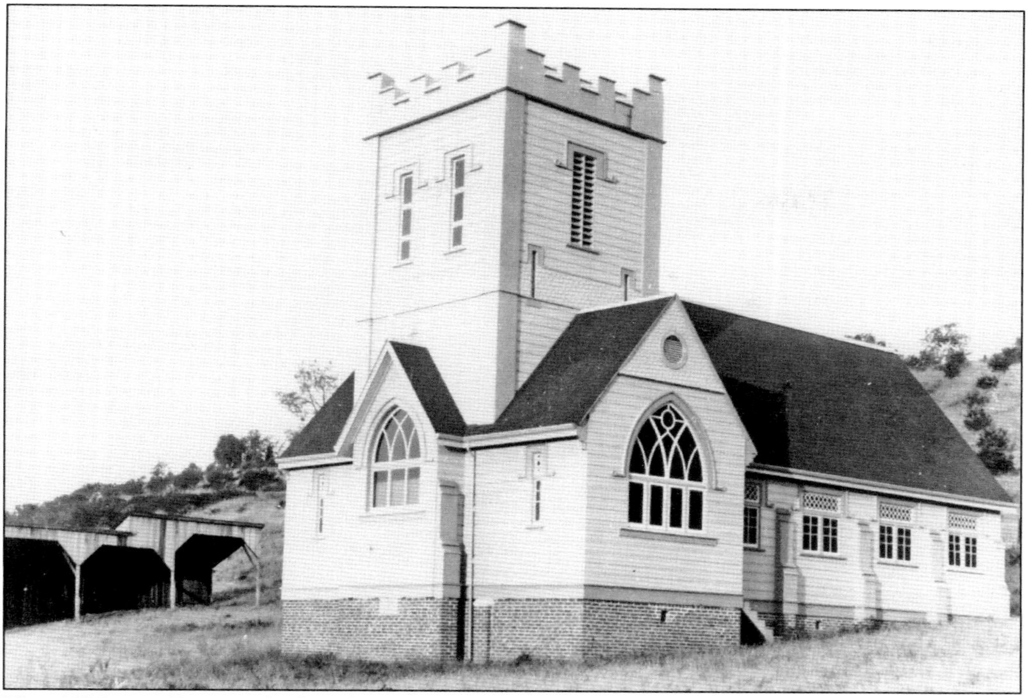

The All Saints Episcopal Church was originally located in the Citrus Colony on the ridge near Sierra College Boulevard. The building was moved in three pieces to the corner of Webb Street and Laird Street in Loomis before 1908.

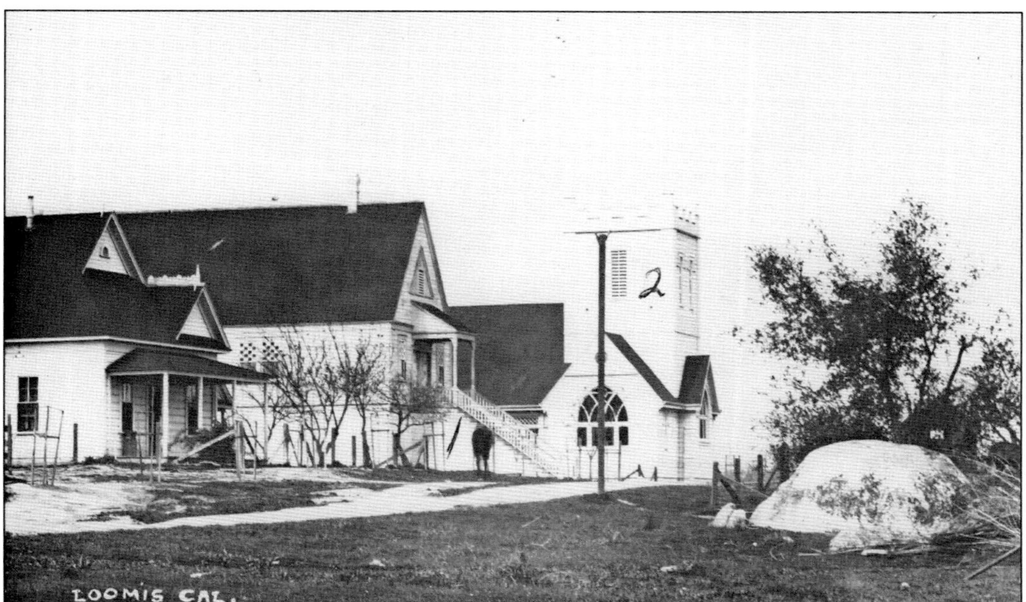

This original postcard belonging to Ida Flesher shows the Loomis Guild Hall and the All Saints Episcopal Church about 1910. This was behind the Hardware Emporium.

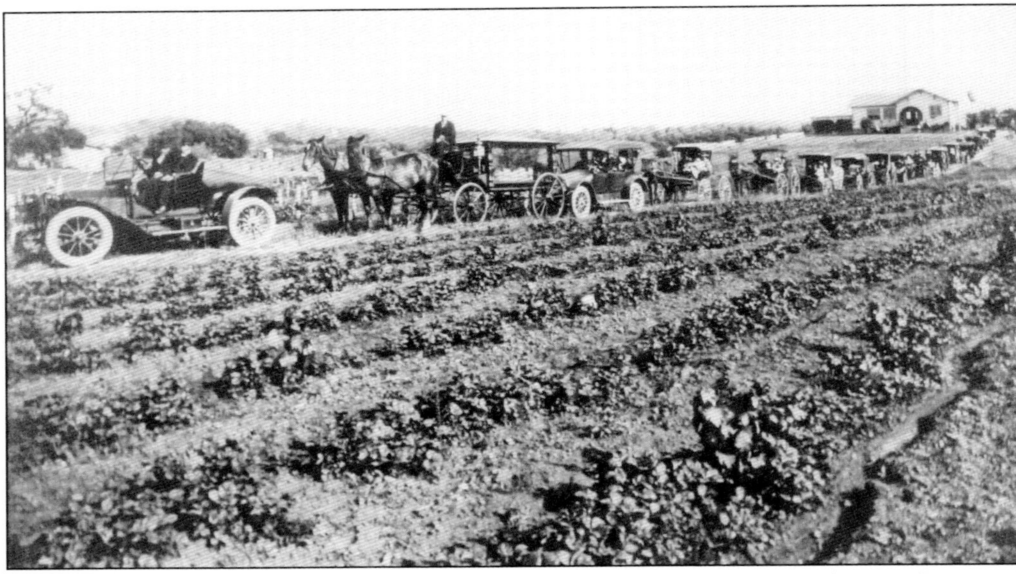

The Loomis Methodist Church was built in 1904 at the intersection of what became Brace and Barton Roads. This photograph shows a funeral procession. The building in the right background is the original one constructed by the Issei. The road with all the cars and buggies goes through the strawberry fields.

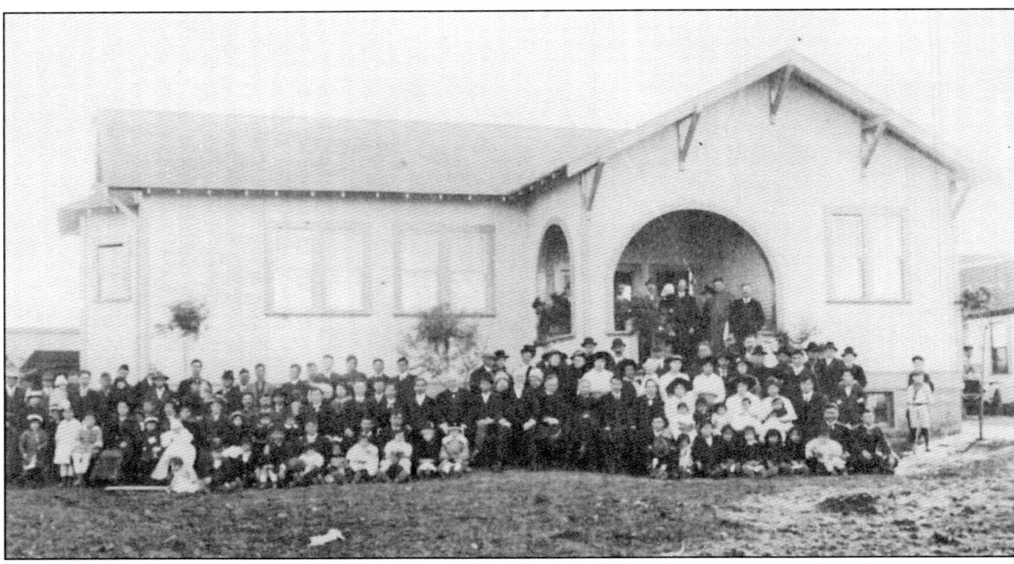

This photograph was taken at the Loomis Methodist Church's Founders Day Anniversary in November 1916. This building is still in use at the church.

Eight

Organizations and Sports

There were many organizations in the area in the good old days. There were many card clubs that played bridge and whist. There was the Men's Club, which helped the Women's Club; the Poppy Club; and the Boys Scouts of America; 4-H was very prominent in the area. There was the Levis and Lace dance club. The fire department held annual dances. Sports were not left out, either. There were school baseball and basketball teams. The Loomis Reds, the men's baseball team, were league champions. When the interest in baseball was strong, the town got together and built a diamond. Most unique was the sport of blue jay hunting. The huge amount of birds that flocked to the newly planted fruit trees caused havoc with the fruit. To slow the problem down, there were competitions where men and boys competed to see who could drop the most birds. Prizes were awarded, and the bird problem was lessened. Many of the clubs were based on community beautification and making the community a better place to live. A ladies aid society started in 1911. The Japanese American Citizen's League formed in the 1930s. The Loomis Junior Women's Club was organized on December 7, 1951. The schools had the support of the Parent Teacher Association. The John A. Stacker Post of the American Legion met at the Veteran's Memorial Hall. The Lions Club organized. The Farm Bureau was an active group. The Masonic organizations were also represented, meeting at the Penrhyn Masonic Lodge in Penryn.

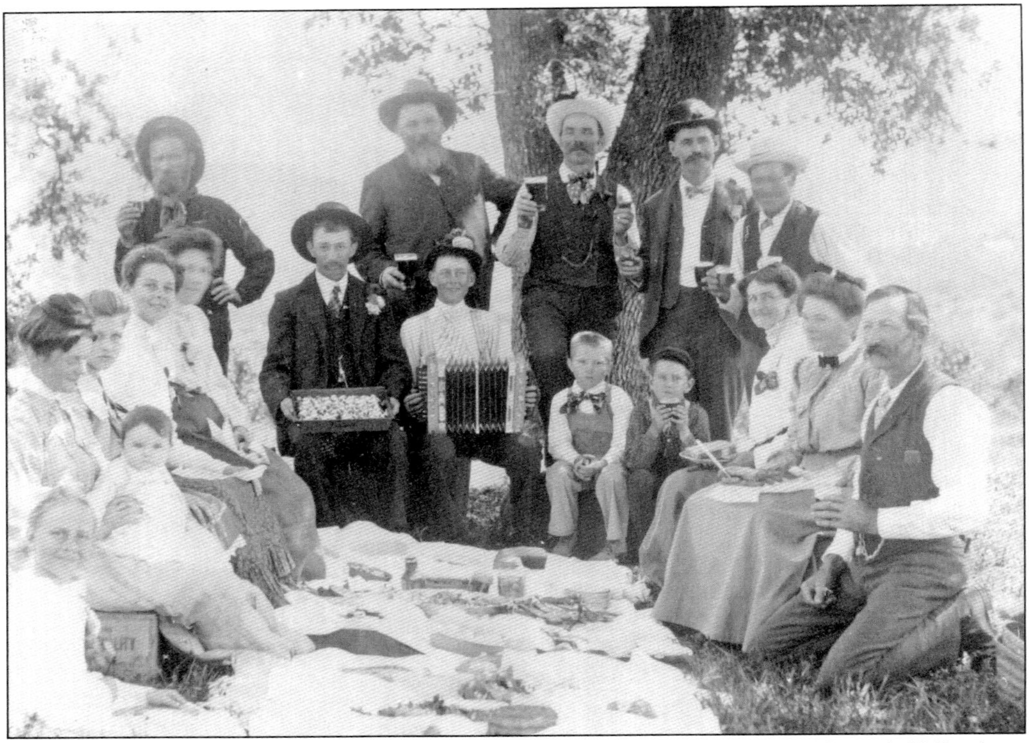

This *c.* 1905 photograph shows an early day Danish and German picnic on Hergot's Hill, where the Valley View Clubhouse was located. From left to right are Mae Fieser Mehl, Zella Reineck holding baby Gladys Reineck, Olga Arnold, Kate Fieser Leak, Mary Kutschker, Charles Schultz, William Prisser holding cake, Freddy Fieser with his accordion, Professor Reineck, Fred Fieser Sr., Zeno Kutschker, Jake Hergot, Frank Stark and Albert Fieser (the two little boys), Caroline Fieser, Anna Marie Rasmussen, and James Rasmussen.

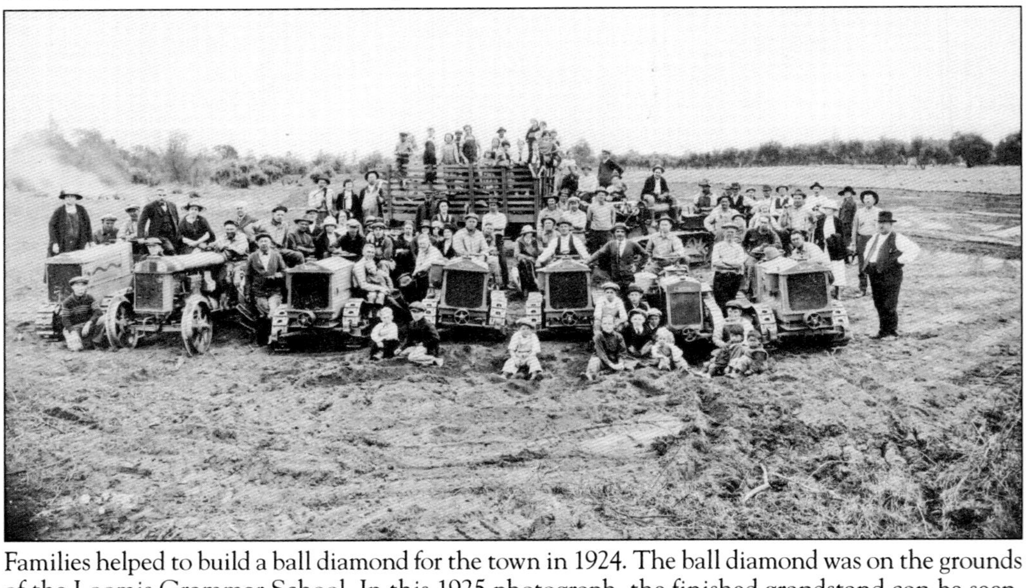

Families helped to build a ball diamond for the town in 1924. The ball diamond was on the grounds of the Loomis Grammar School. In this 1925 photograph, the finished grandstand can be seen.

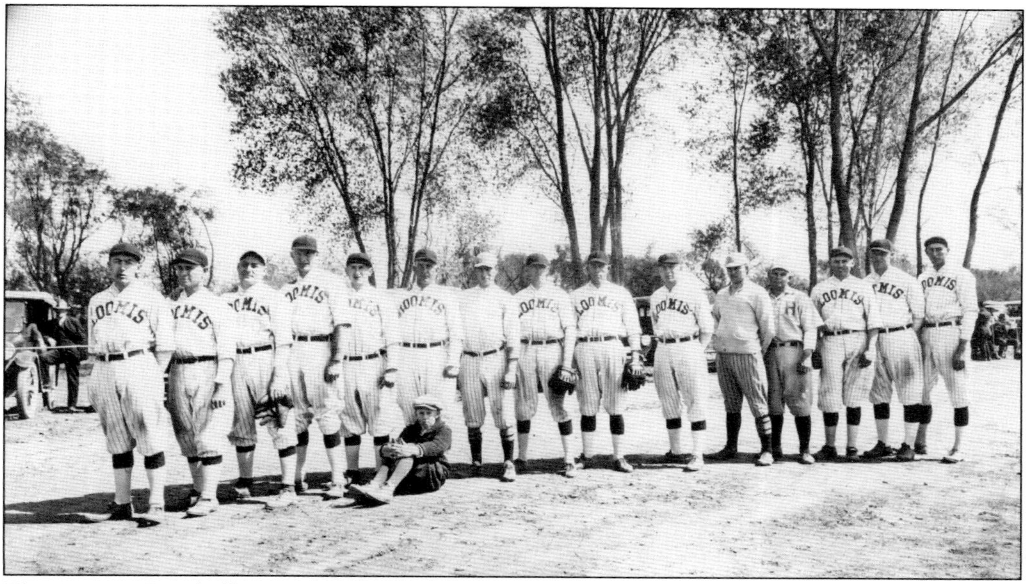

The Loomis Baseball team of 1924 included, from left to right, Ted Gordon, right field; Troy Barr, left field; Roscoe Schuler, center; Fenn Laird, manager and first baseman; Otto Bischoff, third base; Hjalmer "Del" Alexson, catcher; unidentified; Jimmy Brennan, shortstop; Bill Coten, pitcher; Vince Horton, second base; unidentified; Lorry Hendrickson, substitute catcher; Harold Siever, catcher; Ed Horton, right field; and Al Fieser, utility and outfielder. Their mascot was Barton Smyth.

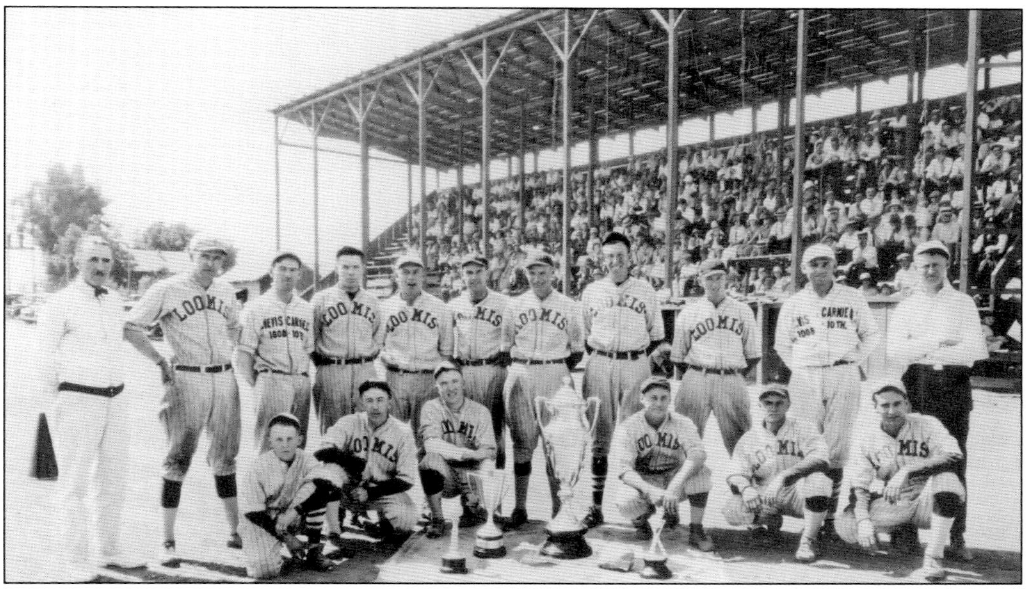

The 1925 Loomis Reds were the Champions of the Valley. From left to right are (kneeling) Irv Smyth, batboy; Ted Gordon, center and right field; Johnny Lane, catcher; Roscoe Schuler, left field; and pitchers Bub Wales and John Mealia; (standing) Chet Hall, announcer; Jim Oates, left field; Bob Gordon, utility; Irv Elliot, catcher; Vince Horton, second base; Adie Chase, shortstop; Fenn Laird, manager and first base; Verne Hodge, first base and right field; Jim Brennan, third base; Hal Siever, utility; and Fenn Bock, secretary.

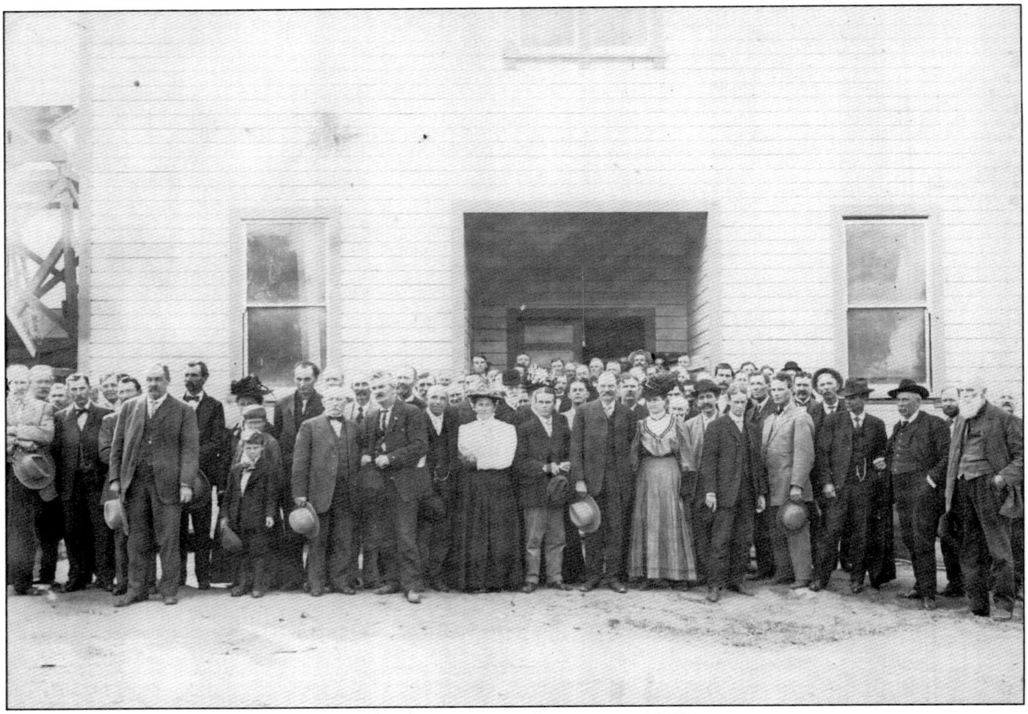

This was a typical gathering outside the Loomis Grange in 1908.

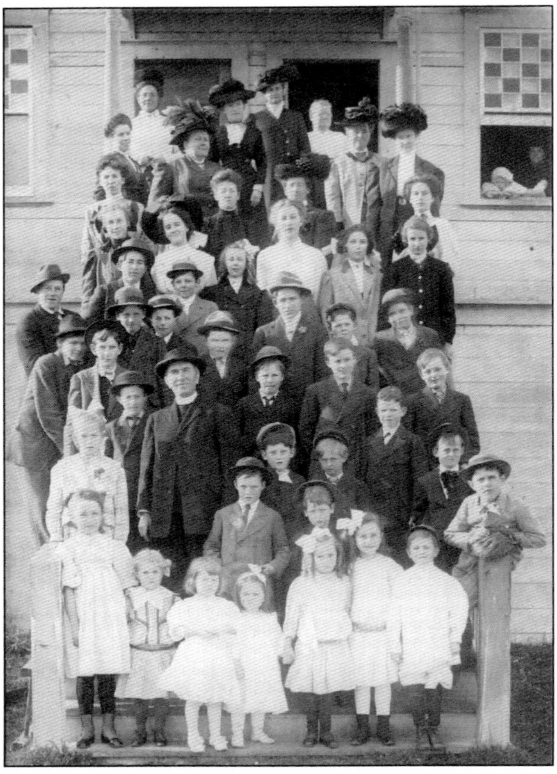

This is a 1905 gathering of the Episcopal Sunday school class at the Loomis Guild Hall. The photograph only lists the names, not their position in the photograph. Included are Mae Fieser, Mildred Brainerd, Olga Jensen, Thelma Johnson, Marian Nixon, Harold Misley, Audrey Cook, Beryl Tudsbury, Rudolph Brahm, John Blemmer, Harold Brainerd, Thomas Ryan, Ed Larsen, Fred Turner, Charles Turner, George Bock, Ed Aymer, Robert Aymer, Frank Gallaway, William Cook, William Bock, Norman Pendleton, Theresa Brahm, Albert Gallaway, Clarence Cook, Carl Dunn, Alice Swetzer, two Locket family members, Carmen and Gwendolyn McGovern, Austin Plaus, Mrs. McGovern, Mrs. A. Lyle, Mrs. Fieser, Martha Turner, Ada Swetzer, Carrie Turner, Belle Tudsbury, Alice Law, Birdie Nixon, Mrs. Eckles, Mrs. Whitaker, Mrs. Locket, Albert Fieser, Rev. J. T. McGovern, and Kate Fieser.

This is a program from September 20, 1895, for the Y. P. Club of Loomis. Admission was 25¢ for adults and 10¢ for children.

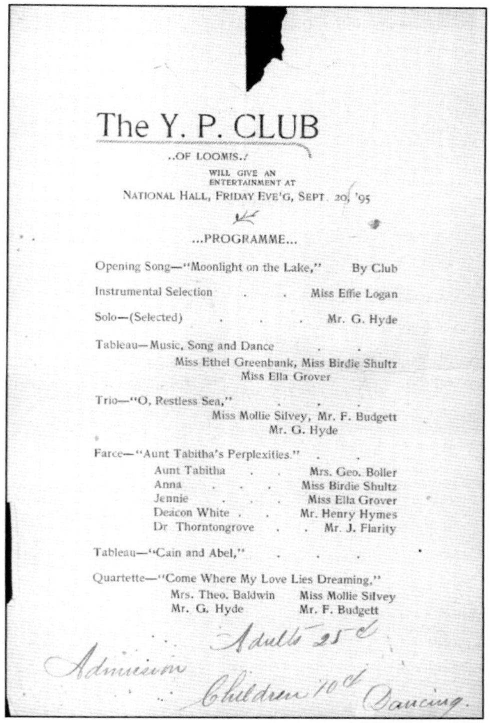

The Y. P. CLUB

..OF LOOMIS..

WILL GIVE AN
ENTERTAINMENT AT
NATIONAL HALL, FRIDAY EVE'G, SEPT. 20, '95

...PROGRAMME...

Opening Song—"Moonlight on the Lake," . . . By Club

Instrumental Selection . . . Miss Effie Logan

Solo—(Selected) . . . Mr. G. Hyde

Tableau—Music, Song and Dance . .
Miss Ethel Greenbank, Miss Birdie Shultz
Miss Ella Grover

Trio—"O, Restless Sea," . . .
Miss Mollie Silvey, Mr. F. Budgett
Mr. G. Hyde

Farce—"Aunt Tabitha's Perplexities." . .

Aunt Tabitha	Mrs. Geo. Boller
Anna	Miss Birdie Shultz
Jennie	Miss Ella Grover
Deacon White	Mr. Henry Hymes
Dr Thorntongrove	Mr. J. Flarity

Tableau—"Cain and Abel," . . . .

Quartette—"Come Where My Love Lies Dreaming,"
Mrs. Theo. Baldwin Miss Mollie Silvey
Mr. G. Hyde Mr. F. Budgett

Admission Adults 25¢
Children 10¢ Dancing.

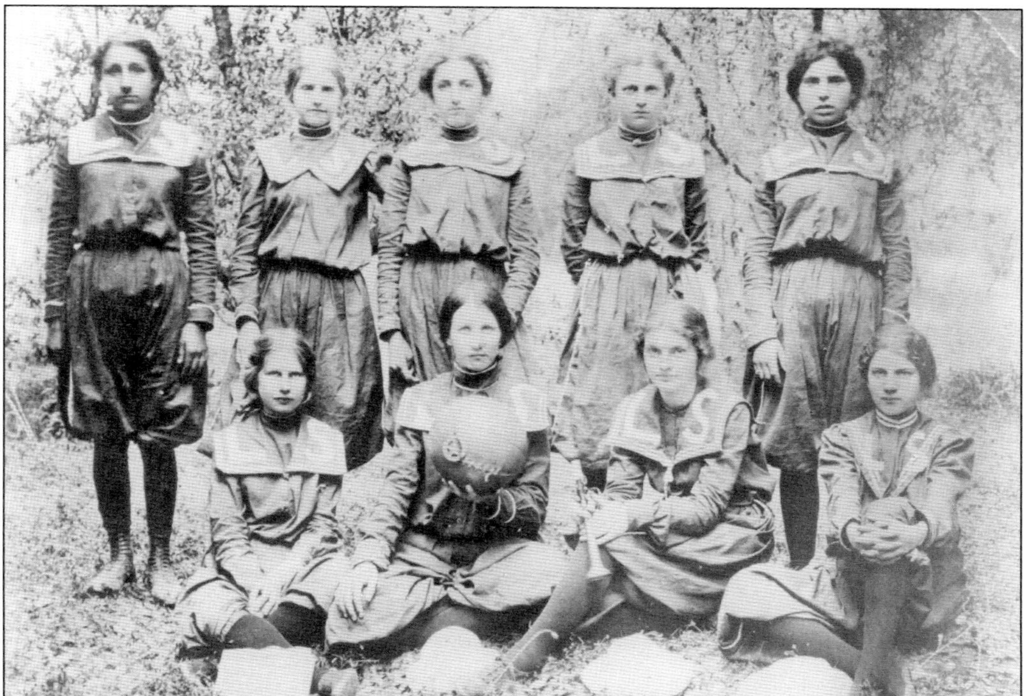

Pictured are players on the 1903 girls basketball team from Loomis School. The identities of the players are, sadly, unknown.

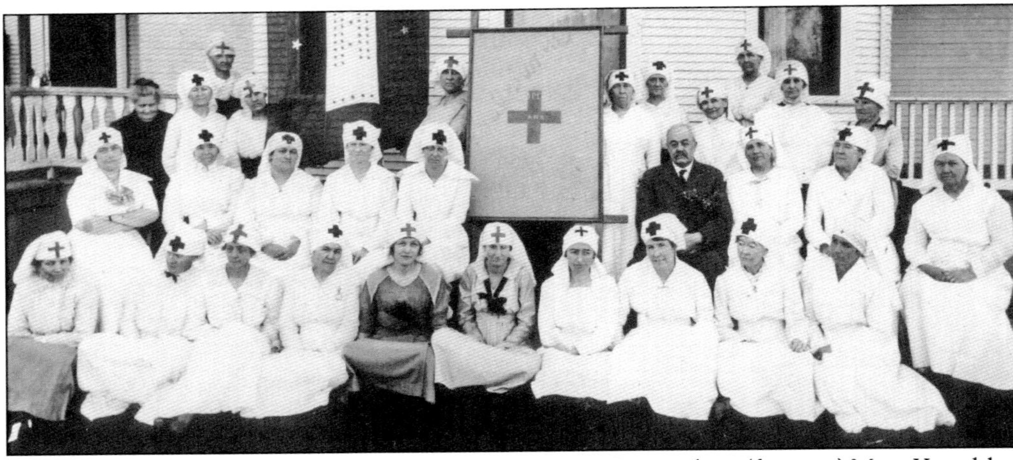

Loomis had a large group of Red Cross volunteers in 1918. Pictured are (first row) Mary Kutschker, Hattie Smyth, Ella Brainerd, Mattie Nelthorpe, Olga Kutschker, Marion Denton, Sadie Callison, Mamie Cook, Sarah Kirk, and Mary Williams; (second row) Mabel Ritchie, Caro Plaus, Clara Cook, Magdalena Eckhardt, Helen Dearborn, Dr. Orren Barton, Beatrice McGovern, Mamie Brennan, and May Wilson; (third row) Mrs. Federoff, Agnes Kinney; Mrs. Pete Kelly, Lulu Rippey, Lillian Reeves, Belle Balmer, Nell Boller, Ada Barton (the doctor's wife), Blenda Goddard, Ida Belle Plank, and Caroline Lyall. These women knitted socks, sweaters, and blankets for soldiers wounded in action in World War I.

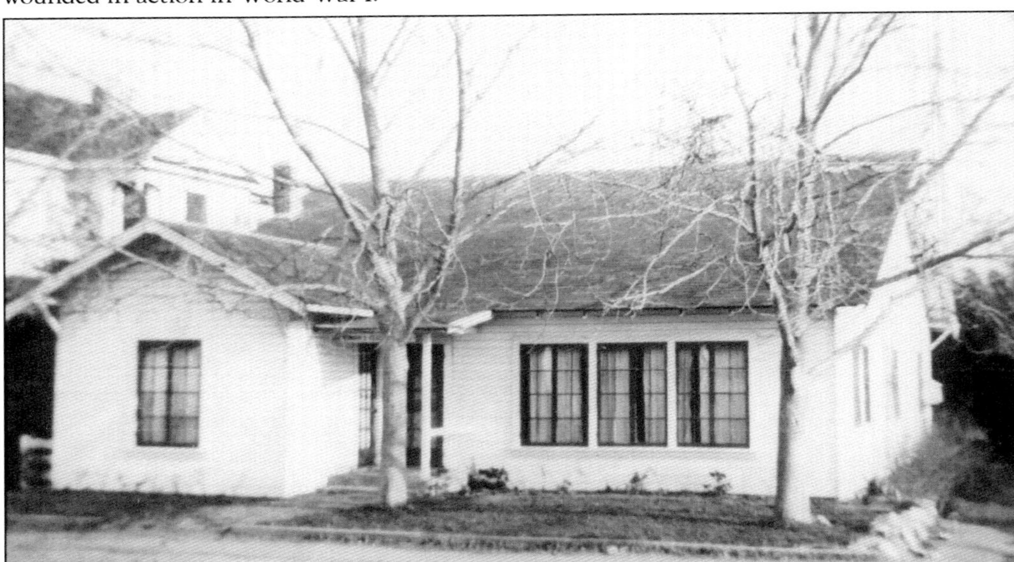

The Woman's Club of Loomis was organized on February 17, 1917. They originally met in the Guild Hall, which was built for social and business gatherings. The first floor included open stables for the horses and buggies of those attending meetings at the hall. Charter members included Hilda McFall, Minta Bassett, Ethel G. Law, Mable Ritchie, Mildred Scroggs, Helen Dearborn, Magdalena Eckhardt, Caroline Lyall, Alice Howse, Mary Kutschker, L. Hunter, Ellen Barton Tufts, Cora Whittimore, Belle Balmer, Cara Plaus, Amalia Rivarde, Beatrice MacGovern, Winifred Hall, Amalia Nicholls, Hazel Ostrom, Mary Flaridon, Mamie Brennan, Loretta Branstetter, Agnes Kinney, Ada Vail Barton, Claire Rasmussen, Edith Lockett, Melissa Branstetter, and Aileen Parsons. During World War I, club members were active in Red Cross and other patriotic activities.

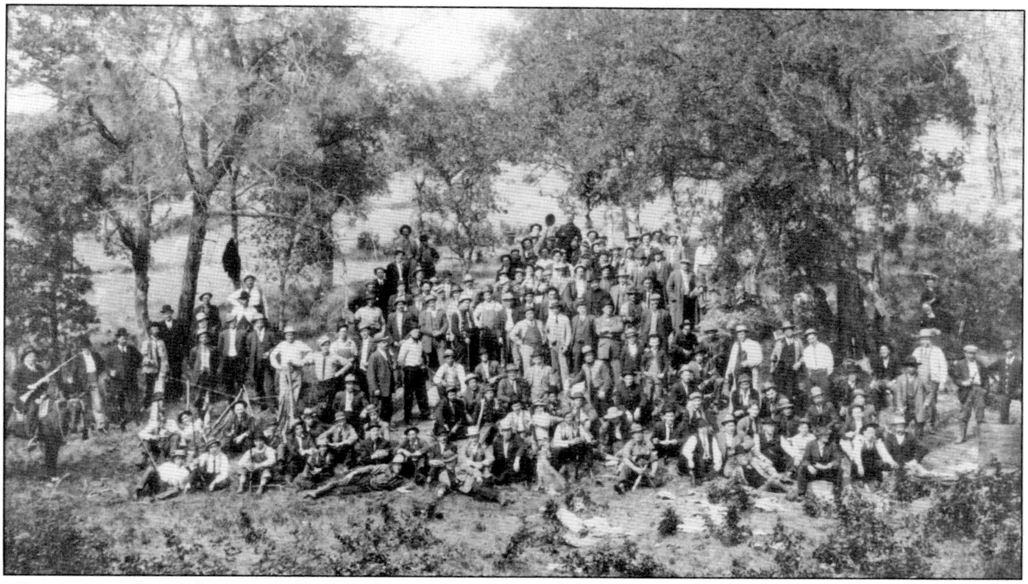

The new orchards became a haven for birds, especially blue jays. The birds came by the thousands, and much of the fruit was ruined. Damaged fruit could not be shipped to market. It was decided to have blue jay hunts in the early summer, when the cherries were beginning to ripen. The first hunt was in 1902. Hunters started from their homes and ranches, walking and hunting toward the appointed gathering place. Originally they gathered at the Angelo Orsolini ranch off Barton Road. Later hunts were held on the Cordell ranch off Laird Road. There were many good hunters, and hundreds of birds were brought in. The merchants of the town furnished prizes, which generally included shotgun shells, a hand ax, or a hammer and 10 pounds of nails for the most birds.

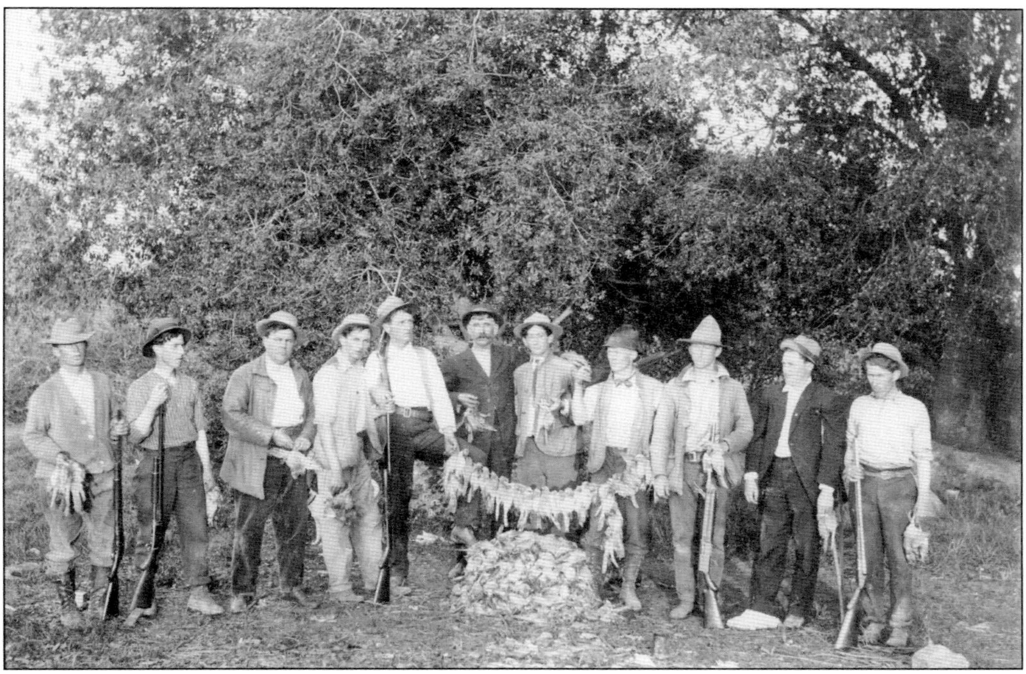

The prizewinners from one of the blue jay hunts are pictured.

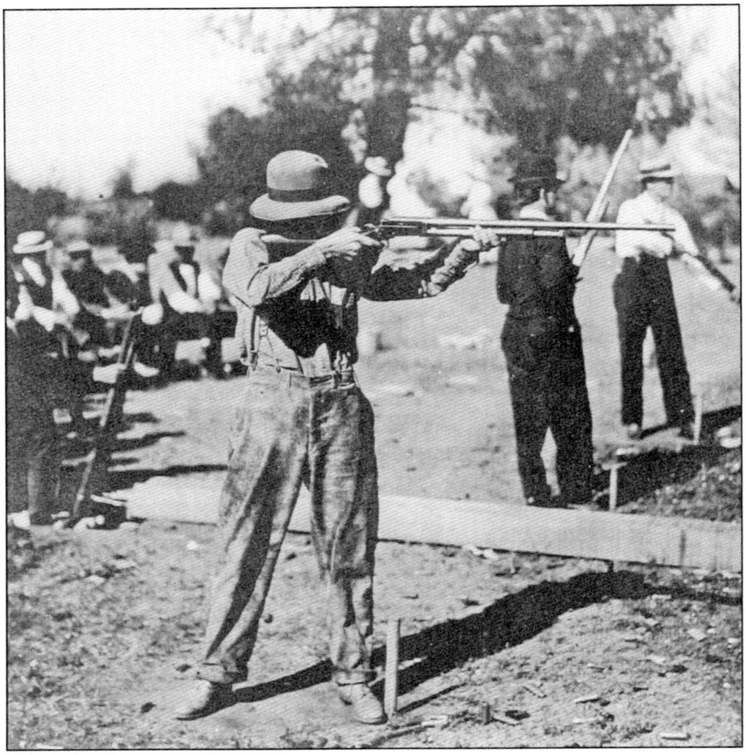

William Crossley takes part in a sharpshooter's competition. Note the style of dress on the other men. The women are in the background in fancy dresses.

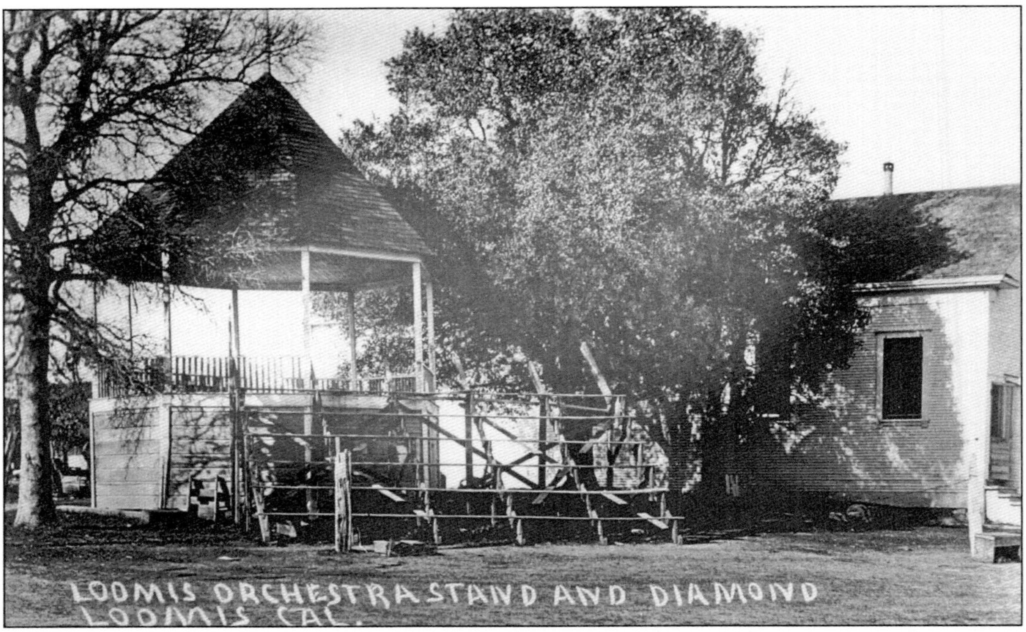

The orchestra stand was just south of town. This photograph was taken in 1912. The Loomis Cornet Band had concerts here.

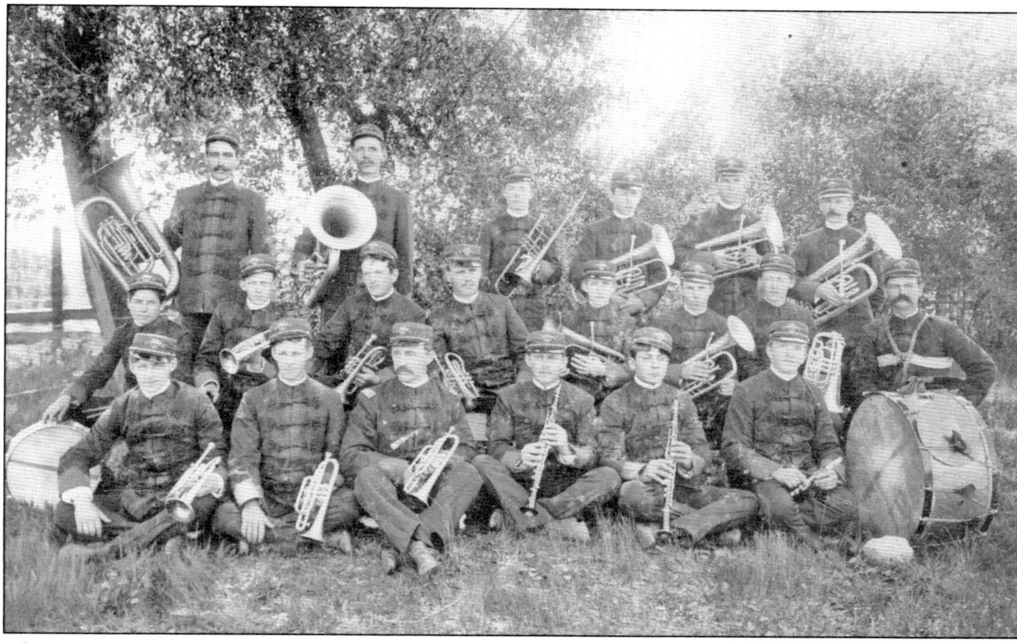

The Loomis Cornet Band included, from left to right, (first row) George Pendleton, George Higson, leader Dan McKelips, Jack Swetzer, Charley Dolce, and Clarence Tufts; (second row) Charley Cook, Al Pendleton, Frank Tufts, Pete Swetzer, Warren Boller, Bart Frazer, Bill Pendleton, and drummer Elmer Caldwell; (third row) Arthur Howard, Henry Swetzer, Harry Winton, Bill Frazer, Leonard Frances, and William Turner. This photograph was taken around 1895.

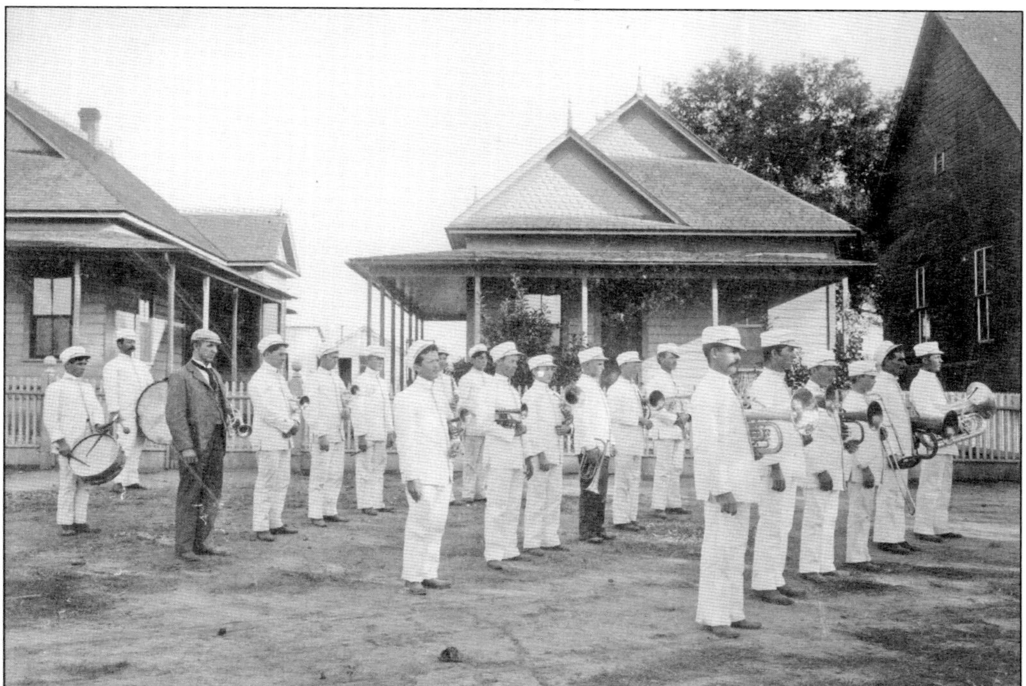

The Loomis Cornet Band is pictured in their lighter weight uniforms.

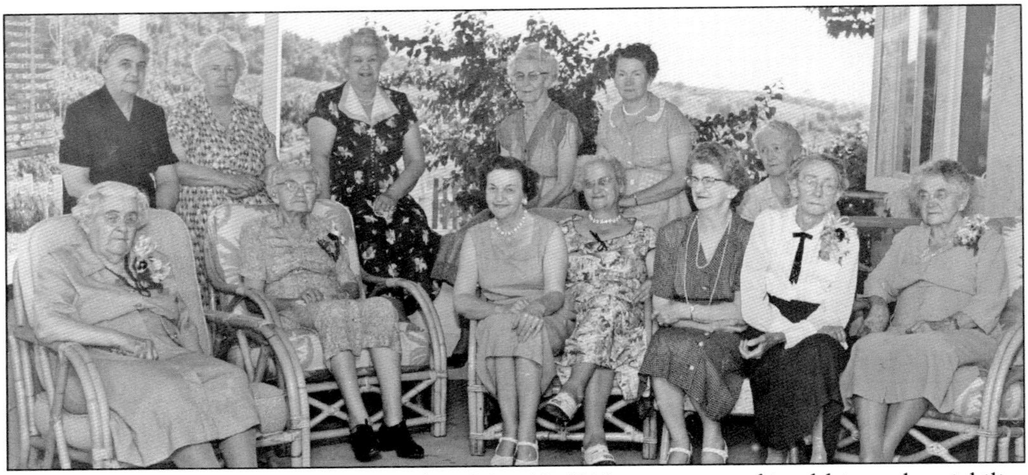

The Loomis Poppy Club was organized on May 10, 1910, to promote friendship and sociability among the women of the neighborhood. Embroidery was taken up as a diversion. Eventually the meetings were given over to games, sociability, and fancywork of many kinds. The first meeting took place at the Earl home on the Crocker ranch near the American River. The 12 charter members were Etta Earl, Ella Woods, Mabel Longstreth, Mamie Brennan, Bella Tudsbury, Bertha Nixon, Ida Brown, Blenda Goddard, Mattie Nelthorpe, Sarah Kirk, Katherine King, and Grace Day. This group is believed to be the first Poppy Club and known to be the first club for women in Placer County. During World War I, the group engaged in Red Cross, Belgian Relief, and Junior Red Cross work and also purchased a liberty bond as part of their war efforts. At the 45th anniversary celebration, Mattie Nelthorpe was the only surviving charter member present. The club celebrated its 50th anniversary as guests of Adaline Hansen at a luncheon near Colfax on April 25, 1960. After the summer vacation, the club disbanded because of so much illness among the members.

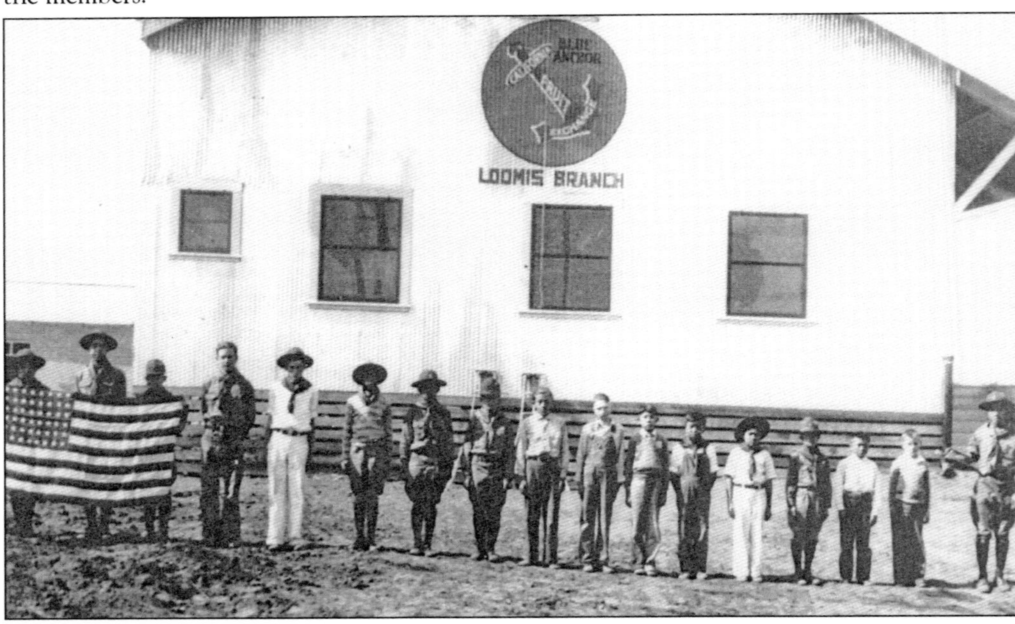

The Boy Scouts of America have always been very active in Loomis. Here is Troop 12 in front of the California Fruit Exchange in the 1930s.

Nine

Quarries of the Loomis Area

Granite quarries were also active in the area. The Carlow brothers' 15-acre, six-man quarry started in 1878 and was located near Pino on the Turner property. They had excellent quality dark granite, which was perfect for cemetery and building purposes. Carlow granite was used in the San Francisco City Hall, the old post office in Sacramento, and the Van Voorhies Mausoleum in the Sacramento City Cemetery. George Turner worked at the Carlow quarry for years; wages were 25¢ an hour for a 10-hour day. James Grant, born in Ireland in 1819, worked at Carlow for a time, but he also owned other quarries. The Grant quarry is one of the oldest in the area, developed by Andrew Grant and continued by his son James. Their quarries were located near Brace and Barton Roads, including land that much later became the golf course. The original 160-acre land purchase from the Central Pacific Railroad Company was signed by Leland Stanford. Their granite was used in the Placer County Courthouse in Auburn and in the California State Capitol building in Sacramento. The Healy quarry was also located in Pino. The quarry had a large open cut and was 65 to 75 feet deep. Michael Healy, the owner of the property, was also an Irishman. He became an American citizen in Berkshire County, Massachusetts, on October 30, 1876. The start date for this quarry is unknown, but it was doing a good business in 1887 and lasted until about 1909. It furnished a large order of dry dock materials for Mare Island. A spur track ran from the main line of the Central Pacific to the quarry. It employed 25 to 30 men, including Ed Naramore of Penryn. Alfred Nassi, a native of Finland, worked in the quarry around 1887; he moved to Rocklin to become a stone cutter. The Cook quarry was located off Horseshoe Bar Road, not far from the Carlow quarry. William Cook was an Englishman who came to America in 1855 with his wife, Ellen Graham Cook. Cook started in a quarry that he developed in Folsom. In 1865, he came to Smithville (later Loomis). Here he owned his own quarry and built his home. He sold granite for building and monument purposes. Some of the granite rock was used in the building of the California State Capitol.

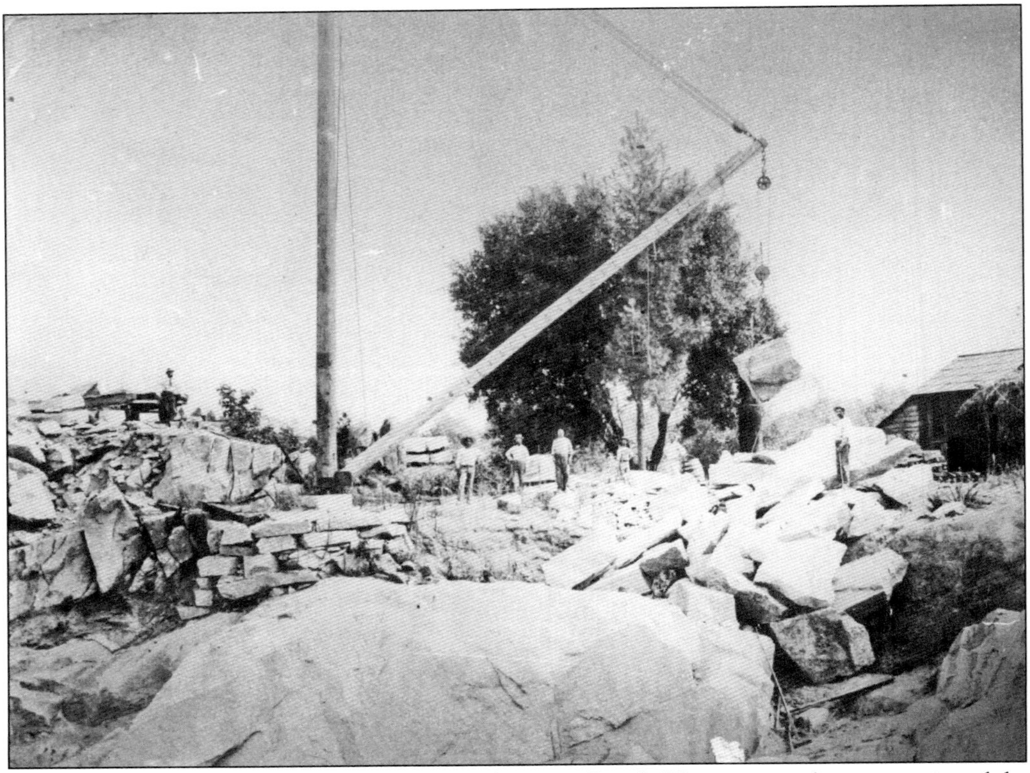

The Carlow Quarry was located on Horseshoe Bar Road. The crew is shown moving slabs of granite.

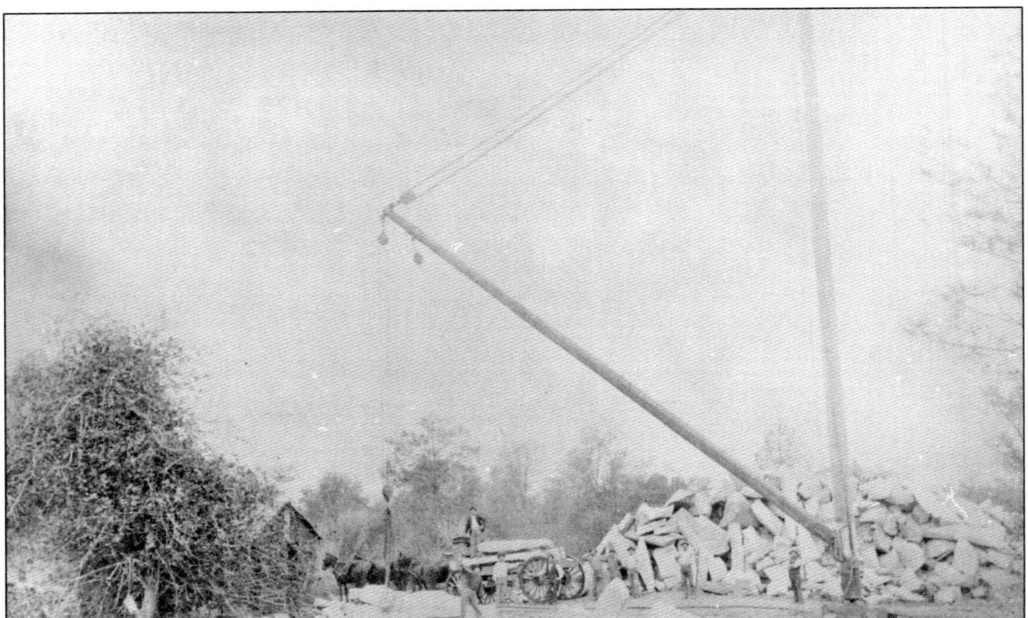

The James Grant granite quarry employed a similar method to move the granite.

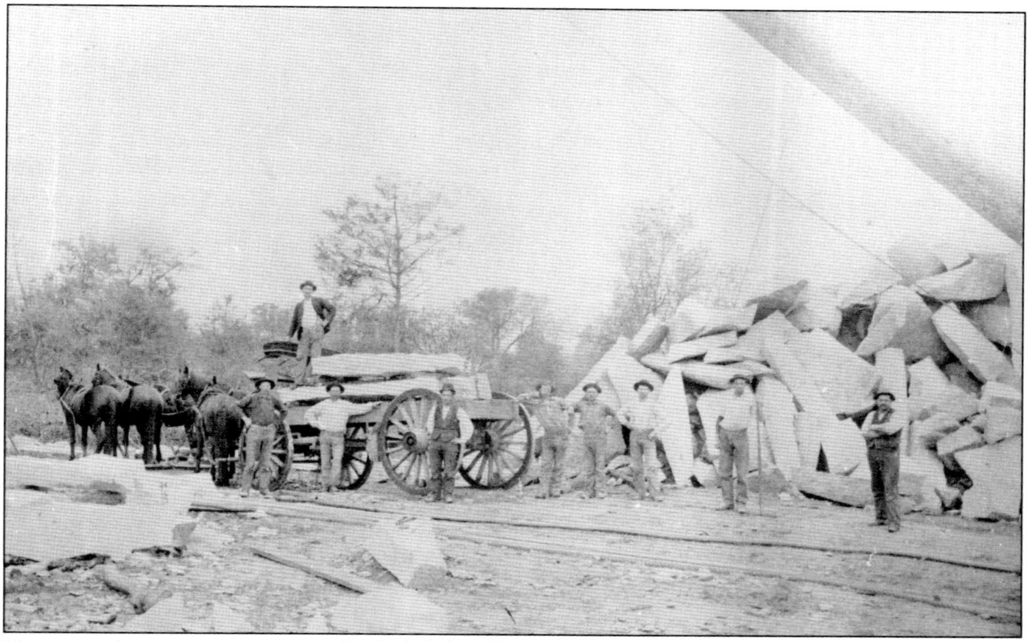
Horses and wagons are moving loaded slabs of granite at the Grant Quarry.

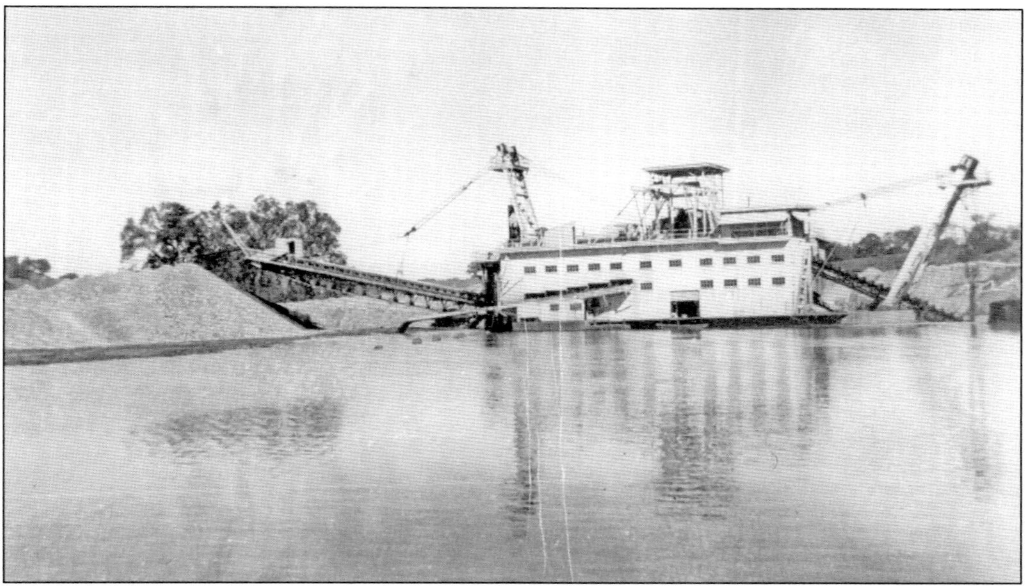
A gold dredger works between Humphrey and Swetzer Roads in the 1920s.

Loomis through the Years

Loomis was named for pioneer James Oscar Loomis, but the community had many names when it was originally located 1 mile southeast of the present site, to which it was moved in 1869 when the Central Pacific Railroad came through:

Pine Grove	1850, mining town
Placer	October 4, 1861
Smithville	January 2, 1862
Pino	December 6, 1869
Loomis	May 28, 1890

About the Loomis Basin Historical Society

The Loomis Basin Historical Society was founded in 1993 for the purpose of discovering, collecting, preserving, and making accessible the history and the heritage of the Loomis Basin Area.

The members of the society work to identify and preserve places of historical interest and promote public awareness of the history of the Loomis Basin; educate the public on the importance of the Loomis Basin's role in the history of California and the United States; and encourage the development of a Loomis Basin history museum.

The membership is open to all persons interested in the history of the Loomis Basin. The group meets the third Wednesday of the month at the Loomis Library, 6050 Library Drive, Loomis, California.

The photographs in this publication belong to the Loomis Basin Historical Society. Families mentioned in the acknowledgements loaned the photographs to the organization to use as needed by the organization for publication.